MATTHEW FOX

A SPIRITUALITY NAMED
COMPASSION
AND THE HEALING
OF THE GLOBAL VILLAGE,
HUMPTY DUMPTY AND US

Winston Press

Acknowledgment is gratefully given to the following publishers: W.W. Norton & Co. for permission to cite from Adrienne Rich's poems, "Planetarium" and "The Phenomenology of Anger" in *Adrienne Rich's Poetry* copyright © 1975; and "Stepping Backward" from Adrienne Rich, *Poems, Selected and New* © 1975; Beacon Press for permission to cite from Robert Bly, *The Kabir Book* copyright © 1977; to Chuck Lathrop for permission to cite from his poem, "In Search of a Roundtable" in Chuck Lathrop, *A Gentle Presence* copyright © 1977; to World Poetry Inc. for permission to cite from Constance Urdang's poem, "Living in the Third World," in *The American Poetry Review*, vol. 6, no. 2, copyright © 1977 and Jane Rohrer's poem, "In the Kitchen Before Dinner," in *The American Poetry Review*, vol. 6, no. 5 copyright © 1977. Excerpts from *The Jerusalem Bible*, copyright © 1966 by Darton, Longman & Todd, Ltd. and Doubleday & Company, Inc. Used by permission of the publisher.

Book design by Bill Davenport Studio/JPR Associates

Cover design by Keith McCormick

9 8 7 6 5 4 3 2

Printed in the United States of America

Library of Congress Catalog Card Number: 79-63231
ISBN: 0-03-051566-1

Winston Press, Inc.
430 Oak Grove
Minneapolis, Minnesota 55403

"The whole idea of compassion is based on a keen awareness of the interdependence of all these living beings, which are all part of one another and all involved in one another."

— Thomas Merton, from his final talk, delivered two hours before his death.

This book is dedicated to all those who are actively engaged in trying to mend the cracked world egg and especially to two citizens of the world who died in the summer of 1977, but not before leaving behind waves of compassionate energies: Zuita Giordiani and E.F. Schumacher.

CONTENTS

Compassion is not pity but celebration/Compassion is not sentiment but is making justice and doing works of mercy/Compassion is not private, egocentric or narcissistic but public/Compassion is not mere human personalism but is cosmic in its scope and divine in its energies/Compassion is not about ascetic detachments or abstract contemplation but is passionate and caring/Compassion is not anti-intellectual but seeks to know and to understand the interconnections of all things/Compassion is

Contents

Contents

PREFACE

RETRIEVING COMPASSION FROM ITS LONELY EXILE

Compassion is everywhere. Compassion is the world's richest energy source. Now that the world is a global village we need compassion more than ever—not for altruism's sake, nor for philosophy's sake or theology's sake, but for survival's sake.

And yet, in human history of late, compassion remains an energy source that goes largely unexplored, untapped and unwanted. Compassion appears very far away and almost in exile. Whatever propensities the human cave dweller once had for violence instead of compassion seem to have increased geometrically with the onslaught of industrial society. The exile of compassion is evident everywhere—the oil globules piling up in our oceans and on the fish who inhabit the oceans, the teeming masses of persons pouring into already congested cities, the twenty-six million persons who live poor in the midst of affluent America, the 40% of the human race who go to bed hungry each night, the maldistribution of food and of research for energy, the mechanization of medicine that has reduced the art of healing to the engineering of elitist technologies, unemployment, overemployment, violent employment, the trivialization of economics and the proliferation of superfluous luxuries instead of basic needs for the needy, the deadening bureaucratization of our work, play and educational lives. The list goes on and on.

Rev. Sterling Cary, former president of the National Council of Churches, assesses the moral conscience of humanity in our time in this way: "We are losing our capacity to be human. Violence and oppression are becoming so commonplace that the modern victims of injustice are reduced to mere statistics." [1] And Robert Coles, commenting on the state of humanity in present-day Harlem, asks the question: "Does our country, by virtue of what it permits, still, in such places as Harlem, have a morally impoverished culture?" [2] What makes injustices so unacceptable in our time is the fact that we now possess the know-how to feed the world and provide basics for all its citizens. What is lacking is the will and the way. What is lacking is compassion.

In acquiescing in compassion's exile, we are surrendering the fullness of nature and of human nature, for we, like all creatures in the cosmos, are compassionate creatures. All persons are compassionate at least potentially. What we all share today is that we are victims of compassion's exile. The difference between persons and groups of persons is not that some are victims and some are not: we are all victims and all dying from lack of compassion; we are all surrendering our humanity together. The difference is in how persons react to this fact of compassion's exile and our victimization. Some persons react by joining the forces that continue the exile of compassion and joining them with a single mindedness and tenacity that guarantees still more violence, still more of compassion's exile; others react by despair and cynicism—drink, eat and be happy for tomorrow we exterminate ourselves; still others react with what Ned O'Gorman calls the "abstract calm" of intellectuals and other too-busy people who want it both ways and advocate political change while living high on the hog. Others are reacting by fleeing to fundamentalist religions and spiritualisms. Spiritualist and fundamentalist spiritualities that forsake the tradition of *imago dei* and humanity's deification in favor of the preaching of sin and redemption will have virtually nothing to say about compassion, for compassion is a divine attribute (see chapter one) and a creative energy force and will not be learned by a cheap religious masochism.

This book is an introduction to an analysis of compassion. It is meant to support those many persons who are moving to a fuller and fuller holistic life style—and there are many. It is also meant as an invitation to those still involved in the ladder-climbing dynamic of so much of our society to consider another way, a better way, called compassion. A more fun-filled and more justice-oriented way. A way of getting in tune with the universe at a time when, intellectually and at the level of scientific discovery, we are confirming the fact that mystics have preached for centuries—namely, that the universe is a very finely tuned organism indeed. And yet, at the level of life-styles and social structures, we are hardly in tune with the universe at all.

It is important that compassion be analyzed and treated critically. One of the guile-filled wiles of the anti-compassionate forces has been to sentimentalize compassion so that its exile is assured regarding any important decisions of our lives, decisions regarding economics, work, sexuality, energy, our bodies, our soil, our food, our air, our transportation, our art, our medicine, our education. For this reason this book is as much an analytic as it is a synthetic treatment of compassion. Like compassion itself, it is interdependent.

After the activism of the 60's, after the quietism of the 70's, there comes—hopefully—the mature spirituality of the 80's which will be characterized by a marriage of mysticism and social justice and whose proper name is compassion. The words *linkage* and *bonding* are emerging in our vocabulary for the 80's just as *consciousness* and *consciousness raising* emerged from the 60's. This book is about linkages (inter-connections) and about bonding (healing by making the connections). It must be so for it is about compassion which is a healing by way of making connections. The linkage is made in the book between sexuality, theology, art, psychology, science, economics, politics, childhood nursery rhymes, and compassion. I dialogue with feminists and artists, bankers and physicists, biologists and economists, doctors and animal lovers, theologians, artists and children. This is as it should be, for compassion is not elitist, but everyone's energies. It constitutes our common humanity.

As the world becomes more of a global village and world religions become better known in localities far from their origins, the question arises as to what, if anything, these religions do for the globe. It is more and more certain to me that religion's purpose is to preach a way of life or spirituality called compassion and to preach it in season and out of season. This is surely the case with Judaism and with Jesus Christ. It also appears to be the case with Buddha, Muhammad, Lao Tzu, Confucius and Hinduism. People can indeed learn compassion from religious traditions, provided those traditions are in touch with their truest roots and have not themselves fallen victim to ignorance regarding their origins. Compassion will also be learned from nature and the universe itself. Yet these two sources of wisdom, faith and nature, are intimately related, for the God of one is the God of the other. As Simone Weil has put it, "How can Christianity call itself catholic if the universe itself is left out?" [3]

This book attempts to explore the wisdom of compassion as learned from religious traditions and from nature and the scientific study of nature. It also explores those obstacles in human culture that prevent compassion, so familiar a law of the universe, from happening in human history. Much healing is accomplished by removing pressures and obstacles and letting nature itself do the healing. Our ancestors called this kind of cause and effect *removens prohibens*—removing the obstacles. Getting out of the way so that nature and the Creator of nature might act. Thus, much of the book is about healing as the act of removing the obstacles to compassion. Chapter two deals with removing the sexual mystification that has contributed so substantially to compassion's exile; chapter three deals with the psychological obstacle of control that blocks compassion's more celebrative energies; chapter four explores the fears that prevent what may well be the essence of being human, namely creativity, and how these fears keep compassion in exile. Chapter five treats the obstacle that an overly Newtonian science sets up against compassionate awareness; chapter six considers the need to translate compassion into the very way we keep this house called the global village (since the name for keeping house is economics); chapter seven considers three political issues that urge us today to retrieve compassion in order that they be: namely, energy, health care and education. Finally, in chapter eight, I deal with an emerging symbol for our shared task of recreating the world and ourselves into a fuller whole and I borrow from a childhood nursery rhyme to develop that symbol of world, cosmic, human and divine egg.

In many respects this is an off-the-wall book. Its purpose is to get Humpty Dumpty—our psyches, our global village, and our cosmic consciousness—off the wall: the wall of division and separation, of possessiveness, of hoarding. Off the wall and down to earth where we can dance eye-to-eye once again.

I sense a growing awareness among numerous alive and awake persons today that something is wrong with the dualistic mystical traditions that Christianity has so often endorsed in our past. This tradition simply blocks out too much—it blocks out body, the body politic, the ecstasies of nature and work and laughter and celebration, the love of neighbor and the relieving of the suffering of others, the wrestling with political and economic evil spirits. In this tradition, as I explain in chapters one and two, compassion is effectively exiled for the sake of contemplation. And yet, strange to tell, Jesus never said to his followers: "Be contemplative as your Father in heaven is contemplative." He did say, however, "Be compassionate as your Father in heaven is compassionate." In doing so he was reiterating what Rabbi Dressner calls the "cornerstone" of the way of life or spirituality of Israel. For in Biblical spirituality (as distinct from Neoplatonic spirituality) believers are taught "that the holy and awesome name of the Lord, YHWH, which remains secret and unpronounced, signifies compassion." [4] The Bible, unlike Neoplatonic spirituality, suggests it is in compassion and not contemplation that the fullest spiritual existence is to be lived, enjoyed and passed on. What is at stake in recovering compassion as the center of our spiritual existence is the remolding of contemplation after compassion's image. Thus I suggest in chapter eight that a meditation on that art of creation we know as the Global Village is truly an experience of a New Mandala when it leads to compassionate consciousness and action.

In my opinion there are three major developments in spirituality today that are urging us all to deep changes of heart, symbols and structures. These are 1) the recovery of the Biblical, Jewish categories and therefore our practice of detaching ourselves from hellenistic ones. 2) The feminist consciousness and movement among women and men alike and its discovery of new images and symbols for our shared, deep, common experience. A feminist consciousness requires our detaching ourselves from more one-sided and patriarchal symbols, images and structures. 3) The emergence of critical, global thinking urged upon us all by the brevity of time that our planet has remaining if it is to survive beyond the twentieth century. All three of these developments in spirituality are very much in evidence in this book. They are like threads that weave in and out of its entire fabric. They enter and re-enter all the chapters of this book like waves moving the ocean — or does the ocean move the waves?

This book is the third in a trilogy on contemporary spirituality that I have found myself writing quite unaware in any conscious sense that I was writing a trilogy. Integral to my writing has been the deeply felt need to recover our spiritual language by a critical treatment of it. Thus the first book, *On Becoming a Musical, Mystical Bear: Spirituality American Style*, concentrated on the meaning of the word "prayer" and its relationship to the personal and psychological — when it is so related it is called "mysticism" — and to the social — when it is so related it is called "prophecy". There exists a necessary dialectic between the mystical and prophetic for adult prayerful or spiritual people. In that book I define prayer as "a radical response to life." The second book to this trilogy, *Whee! We, wee All the Way Home: A Guide to the New Sensual Spirituality* dealt with the recovery of non-elitist understanding of spiritual experience, both from the practical and theoretical viewpoints. I concentrated on the experience called *ecstasy* and how our ecstasies, whether of orange or blue coloring, are indeed our experiences of God and how we all have a right to them. Necessarily, this kind of non-elitist spirituality leads to a re-examination of the roles of body and body politic, of pleasure and the sharing of pleasures that make up our spiritual journeys. (I understand justice to be the structured struggle to share the pleasure of God's good earth.) In retrospect I can now see how essential it was that a study of passion precede this study on compassion. Thomas Aquinas writes that "compassion is the fire which the Lord has come to send on the earth"; and Rabbi Heschel, commenting on the prophets' experience of God, says: "To sense the living God is to sense infinite goodness, infinite wisdom, infinite beauty. Such a sensation is a sensation of joy." [5] Joy and celebration are integral to compassion, as I point out in chapter three of this book where I suggest that only a psychology of celebration can yield a compassionate consciousness. Compassion, the theme of this study, seems to be the proper name and the correct energy for spiritual living in the Global Village, the new word for a new soul. (See chapter eight.)

I began this trilogy on contemporary spirituality with a line from a poem by T.S. Eliot: "Perhaps it is not too late and I must borrow every changing shape . . ." There are some today who say that it is in fact already too late, that industrial society's greed and violence have already polluted the global village beyond repair. Others are not quite so pessimistic. What I am sure of is this: that if it is not too late already, the only energy and direction that we can take in the brief time left is the way of life called compassion. Compassion alone can save us and our planet. Provided it is not too late. Compassion is our last great hope. If compassion cannot be retrieved from its exile, there will be no more books, no more smiles, no more babies and no more dances, at least of the human variety. In my opinion, this might be a great loss to the universe. And to its admittedly foolish Maker.

From the point of view of methodology, this book employs two classical motifs in Western spirituality: that of the *via negativa* and that of the practice of detachment. The *via negativa* is employed as a method in chapter one where I try to sort out the wrong definitions that we have assigned, wittingly or unwittingly, to compassion. By exploring What Compassion Is Not we begin to delineate what it might mean in the positive sense. The detachment motif is carried out in the subsequent chapters (two to seven) where I urge a more critical understanding of sexuality, psychology, creativity, science, economics and politics in light of the fuller meaning of compassion. What effect will the recovery of compassion have on all these important aspects of world living today? One effect is that we need to re-think all of them, thus detaching ourselves from their presumed meanings during an era when compassion was exiled. Language is the first victim of cover-up and corruption. In this sense, this book is about redeeming a word that has been abused, used, forgotten, lost, and too rarely practiced. With the redemption of the word compassion, perhaps, will come a new birth of its practice. And with compassion's rebirth there may emerge a rebirth of meaning for "soul," which constitutes the subject-matter for chapter eight.

The footnotes in the book are there for at least two purposes: 1) to share a bibliography with the reader so that she or he might pursue areas of interest in greater detail, and 2) to acknowledge my own indebtedness and intellectual interdependence to others, living and dead. Of course no one is obligated to read the footnotes. Special mention must be made of a great spiritual teacher whom I cite often but without footnoting. His name is Meister Eckhart; he is a good friend of mine as I am sure he will become a good friend of the reader. The references for his keen observations on compassion may be found in other works I am publishing about him.[6] As will be evident from the citations from Eckhart in this book, his is a refreshingly non-elitist, creation-centered and compassion-oriented spirituality.

In addition to footnoting those thinkers that have stirred my reflections on compassion, I wish to acknowledge some other individuals and groups who have assisted me in the living and articulating of this book. To those who invited me to speak and responded critically to many ideas contained in this book I am grateful, especially to the organizers of the Symposium on "Revolutionary Alternatives for the Future" at the University of Oregon, Ashland, Oregon; for the George Jordan Memorial Lecture Series at the University of Washington; for the Willson Lectures at Southern Methodist University; and for the invitation to address the Religious Education Association Convention in St. Louis. Ideas contained in this book matured as a result of feedback I received from these and other lecturing opportunities. To Sister Mary Anne Shea, o.p., for her steadfast research assistance, and to

Brendan Doyle for his steady compassion toward the universe in the
midst of institutional violence, thank you. To Sister Martha Curry,
RSCJ for her encouragement and her reading of the text and to Judy
and Tim Rowan for its typing, I am indebted.

Institute of Creation-Centered Spirituality,
Mundelein College, Chicago
September, 1978

1

TOWARDS A MEANING OF COMPASSION:

FROM EXILING COMPASSION AS SENTIMENT TO LIVING COMPASSION AS A WAY OF LIFE

God created a reminder, an image.
Humanity is a reminder of God.
As God is compassionate,
Let humanity be compassionate.

Rabbi Abraham J. Heschel [1]

Compassion has been exiled in the West. Part of the flight from compassion has been an ignorance of it that at times borders on forgetfulness, at times on repression, and at times on a conscious effort to distort it, control it and keep it down. This exile of compassion leads to the poison and pain that becomes incarnated wherever people

[1]

are treated unjustly. Who can number the victims, living and dead, of the exile of compassion, sacrifices of human flesh to all the gods that humanity worships ahead of compassion.

In this chapter I want to explore the meaning of compassion, since its very meaning has been forgotten and distorted. I am using the well-tried method of dealing with spiritual terms which is the *via negativa*. By this I mean that I am proceeding cautiously at first by separating true compassion from its numerous imposters, thus the emphasis on What Compassion is Not—an emphasis that gradually leads to a fuller unveiling of What Compassion Might Mean. In considering these nine dimensions to compassion, themes will emerge which will play throughout the remainder of this book.

COMPASSION IS NOT PITY BUT CELEBRATION

Compassion is not pity in the sense that our culture understands pity. It is not a feeling sorry for someone, nor is it a preoccupation with pain.

Compassion is not pity

To reduce compassion to pity and to pitiful feelings is to exile compassion altogether from adult living. The word "pity" has evolved to mean something very different from compassion. What is the difference between pity and compassion? Pity connotes condescension and this condescension, in turn, implies separateness. "I feel sorry for you because you are so different from me." Gestalt therapist Frederick Perls emphasizes that pity and compassion present shades of meaning that, "while subtle from the linguistic standpoint, are profoundly significant from the psychological." What are the differences? Pity "sometimes regards its object as not only suffering, but weak or inferior." There is less participation in the sufferings of another in pity than in compassion—compassion never considers an object as weak or inferior. Compassion, one might say, works from a strength born of awareness of shared weakness, and not from someone else's weakness. And from the awareness of the mutuality of us all. Thus to put down another as in pity is to put down oneself. "Most of what passes muster as pity is actual disguised gloating," warns Perls.

Pity works out of a subject-object relationship where what is primary is one's separateness from another. It presumes ego differences as a basic way of relating to reality. As such, it is about emoting and feeling without including actual relieving of the causes of another's pain. It involves what Perls calls "the luxury of sentimental tears" which "is mostly a masochistic enjoyment of the misery." Such tearful pity leads to philanthropy and what has come to be known as "good works of charity."

> Such pity is condescension. We apply it to those who are in such a low estate that they are not or have ceased to be our own serious rivals. They are 'out of the running.' By pitying them we emphasize the discrepancy between their lot and ours. Such attitude, we believe, motivates much so-called charity.[2]

The origin of the word pity is from the words piety and pious (*pietas* in Latin; *pius* in French) whereas the root of the word compassion is from the words *cum patior* meaning to suffer with, to undergo with, to share solidarity with.

Compassion is celebration

The surest way of discerning whether one has pity towards or compassion with another is to answer this question: Do you celebrate with this same person or these same people? Max Scheler, in his study on *The Nature of Sympathy*, takes for granted not only the fact that true "fellow-feeling" or compassion includes joy but also the fact that joy and celebration constitute the better half of the whole that compassion is about. He cites approvingly the German proverb, "a sorrow shared is sorrow halved; joy shared is a joy doubled," suggesting that it is "one of the few proverbs which brook examination from the moral point of view"; and he comments on the two directions of compassion. "In respect of its quality as an emotional act, the purely ethical value of rejoicing is quite equal to that of pity. As a *total act*, however, it [rejoicing] contains *more* value, as such, than pity, for joy is preferable to sorrow. The value of its occurrence is likewise the greater, as evincing a nobler disposition, by the very fact of its greater liability to frustration through possible envy." [3] One is reminded of Jesus' expression of compassion as joy when he heard from his disciples that their preaching was being well received. "The seventy-two came back rejoicing. 'Lord,' they said 'even the devils submit to us when we use your name.' . . . It was then that, filled with joy by the Holy Spirit, he said, 'I bless you, Father, Lord of heaven and earth, for hiding these things from the learned and the clever and revealing them to mere children. Yes, Father, for that is what it pleased you to do.'" (Lk. 10. 17, 21)

Compassion operates at the same level as celebration because what is of most moment in compassion is not feelings of pity but feelings of togetherness. It is this awareness of togetherness that urges us to rejoice at another's joy (celebration) and to grieve at another's sorrow. Both dimensions, celebration and sorrow, are integral to true compassion. And this, above all, separates pity from compassion for it is seldom that we would invite someone we had pity *on* to a common celebration. (Notice the preposition *on* as in "patting one *on* the head".) Yet the passion-with of true compassion urges us to celebration.

Celebration is a forgetting in order to remember. A forgetting of ego, of problems, of difficulties. A letting go. So too is compassion a letting go of ego, of problems, of difficulties, in order to remember the common base that makes another's suffering mine and in order to imagine a relief of that suffering. There can be no compassion without celebration and there will be no authentic celebration that does not result in increased compassionate energies. A person or a people who cannot celebrate will never be a compassionate people. And a person or a people who do not practice compassion can never truly be celebrating. Such people only wallow in superficial feelings of pious and pitiful energies.

The Biblical teaching on compassion is not about pity as our culture understands that word. "Israel has never regarded pity as mere condescension, but rather as a feeling of kinship with all fellow creatures." [4] Compassion is about what I have called feelings of togetherness, suspended egos, or the "feeling of kinship with all fellow creatures." This kinship in turn urges us to celebrate our kinship. Compassion, then, is about celebration.

COMPASSION IS NOT SENTIMENT BUT IS MAKING JUSTICE AND DOING WORKS OF MERCY

Compassion is not pure feeling or sentiment. It involves the relief of the pain of others. This emphasis on action and doing is found in the Biblical tradition of the *works of mercy*.

Compassion is not sentiment

The word "compassion" has been so much in exile in Christian circles that in the first thirteen major theological encyclopedias of both

Protestant and Catholic origins that I have investigated only one had an entry under the word "compassion." In contrast, all four of the Jewish encyclopedias I investigated had a substantial article on compassion. The one article that was available on compassion in one Catholic encyclopedia reveals what happened to compassion in its exile in the West. In one word, it has turned into sentimentalism, into "emoting with Mary at the foot of the cross" as this article explains it. Defining compassion as "the movement of the soul," the author continues.

> In the vocabulary of Christian spirituality it designates the hearty participation of Mary in the Passion and the redeeming sacrifice of Jesus. It also applies to the sentiments and the acts of love of all those who, by intention or by fact, follow the example of the sorrowful Virgin and associate themselves with our suffering and dying Lord.

> Compassion can be understood in a narrow or broad sense. In the first sense, it is properly affective love, the sympathy, the sorrow experienced before the sufferings of Jesus. In the second sense, it understands, moreover, the compensations and reparations which, as follows from these sentiments, the Christian desires to offer to God, the object that Our Lord asks for his Passion and which the faithful try to give to him.[5]

Finally, after continuing for over twenty-three lines about such matters, the author concedes that compassion can be exercised "before the sufferings and experiences of one's neighbor." It is evident that, where compassion is alluded to at all in much Christian writing, it has become rankly sentimental.

In the late Middle Ages a sentimental piety was developed that sidetracked the true meaning of compassion, and instead of celebrating and relieving one another's pain together the people "drew up a minute inventory of the torments inflicted on Christ; they enumerated the steps that he made on the *Via dolorosa*, the bruises of his body and the drops of his blood." [6] One can explore how much of this masochistic and sentimental energy of pity is still present in pieties and hymns, in sermons and in petrified languages of Christian churches, Protestant and Catholic.

Sentimentalism is a very powerful energy. Anne Douglas, in her monumental study of sentimentalism in modern culture, defines it as the "political sense obfuscated or gone rancid . . . (that) never exists except in tandem with failed political consciousness." [7] Thus sentimentalism is not only a block to social justice and a thorn in the side of love-justice — it is in fact their opposite. Sentimentalism, a rancid political consciousness, blocks authentic spiritual development. It actually interferes with the natural flow of energy outwards that all persons are born with. It is a flight from action, a flight from politics and a flight from justice-making. And yet, sentimentalism has become a common definition for compassion in the West as witnessed by the lengthy article just cited. Here we have a clear example of the exile of compassion and its reduction to rank feeling, thus its elimination from true adult living and adult structures and history. To sentimentalize compassion is to destroy compassion; powerful persons and groups who have known this for some time have not hesitated to utilize such knowledge. Whether one speaks of the mass-media of nineteenth century post-industrial society as Douglas does in exploring the novels and journals of that period for their sentimentalism, or whether one criticizes the trivialized sentimentalism of television shows and mass circulation newspapers and magazines like *The National Enquirer, The Star* and *People*, we see this energy to sentimentalize still very much at work. Such energies also mean the continued exile of compassion.

In the nineteenth century the philosopher Schopenhauer reduced compassion to a sentimental preoccupation with suffering, and Nietzsche attacked compassion especially from this standpoint. Nietzsche wrote:

> Through pity, suffering itself becomes infectious; in certain circumstances it may lead to a total loss of life and vital energy which is absurdly out of proportion to the magnitude of the cause (—the case of the death of Nazarene). This depressing and infectious instinct thwarts those instincts which aim at the preservation and enhancement of the value of life; by *multiplying* misery quite as much as by preserving all that is miserable, it is the principle agent in promoting decadence." [8]

Max Scheler rightly comments on this text of Nietzsche when he says that compassion would be a " 'multiplier of misery' only if it were identical with emotional infection". (18) But that is exactly what compassion becomes under sentimental influences that divorce it from action! Nietzsche's critique of compassion is altogether accurate vis a vis the article from the Christian encyclopedia with which I began this section. In other words, many of Nietzsche's objections to compassion are correct to the extent that Christians have sentimentalized compassion. Scheler distinguished true from pseudo compassion by the criterion of action, for he says: "It is one of the marks of genuineness in pity, that it should lead to acts of beneficence" and sentimental pity "has nothing whatsoever to do with pity." (13, 15)

Compassion as Doing Works of Mercy

Biblical compassion resists the sentimentalizing of compassion. In Biblical spirituality the works of mercy are *works* and the word for compassion in the Bible is more often employed as a verb than as a noun or an adjective. Compassion is about doing and relieving the pain of others, not merely emoting about it. Perhaps no one has put this more directly than John in his first epistle:

> If a person who was rich enough in this world's goods
> saw that one of his brothers or sisters was in need, but
> closed his heart to this person,
> how could the love of God be living in him or her?
> My children, our love is not to be just words or mere talk,
> but something real and active.

The so-called corporal works of mercy are found in the Hebrew Bible, especially in the prophet Isaiah.

> Is not this the sort of fast that pleases me
> — it is the Lord Yahweh who speaks —
> to break unjust fetters
> and undo the thongs of the yoke,
>
> to let the oppressed go free,
> and break every yoke,
> to share your bread with the hungry,
> and shelter the homeless poor,
>
> to clothe the man you see to be naked
> and not turn from your own kin? (Is. 58.6–8)

Here Isaiah speaks to four of the works of mercy: feeding the hungry, clothing the naked, sheltering the homeless poor, and breaking unjust fetters or what became narrowly defined as "ransoming the captive." Other corporal works of mercy have traditionally been these three: giving drink to the thirsty as Rebecca did to Isaac (Gen. 24.18); visiting the sick as Ahaziah did when Jehoram became ill from his wounds in battle (2 Kings 8.29); and burying the dead as the inhabitants of Jabesh-gilead did for Saul when they heard of the death of Saul at the hand of the Philistines (1 Sam. 31.11f.).

The spiritual works of mercy are the following: To instruct the ignorant as Jehoshaphat did to the towns of Judah (2 Chronicles 17.7); to counsel the doubtful as Sennacherib did in sending messengers to King Hezekiah who was wavering in his steadfastness to Yahweh's law (Is. 37.6, 10); to admonish sinners as Samuel dares to do to Saul (1

Sam. 15.16ff.); to bear wrongs with patience as David did when he was cursed repeatedly by Shimei son of Gera (2 Sam. 16. 5–14); to forgive offenses willingly as Joseph did on revealing his true identity to his brothers who had tried to kill him (Gen. 45.1–5); to comfort the afflicted and those who mourn as Jeremiah did to Baruch (Jer. 45.1ff.); to pray for the living and the dead as Abraham did for the inhabitants of Sodom (Gen. 18.22–33).

What is clear in all fourteen of these traditional "Works of Mercy" is that they are works. Compassion leads to works. Feeding, clothing, sheltering, setting free, giving drink, visiting, burying, educating, counseling, admonishing, bearing wrongs, forgiving, comforting, praying: all these acts of mercy are acts indeed. Though they come from the heart and go to the heart, they are not restricted to sentiment or heartfelt emotions, however powerful. They all involve other people which is to say they are political activities. They are also works of justice-making as we shall see below.

One has to inquire as to whatever happened to these works of mercy. Are the efforts by the contemporary state to educate, to house, to employ or to support by welfare at all comparable to the faith-demand to express compassion by these works of mercy? Indeed, is the state capable of compassion at all? And should it be? Is philanthropy an expression of the works of mercy? To all these questions I would reply: No. The state, with its idolatry of national security, has proved itself incapable of performing these works as works of mercy and compassion in a global-village context, and in that failure lies much of the pain in our world. It is time that persons and groups of persons of faith re-imagine how these works of mercy will become incarnate in our culture and history. In many respects that imagining is what the remainder of this book is all about.

The New Testament continues the action orientation of the works of compassion that the Hebrew Bible initiates. Jesus insists that compassion involves action and not mere sentiment as, for example, in his parable about the Good Samaritan. In that parable Jesus says: "He had compassion and went to him and bound up his wounds, pouring on oil and wine; then he set him on his own beast and brought him to an inn and took care of him." (Lk. 10.35) For Jesus to "define" compassion took him an entire story including the activities of going to him, binding up wounds, pouring on oil, putting him on his beast, bringing him to an inn and caring for him. All these activities constitute for Jesus the meaning of compassion. Clearly compassion in the Biblical understanding is about relieving the pain of another and not merely feeling sentiment over it. Similar lessons are revealed in his parables about the Good Shepherd (Jn 10.1–18), whose act of compassion is actually one of "laying down his life for his sheep," and the Lost Coin (Lk. 15.8–10), where Jesus insists that the angels of heaven rejoice at a lost sinner who is repentent just as a woman who loses a coin holds a celebration on finding it.

Jesus addressed himself to six of the corporal works of mercy in an explicit way in Matthew's Gospel (25.34–46).

> Then the King will say to those on his right hand, 'Come you whom my Father has blessed, take for your heritage the kingdom prepared for you since the foundation of the world. For I was hungry and you gave me food; I was thirsty and you gave me drink; I was a stranger and you made me welcome; naked and you clothed me, sick and you visited me, in prison and you came to see me. Then the virtuous will say to him in reply, 'Lord, when did we see you hungry and feed you; or thirsty and give you drink? When did we see you a stranger and make you welcome; naked and clothe you; sick or in prison and go to see you?' And the King will answer, 'I tell you solemnly, in so far as you did this to one of the least of these brothers of mine, you did it to me'. Next he will say to those on his left hand, 'Go away from me, with your curse upon you, to the eternal fire prepared for the devil and his angels. For I was hungry and you never gave me food; I was thirsty and you never gave me anything to drink; I was a stranger and you never made me welcome, naked and you never clothed me, sick and in prison and you never visited me.' Then it will be their turn to ask, 'Lord, when did we see you hungry or thirsty, a stranger or naked, sick or in prison, and did not come to your help?' Then he will answer, 'I tell you solemnly, in so far as you neglected to do this to one of the least of these, you neglected to do it to me'. And they will go away to eternal punishment, and the virtuous to eternal life.

It is clear from this passage that God is to be loved through the relief of the pain of others. "Hungry, thirsty, a stranger, naked, sick, in prison—these are the realities of pain. God becomes *immanent* in these realities of pain: he says, 'for I was hungry.' " [9] Thus our works of compassion are works of God-love as well, for God suffers and not only others when others suffer. The term "good works" is a technical term in the Scriptures, as Biblical scholar Walter Grundmann indicates. "Good works are actions of mercy on behalf of all those in need of them, and they are works of peace-making that eliminate discord among people." This is the meaning of Jesus' story of the Last Judgment that we have just read from Mt. 25. In this passage on compassion that we have considered from Matthew's Gospel, it is highly significant that, as Miranda points out, "the only criterion of judgment is stated to be good or evil works," and that this passage constitutes "the only description of the Last Judgment in the New Testament." [10]

It has been pointed out that the feeling of compassion in Jesus "always gave rise to an outward act of succor." [11] His compassion urged him to heal the blind (Mt. 20.34), to cleanse the leper (Mk. 1.41), to teach the ignorant (Mk. 6.34), to raise the dead (Lk. 7.13), to feed the hungry (Mt. 15.32, Mk. 8.2), and when he was pressed by John the Baptist's followers to tell what his mission was about, his reply was in terms of his relief of these pains of others (Mt. 11.4,5). Compassion as feeling separated from action is inconceivable to Jesus. When he talks about being "compassionate as your Father is compassionate" he talks about *giving:* "Give, and there will be gifts for you: a full measure, pressed down, shaken together, and running over, will be poured into your lap; because the amount you measure out is the amount you will be given back" (Lk. 6.36,38). Compassion is giving and not only feeling for Jesus. Jesus' teaching on the works of compassion underlines the starting point of all compassion: namely, that I am not only I but we are one another. And he brings in still a new and deeper mystery: that we are also God. That God suffers as we suffer. That God is relieved as we relieve the pain of one another. Other examples of both the spiritual and corporal works of mercy can be found in abundance in the New Testament.[12] The Beatitudes, too, are Jesus' teaching on compassion and we will consider them later.

Compassion as Justice-making

Given this evidence of compassion as action in the New Testament, the sin of sentimentalizing that Christians have performed on compassion becomes even more startling and shocking. Reasons for this sin include the sentimentalizing of the word love in the West and its divorce from justice and the relation of love and hate to the structures of injustice. Jose Miranda has put the situation bluntly: "One of the most disastrous errors in the history of Christianity is to have tried—under the influence of Greek definitions—to differentiate between love and justice." [13] In the Biblical tradition all experience of God is to lead to creative compassion to neighbor. Being alone with the Alone is not a Biblical ideal. Nor is pining with the divine à la the sentimental spiritualisms that have racked Christian mysticism for centuries. "To know Yahweh is to do justice," says the prophet Jeremiah. To know the compassionate one is to do compassion. Tres-

montant puts it this way: "Justice in the Bible is not opposed to charity. It *is* charity. The theological virtue of justice expresses itself in
justice toward neighbor, which is also love, and in social justice." [14]

The distinction between love and justice follows upon the gnostic
distinction between a good God and a just God. "The most important
antithesis" in the schemes of the gnostic Marcion, according to Hans
Jonas, is "that of the '*just*' God and the '*good*' God." But here lies the
destruction of all compassion, namely in separating good and just.
"From the Christian point of view this is the most dangerous aspect of
Marcion's dualism: it sunders and distributes to two mutually exclusive
gods that polarity of justice and mercy whose very togetherness in one
God motivates by its tension the whole dialect of Pauline theology." [15]

How does one work to relieve the pain of others that can be relieved? The contemporary word for that relief of pain is justice-making. Psychologist William Eckhardt defines compassionate justice as
"moving towards equality, guided by the assumption that human
beings are equally human." [16] But justice-making is not only a contemporary term for compassion, it is a Biblical word as well. "The Hebrew idea of justice approaches our notion of holiness, piety, and
righteousness ... This justice, as the basis of human conduct, must
embrace all activity, especially in the relationship of an Israelite with
his neighbor." [17] We see works of mercy becoming acts of justice in
the Hebrew notion of *zedakah*, which literally means "righteousness"
or "justice" but which is usually translated as "charity." In this kind
of charity the action taken is not "a favor to the poor but something to
which they have a right, and the donor, an obligation." Thus rabbis
teach that "the poor man does more for the householder (in accepting
alms) than the householder does for the poor man (by giving him the
charity)." [18]

A Biblical word which is translated sometimes as "compassion",
sometimes as "mercy" and other times as "pity" is the Hebrew word
hesed. It also means grace to the believing Israelite. Yet all scholars
agree that there is no adequate one-word translation into English.
Greek Bibles translated *hesed* as *eleos* and the Latin vulgate translated
it as *misericordia*. What is lacking in all these translations is the dimension of action that the Hebrew word implies. The Hebrew talks of
"*doing hesed* with someone" and hesed is frequently associated with
the word *mispat* or right.[19] It implies the doing of deliverance that justice is about. It implies liberating self and others, as Micha speaks of
"What does Yahweh ask of you except to do *hesed* (i.e. compassion)
and love *mispat* (i.e. justice)?" (Mi. 6.8) When Jesus comes announcing
that "The Kingdom of God is at hand," he is suggesting that the mes-

sianic time of justice-making and compassion is ready to begin, much as Isaiah had foretold. "I am bringing on my justice, it is not far off; my salvation shall not tarry." (40.13)

In Judaism an atheist is not one who denies God's existence but one "who maintains that there is neither justice nor Judge in the world." The Jew is exhorted to justice by the Torah: "Justice, justice shall you pursue" (Dt. 16.20). And the prophets call the Jewish people back to this fundamental law of Torah: "Let justice roll down like waters and righteousness like a mighty stream" (Amos 5.24). We see how far Christian speculation on interior righteousness and on striving for a life of perfection has come from the outward-oriented holiness that Jewish faith expected in acts of justice. "A holy man in Judaism is a 'just man'; his characteristics are consideration for others, integrity, truthfulness, *compassion—all social traits.* In Jewish thought, justice is 'akin to holiness'; it is a recognition of the sacred, inalienable rights of every individual, group, and people. Justice, in Judaism, demands removal of all discrimination; it calls for a continuous battle against hate, prejudice, or defamation of any people or group ... No Jew can be morally neutral." [20]

Latin American exegete Jose Miranda makes a strong case for translating *hesed* as "interhuman compassion" as for example in the prophet Hosea.

> What I want is compassion, not sacrifice; knowledge of God, not holocausts. (Hos. 6.6)

The prophet in this context is complaining about the rank injustices among the People. The prophet is putting compassion ahead of worship and liturgy and is also equating knowledge of God with compassion, an equation that we have seen the prophet Jeremiah making and that John in both his Gospel and his epistles continues to make. This passage from Hosea is taken up also in Matthew's Gospel, when Jesus defends himself against those who were scandalized by his eating with tax collectors and sinners (9.13), and again when he defended his disciples' action of picking and eating corn on the Sabbath (12.7). Miranda approves of the translation of *hesed* as *eleos* or compassion because "this is a compassion strictly related to a sense of justice. . . . It is a compassion-for-the-poor-and-oppressed, which can be indentified with the indignation felt before the violation of the rights of the weak" and he demonstrates how frequently *hesed* appears with justice (*sedakah*) or right (*mispat*) in Biblical parallelisms.[21] Miranda is convinced that compassion best translates the word *hesed* (often translated as grace) "in spite of the degeneration into paternalism that the term 'compassion' has suffered over the last twenty centuries. . . . The paternalistic sense of compassion is foreign to both Old Testament and the New . . . Biblical compassion is not condescension; it is unreserved commitment to the weak, the poor, and the oppressed. It acknowledges their rights; it is identical to an absolute sense of justice." (Being, 152)

The institutionalization of sentimental compassion as mercy will be discussed in the next chapter in the context of the paternalism generated by ladder symbols in Christian mysticism. It is worth noting here, however, that justice-making is not an easy or superficial task. It implies a kind of power on behalf of the oppressed. Thus we have Biblical images of the "Yahweh the Warrior" (Judges 5) who wages war against oppression, and we have the image of the "savior hero" (Zephaniah 3.1, 17).

One objection that Miranda has to translating *hesed* as love is that *hesed*, like compassion, demands a "volitional attitude." *Hesed* is more than sentiment, which is in fact what so many in our sentimentalized culture imagine love to be. Biblical love, insists Miranda, really means love-justice. Lutheran theologian and exegete Krister Stendahl appears very much in agreement with Miranda when he insists, in an essay on "Judgment and Mercy" that "it is important to revive and revitalize the biblical meaning of judgment (*krisis*) as that establishment of justice which by necessity means mercy for the wronged and loss for those who have too much." The English and German languages are dualistic, he points out, in the distinctions they make between the words "justice" and "righteousness" whereas the Biblical languages of Greek and Hebrew make no such dichotomies. "Righteousness and justice—are the one and only *justitia*" he declares. We ought not to be busy about balancing judgment and mercy, for they are much more closely aligned than we had imagined: "We must resist all homogenizing, neutralizing, dialecticizing and balancing acts with these terms" he warns. For what is mercy for the have-nots is judgment for the haves.[22] Thomas Aquinas also made the point that compassion is not pure feeling but implies *electio* or moral decision-making and doing,[23]

Injustice, then, is a prime enemy of compassion, and this fact is completely covered over by sentimentalisms that never in fact deal with injustice because they are so occupied in wallowing in self-centered emoting. Thus Harriet Beecher Stowe complained of the lack of a "sense of justice" in nineteenth century America and observed that the "utter deadness to the sense of justice" was actually promulgated by religionists "as a special grace and virtue" for persons to imbibe in (in Douglas, 380, n. 76). Rabbi Dressner calls us back to Biblical compassion which is justice when he observes that many Westerners "forgot justice in the midst of an over-extended, loosely-conceived, compassion, there is also justice—the exacting, demanding, stern call to justice." (D, 208f.) And the epistle of James takes up the same theme, linking the works of mercy with justice.

> If one of the brothers or one of the sisters is in need of clothes and has not enough food to live on, and one of you says to them, 'I wish you well; keep yourself warm and eat plenty', without giving them these bare necessities of life, then what good is that? Faith is like that: if good works do not go with it, it is quite dead ... You see now that it is by doing something good, and not only by believing, that a man is justified ... A body dies when it is separated from the spirit, and in the same way faith is dead if it is separated from good deeds. (James 2. 15,16,24,26)

COMPASSION IS NOT PRIVATE, EGO-CENTRIC OR NARCISSISTIC BUT PUBLIC

Compassion, far from being a privatizing energy, actually frees us from too privatized a way of feeling and acting. Or at least it ought to. Jewish scholars have complained about how this has not been the case at all in Christian history, calling Christian morality for the most part "unlimited and unconditional individualism" lacking entirely "an ideal for humanity."[24] What a far cry such individualism is from the Hebrew notion of *hesed* or deeds of love. The domestication of compassion took place especially with the industrial revolution when morality came to mean bedroom morality because the real issues of injustice, such as work, unemployment, child labor, were removed entirely from home or church into the market place. Indulgence became a substitute for justice, remarked an English radical, Harriet Martineau, and middle class women evolved from being makers of cloth to being purchasers of clothing. Anne Douglas comments that "women no longer marry to help their husbands get a living, but to help them spend their income" and henceforth the lady's "preoccupation is to be with herself," her clothes, her manners, her feelings, her family." (52, 57)

This domestication of moral energy and of compassion results in an idolatry of the family that Jesus himself was very harsh in repudiating. He said: "Anyone who loves father or mother more than me is not worthy of me." (Mt. 10. 37) Japanese theologian Kazoh Kitamori remarks how, even though parents are to experience compassion for their children and vice versa, "if their concern is centered on their own pain and their indulgence in it," sin is involved. (54) Sin being a flight from compassion. Family then becomes the nucleus of a rotten society, the "cell" of a cancerous sickness, for it buttresses what is essentially an egocentric way of life. Such a way of life is narrow and parochial and bent on the idol named security, which is meant to keep at bay all suffering and celebration that is not in one's own family. Max Scheler defines egocentricity as "the illusion of taking one's own environment to be the world itself." (58) The Global Village becomes reduced to the myopic experience of one's own nation or family or business or religion. This is why such thinking is an "illusion" to Scheler—it is a lie.

But egocentricity is an ugly energy that runs even deeper than do lies. It becomes a pathological state of ego-defense and invulnerability. "As an apprehension of the reality to volition and practical behavior, it is egoism; and as an attitude of love it is auto-erotism." (58) Privatized compassion then becomes a titillating affair of self-indulgence in the pain of others. An emotional infection occurs, says Scheler. "Here there is neither a *directing* of feeling towards the other's joy or suffering, nor any participation in her experience. On the contrary, it is characteristic of emotional infection that it occurs only as a transference.of the *state* of feeling, and does *not* presuppose any sort of *knowledge* of the joy which others feel." (138, italics his) People become objects, not subjects, in such a situation and, as Douglas points out regarding the sentimentalizing of the elderly, "the emotions they arouse in us are more important than the emotions they feel." (196)

Such emotional infection is simply "as a means to one's own pleasure" (17) observes Scheler, and he accuses Schleiermacher and modern Protestantism of indulging in too much concentration on emotion and the subjective, internal states of consciousness at the expense of more outward-oriented thinking which leads to love and action. Solipsism fails to admit the real equality in worth that every person holds for us. "Other people have the same value as you do" insists Scheler, but the solipsist never concedes this. Egoism, which results from a closed heart and mind, can only be eradicated at a root level. True compassion alone will displace it.

Scheler also cautions against the "taste for pain" that attracts some people, such as Schopenhauer, to interest in compassion. Schopenhauer is drawn to compassion, *not* for its dimension of shared experience but because of the suffering that is implied therein. "Schopenhauer's idea of pity is ultimately based on a morbid energy of life in decline, which is taken to be morally positive only through self-delusion . . . he treats pity as having a higher *ethical* value than rejoicing [(and)] . . . betrays a hidden element of sadistic glee in the affliction of others." Scheler wisely warns us to be alert about the sado-masochistic attractions of privatized compassion—especially the masochistic. "The dissolution of the self in a common stockpot of misery eliminates genuine pity altogether" (53–55). Masochism is an indulgence in narcissim, where there is no joy or celebration with others any more than there is true relief of the suffering of others. Narcissistic compassion puts one under the spell of "illusion that he is in loving contact with 'Another,' while in fact it is never anything more than himself that he is adoring—his own face in a glass, darkly" (156).

What is lost when compassion becomes so ego-centric and narcissistic? Transcendence itself, according to Miranda. "Love which is not an acute sense of justice and an authentic suffering-with-my-outraged-brother, such love *does not transcend*. (sic) It is satisfied with itself although with its words it denies that it is so; and thus it remains in itself and does not transcend." (62) Compassion, then, that is truly directed outward is the new word for transcendence. This is what John says in his first epistle, also, when he declares that "no one has seen God" and so God is to be seen only in love of neighbor. It is interesting that in this powerful passage (1 Jn 12–21), the archetype for love is not love of parent for child or even husband for wife, but it is fraternal love. True compassion is fraternal and sororal and not paternal, patriarchal or even parental.

In our time and culture a person has emerged, much as Francis of Assisi did in the thirteenth century, to assist us in redefining compassion. His name was E.F. Schumacher; he died in 1977 but not before leaving behind his own conversion story and with it a powerful testimony to authentic compassion in his book *Small is Beautiful*. E.F. Schumacher has redeemed the word compassion for us, getting it back from the privatizers and sentimentalizers and the morbidly preoccupied and putting it where it belongs: in the public arenas of energy, work, technology, economics, market place, third world and first world countries. His use of the word compassion in that book is truly public and not privatized, and we will have recourse to some of his ideas later in this book. Compassion, he knew, is far too important an energy to be directed inwards and domesticated. Without its active presence in the world of economics and in the arenas of public moral decision-making, we will all perish.

COMPASSION IS NOT MERE HUMAN PERSONALISM BUT IS COSMIC IN ITS SCOPE AND DIVINE IN ITS ENERGIES

Personalism, or the caring of one person for another, may be an instance of compassion and may truly lead to development of compassion, but compassion is far fuller than personalism. This is not only because compassion leads to justice-making and therefore to the re-creation of society's structures but also because compassion is about energy we give and take from all creatures, not just from human beings. After all, Martin Buber explained that I-Thou is not only an experience between people but among people and trees, people and animals, people and music and painting and other arts, and people and God. The selling of psychological personalism has often ignored compassion and reduced it to ego-feeling alone, just as it often tends to ignore the mystery and riches of silence and solitude where so much compassion is learned and developed.

Krister Stendahl characterizes our times as being "cosmically scared," frightened as we are by "principalities and powers where tiny little human beings just know that they cannot do much, that they are not in control, that they are just caught." In such a situation he cautions against still more introspective and individualized religion and implores Christians to return to the cosmic tradition of their faith.

> Even justification by faith—must be subsumed in the wider context of Paul's mission to the Gentiles, part of God's total plan for his creation—Paul's thoughts about justification were triggered by the issues of divisions and identities in a pluralistic and torn world, not primarily by the inner tensions of individual souls and consciences. His searching eyes focused on the unity and the God-willed diversity of humankind, yes, of the whole creation. (KS, 39f.)

Compassion is a spirituality of meat, not milk; of adults, not children; of love, not masochism; of justice, not philanthropy. It requires maturity, a big heart, a willingness to risk and imagination. Yet for many persons with good spiritual intentions spirituality has meant either meditative disciplines or introverted contemplation. Compassion moves beyond these beginning stages of spiritual searching to a fuller stage of dialectical living that experiences both cosmic contemplation and local pain and then gives birth to alternative healing of that pain.

Compassion as cosmic

Biblical compassion carries the energy of compassion far beyond the limited parameters of personalism. First, compassion extends to the entire universe and all of creation according to the Hebrew Bible. "His compassion is over all that he has made" sings the Psalmist (145.9) who insists that "the compassion of the Jew should extend beyond the human race to the lowliest of God's creatures." True compassion extends to all creatures. "Israel has never regarded pity as mere condescension, but rather as a feeling of kinship with all fellow creatures."[25] Thus the cosmic dimension to compassion helps to prevent sentimentalisms in compassion's name. Animals are very much included in the Biblical experience of compassion. Jewish law forbids hunting as a sport or pasttime and the slaughtering of animals for human food was permitted but only within very strict regulations—regulations that are meant to insure "a minimum of suffering" on the part of the animal. The weekly Sabbath day of rest was to be a day of rest for the domestic animals no less than for humans (Ex. 20.10). The ox that treads the corn was to be unmuzzled in order that it might eat and not be tantalized (Dt. 22.10). The one time an interruption of the Jewish grace before meals is allowed is if the domestic animals have not been fed. Leo Baeck observes, "In an act without parallel in civilization, the Bible placed animals under the protection of laws devised for man . . . Judaism taught man to treat the animal with a love that was more than pity." Talmudic law develops this principle of kindness toward animals, forbidding as it does mutilation or castration of animals.

Max Scheler insists that it is this love of Nature *for its own sake* that distinguishes true compassion from "its spurious, sentimental form. This is why such things as brutality towards the organic forms of Nature, animal and vegetable, do not become 'wicked' merely through being regarded as a symptom of 'potential' brutality towards men, but are actually wicked in themselves" (155f.). In other words, for Scheler, to fail to act out of our kinship with all of creation is to invite brutality that narcissism so easily entertains. An experience of cosmic awareness is a basic ingredient for true compassion.

Compassion as a divine attribute

Another way in which Biblical compassion goes far beyond personalism is the Bible's emphasis on compassion as an attribute of God. In the theophany to Moses on Mount Sinai, Yahweh is said to descend in the form of a cloud and to speak. "Yahweh passed before him and proclaimed, 'Yahweh, Yahweh, a God of tenderness and compassion, slow to anger, rich in kindness and faithfulness' " (Ex. 34.6). The very name Yahweh designates God as Compassion and God is called "The Compassionate One." God is full of compassion (Ps. 103, 11) and promises this compassion toward people (Dt. 30.3) and delivers on this promise (Dt. 13.17). "His compassion fails not, being new every morning" sings one psalm (Lam. 3.22). Time and again God demonstrates compassion (II Kings 13.23; 2 Chron. 36.15) and the divine love is extended especially to the poor, the widow, the orphan and the stranger. God is called the "Father of Compassion" and according to Midrash creation was born of the divine compassion toward creatures.

To say that God is compassionate is to say that God suffers at the sufferings of others. God suffers. God is in pain. Human compassion then becomes the relief of the pain of God as well as the relief of human pain. This theme of God in pain is an ancient one, well developed in Judaism and in certain thinkers but very much underdeveloped in much of Christian spirituality. Augustine, for example, explains away God's pathos as allegorical when he says: "God himself, according to the Scriptures, becomes angry and yet he is never disturbed by any passions whatsoever."[26] Kazoh Kitamori wisely observes that "every form of docetism results in a denial of the pain of God" (p. 35) and this may account for much of the loss of the pain-of-God motif in Christianity—namely the heavy burden of docetism that riddles Christian spirituality. The encroachment of rationalism into theology also drives out the pathos of God in pain as we shall see in the section on anti-intellectualism below.

The theme of God in pain is not a foreign one to the true Biblical thinker. Rabbi Heschel, in an interview given a few days before his death, declared that "There is an old idea in Judaism that God suffers when man suffers. There's a very famous text saying that even when a criminal is hanged on the gallows, God cries. God identifies himself with the misery of man. I can help God by reducing human suffering, human anguish and human misery" (p. 79). We are a long way from the "unmoved Mover" in this Biblical theology. And a long way from God as Apathy. It is the prophet's work, says Heschel, to keep God and people together. "The prophet can hold God and man in one thought, at one time, at all times. This means that whatever I do to man, I do to God. When I hurt a human being, I injure God" (77). According to Kitamori, who has devoted a book to the *Theology of the Pain of God*, God is in pain because God embraces "completely those who should not be embraced" (12) and God's love comes from a love that is rooted in pain. He cites Scheler's opinion of human history: "all of history is virtually an enigma without a concept of an *agonizing God.*"

The mystery of God's pain is also the mystery of God's love, argues Kitamori, using especially the following two texts from the prophets Jeremiah and Isaiah.

> Is Ephraim my dear son? Is he a pleasant child? For since I spoke against him, I do earnestly remember him still: therefore my bowels are troubled for him. I will surely take compassion upon him, says the Lord. (Jer. 31.20)

> Look down from heaven, and behold from the habitation of your holiness and of your glory. Where is your zeal and your strength, the sounding of your bowels and of your compassion toward me? Are they restrained? (Is. 63.15)

God's bowels are said to turn with anguish and with pain. Here lies the origins of true compassion, for the bowels and not the heart form the true seat of deep emotions according to Jewish thinking. God then experiences compassion at the gut level where we all do. Compassion is passionate. The compassionate God is a passionate God. Compassion is about being moved. It is a movement.

Compassion, while not putting down persons or personhood, nevertheless moves one beyond mere personalism to a consciousness of energy everywhere, human and divine, vegetable and mineral, animal and musical, planetary and interplanetary. In this sense one might say that the cosmos becomes personalized through compassion—but this is not what is usually meant by personalism. Compassion is a way of being at home in the universe, with life and with death, with the seen and the unseen. The energy-consciousness that compassion presumes takes one beyond mere psychologies and spiritualities of inter-personalism.

In this sense, too, contemplation—when it is truly cosmic and not overly individualized—is a rich and even necessary grounding for compassion. Compassion grows from cosmic solitude and one's courage to face the fear of the cosmos. Arturo Paoli writes of this kind of cosmic contemplation when he insists that

> the only sign of being 'touched by God' is to be able to see yourself as 'universal brother'—to use a favorite phrase of Father De Foucauld's. And this means to be in communion with people and with all beings. . . . Sinking roots into this wholesomeness demands the courage to accept the world as being in a process of constant creation in which things go on being

liberated from human aggressiveness. . . . Contemplation ma-
tures in communion with Brother Fire, with Sister Water,
with Brother Wolf and discovers a loving and joyful brotherhood. . . . The contemplative design for the future is qualitative change, reconciliation with things. The universe is discovered to be liberated from slavery and weakness in order to
take part in the 'glorious freedom of the children of God.'
(Rom 8, 21)[27]

COMPASSION IS NOT ABOUT ASCETIC DETACHMENTS OR ABSTRACT CONTEMPLATION BUT IS PASSIONATE AND CARING

Compassion is not knowing about the suffering and pain of others. It is, in some way, knowing that pain, entering into it, sharing it
and tasting it in so far as that is possible. As Scheler puts it, compassion "is indeed a case of feeling the other's feeling, not just knowing of it, nor judging that the other has it" (9). But how does one
know another's feeling and not merely know about it? Imagination is
absolutely necessary for such a compassionate learning experience and
that is one more reason why neither ascetic thinkers nor rationalist
ones have much if anything to teach us about compassion. For they
are into controlling the imagination instead of learning from it. Mary
Richards talks of the proper instruction for what she calls Moral Imagination, and links it up with the creative work of pottery-making. "We
are not always able to feel the love we would like to feel. But we may
behave imaginatively: envisioning and eventually creating what is not
yet present. This is what I call Moral Imagination . . . From the child's
ability to imagine grows as well the adult's capacity for compassion:
the ability to picture the suffering of others, to identify. In one's citizenship, or the art of politics, it is a part of one's skill to imagine other
ways of living than one's own." [28] The proper way to learn passion
and caring is by interaction with matter—a transformation of energy
(rather than a control over it) that all artists know well.
    As Bultmann and Miranda both point out, the word "hatred" in
the Bible means "a simple lack of compassion" (M, 128), an apathy, a
coldness, an abstractness that prevents love of neighbor or is indiffer-
ent to it. But the rationalist tradition in the West has inculcated into
our very patterns of thinking and acting, including our theology and
our institutions, an abstractionist approach to living. One might even
say that such an educational system educates us in hatred and how to

be haters and cold-hearted, i.e. noncompassionate people. Miranda is convinced that Western culture, under Plato's and Aristotle's tutelege, "has been inevitably aristocratic, privileged, incapable of perceiving the most massive, tragic, and urgent reality of our history. Its humanism was and is a humanism of thought—a mental, aesthetical humanism. And its 'man' is an abstraction, a Platonic essence valid *semper et pro semper*, not real flesh-and-blood humanity, a humanity of blood and tears and slavery and humiliations and jail and hunger and untold sufferings." (31) Social problems are "new" to the West, he points out, and receive only the status of an addendum or a footnote. Compassion as social justice is indeed a new concept for many, many spiritualities operating in our day.

Kazoh Kitamori, himself a Protestant, calls for a replacing of the "Theology of the Word of God" with a "Theology of the Pain of God" in order to get back to the passion and compassion of the Biblical God. Citing Karl Barth who said that "God is a total person without tearing and pain," Kitamori insists that "we must proclaim the 'theology of the pain of God' against the so-called 'theology of the Word of God' " (I, 23f.) There is insight to his position, for words can be immensely abstract and abstracting. They can alienate us from the Biblical, passionate God, and Kitamori puts his finger on the same sensitive nerve that Miranda exposed when he comments on Hegel's God. "By cunning of reason, Hegel's God never suffers wounds. Thus the abstractness of Hegel's philosophy lies not in his portrayal of God as embracing the world, but in his portrayal of God as being without pain" (28). To deny God divine pathos and passion is to make an abstraction of God. It is here too, in rediscovering the pain and passion of God, that Kitamori sees common ground between Western faith and Buddhist, for Buddha saves by his own sickness at humanity's sickness. "Sickness is saved by sickness" in that philosophy.

Thomas Aquinas, unlike Augustine, saw the important relationship between passion and compassion and did not counsel the putting down of either. To this extent he was Jewish and Biblical in his spirituality just like Rabbi Heschel. Aquinas says: "Compassion ought to be spoken of, that is, at the same time as, passion" and "compassion is a certain kind of passion because no-one becomes compassionate unless he suffers"; "compassion proceeds from a love of God and of neighbor which is a consuming fire while it moves one to relieve miseries of others." [29] Rabbi Heschel contrasts the passionate God of Israel to the absractionist God of the Philosophers. The latter "is all indifference, too sublime to possess a heart or to cast a glance at our world. In contrast, the God of the prophets is all concern, too merciful to remain aloof from His creation. He not only rules the world in majesty of His might: He is personally concerned and even stirred by the conduct and fate of man. 'His mercy is upon all His works'." (D, p. 14) Heschel also comments that the prophets, who know the meaning of compassion, are not ascetics. The goal of life is celebration, Heschel maintains. Tresmontant wisely points out that "contemplation has a different meaning within" Biblical and Neo-Platonic ways of thinking. "To Neo-Platonism it implies flight, whereas to the Bible it is entirely compatible with action and with work" (170). Action and work are integral aspects of compassion. Compassion is the Biblical word for contemplation. Gnosticism, Tresmontant points out, has "confused the abstract and the spiritual." The Greek notion of *theoria* and contemplation was very visually oriented so that contemplation became a kind of gazing at—a vision. But the Biblical understanding of divine experience is more in terms of a Banquet, a celebration, and a participation in celebrating. The Jews were ear-people, not eye-people as were the Greeks. One sees at a distance but does not hear well at a distance. The ears, while they cannot perceive as far as the eyes can see, can perceive more tactilely and more sensually. Contemplation is thus more sensual and proximate for the Jew than for the Greek. It is felt from the guts.

COMPASSION IS NOT ANTI-INTELLECTUAL BUT SEEKS TO KNOW AND TO UNDERSTAND THE INTER-CONNECTIONS OF ALL THINGS

While compassion implies passion, pathos and deep caring arising from the bowels and guts, it also implies an intellectual life. Ideals come from ideas after all and ideas are important. Just as there can be no justice without ideas and an intellectual life, so there can be no compassion without an intellectual life, for compassion involves the whole person in quest of justice and a mind with ideas is an obviously significant portion of any of us. Thomas Merton, in the last talk he ever gave, delivered two hours before his death, spoke on the subject "Marx and Monastic Perspectives." His talk's title is a significant fact in itself, namely that he spoke on so intellectual and not mere journey-to-the-heart kind of topic as his final address to us all. In this address he had the following observation to make about compassion. "The whole idea of compassion," he said "is based on a keen awareness of the interdependence of all these living beings, which are all part of one another and all involved in one another." [30] To develop compassion, then, means to develop an ever keener awareness of the interdependence of all living things. But to develop such an awareness implies deep study, not only of books, of course, but of nature itself. It implies study as a spiritual discipline, as a means to entering more and more fully into the truth of the universe in which we live. It implies a rejoicing on the part of spiritual people at the facts of our universe that science can and has uncovered, and therefore an authentic kind of ecumenical dialog between science and spirituality.

Compassion, being so closely allied with justice-making, requires a critical consciousness, one that resists all kinds of keptnesses, including even that of kept academia and kept intellectuals. It implies a going out in search of authentic problems and workable solutions, born of deeper and deeper questions. For example, some persons are gravely concerned about the influx of migrant workers in America and the consequent lessening of employment for American citizens. But our minds are made to go out to ask bigger questions: namely, *why* are migrant workers streaming into America in such great numbers in the first place? And the answer, one which reveals bigger and more global questions, is the misery and poverty in their own land. Therefore the only true solution to "illegal aliens" is a global perspective on employment, unemployment and poverty. Reasserting nationalistic boundaries is a band-aid solution at best. It is thoroughly non-intellectual. Rhetorical invocations of nationalistic pietisms are mere emotional fodder. Compassion is more whole-oriented and more globally concerned than are platitudes of narrow patriotism.

There is no room for anti-intellectualism in the compassionate person—in fact, as Anne Douglas observes, all sentimentalism is rooted in the fear of ideas and in anti-intellectualism. This "death of the critical instinct" is endemic to all sentimentalism, she warns, and she cites the following example from Eva, the heroine of Harriet Stowe's popular and sentimental novel of the nineteenth century, who was wrestling with Darwin's theories. Says Eva: "I think it is a good deal easier to believe in the Garden of Eden story, especially as that's pretty and poetical, and is in the dear old Book that is so sweet and comfortable to us" (251). Notice too the laziness inherent in anti-intellectualism. It is "easier" to believe in prettiness than to relate ideas of science to compassion. Putting the intellectual life to work to serve compassion and celebrating compassion will take work, effort, discipline and even asceticism at times. But there is no other way for compassion to be learned. Understanding is the product of work and not superficiality. Understanding, warns Scheler, is not born of either shallow imitation or projective empathy—these give birth only to a "delusive understanding." True understanding is the "primary component" of compassion for Scheler and it is born of truth, not ignorance or stupidity. (12) There is an intellectual and rational component to compassion that, if ignored, will confuse the energies of compassion with the kind of infatuation or identification that a schoolboy displays who falls in love with his teacher. Identification is not compassion warns Scheler.

COMPASSION IS NOT RELIGION BUT A WAY OF LIFE, I.E., A SPIRITUALITY

I heard a particularly stimulating lecture this past year by an expert on Jewish spirituality. The opening was especially memorable: "Christians must learn," the speaker said, "that Judaism is not a religion but a way of life." Indeed, they must! And how differently human history would have read these past 2000 years had Christians known exactly that: that Judaism *and* Christianity are meant to be ways of life and not religions. The early Christians followed the lead of Jesus and never spoke of themselves as a religion. Instead, in the *Book of Acts* which is the first book Christians wrote about themselves, Christianity is called "the Way" on numerous occasions (Acts 9.2; 18.25; 19.9; 23; 22.4; 24.14, 22). On all these occasions the early Church called itself a Way—but never a religion.

What is the difference between a Way and a Religion? I believe that a Way of life or a spirituality is the living that spiritual people engage in, whereas religion is what empires need to sustain themselves. General Montgomery in his *Memoirs* comments on how the British Empire could not have been the "great" event it was without the religion of the Church of England that sustained it. One need only visit the heart of that religion, the Cathedral of St. Paul in London, to see the truth of what is being said. Lining the walls are tomb after tomb of British Generals who are extolled for their victories over the infidel natives of India, complete with the numbers of Indians that each General killed at such and such a battle. Yes, empires do need religion. Which may account for one solid reason why religion is on the decrease today (do people sense empires are obsolete?) and spiritualities or ways of living in depth are on the increase.

The distinction between religion and a way or spirituality also helps to explain why, during the Constantinian era of Christianity, which was a marriage of empire and church who were betrothed in 312 with the edict of Milan, there has been so little interest in compassion as integral to spirituality. Empires, you may have noticed, and empire-builders, have very little use or interest in compassion. Other priorities count for much more. It also explains why I or anyone else studying compassion in the West would have to rely so heavily on Jewish spirituality—for the Israelites have never been empire-builders. Indeed they have very often been on the receiving end of the aggression of empire-builders. Their tradition has not lost touch with the Way called Compassion. Compassion, which hardly belongs to religion at all, is the very centerpiece of Biblical spirituality.

Two scientifically developed studies on compassion among religious people, one done by a psychologist and another by a sociologist, have concluded independently of each other that no correlation exists between religion and compassion in contemporary society. Thus the psychologist William Eckhardt writes: "Compassion was not consistent with conventional religiosity . . . (as) conceived and practiced in our culture today" and "compassionate theists are in the minority . . . in the Western world today" (pp. 265, 262). Eckhardt does see, however, a connection between compassion and the teachings of Judaism and Christianity and other great faiths as they were originally taught. James A. Christenson's study on "Religious Involvement, Values, and Social Compassion" concludes that "people who regularly attend church exhibit no greater social compassion than those who do not attend. However, stronger adherence to religious values has a consistently positive relationship with social compassion issues."[31] Both these studies seem to be putting the question: What is the relationship between religiosity or church-going and this Way taught by a Jesus, a Moses or an Amos? What intervened between the lives and teachings of these individuals and those who claim to follow after them? I propose that what has intervened is a commitment to religion in so far as it serves empire-builders and that this commitment has taken precedence over a way of living called compassion. Empire builders are notoriously slow to welcome compassionate persons, much less encourage compassion among the peoples of an empire. Compassionate people do not make docile citizens.

Judaism as a compassionate way of life

Rabbi Dressner has underscored how basic compassion is to the Jewish way of life or spirituality. In that way of life "compassion was a cornerstone and mercy the other side of every act of justice" (236).

Taught to walk in the ways of God who is the Compassionate One, Jews were called *rahamanim benei rahamanim*—"compassionate ones and the children of the compassionate ones" (Yev. 79a). To be compassionate as God is compassionate is to perform the *imitatio dei*, the imitation of God. "Just as God is called compassionate and gracious, so you must be compassionate and gracious, giving gifts freely" (Sif. Deut. 49). The Rabbis exhort the people in the following manner: "Even as God is compassionate and merciful, and is called just and loving, so be you compassionate and merciful, just and loving." [32] Compassion is meant to be the characteristic mark or sign of the Jew. Moses Maimonides declared, "The descendents of Abraham, benefiting, too, by the gift of the Torah, are compassionate and merciful towards all." [33]

Compassion is truly a walking in the way of the Lord for the Jewish people, walking in the way of the divine attribute that is compassion. Thus Rabbi Hama ben Hanina says: "It is written: *After the Lord your God shall ye walk.* How are we to understand this? Is it possible for a man to walk after the presence of God? Is it not written: *For the Lord thy God is a devouring fire?* What it means is that we shall walk after the attributes of the Holy One, blessed be he." (in D, p. 193) God's compassion points the way to humanity's compassion as a spirituality which becomes the art of walking in God's way. This way takes over at a deep, more than conscious level. It becomes an entire attitude toward life, a consciousness or spirituality. "When we are aware" of compassion, remarks Rabbi Dressner, "not necessarily in any conscious fashion, but in the intuitive style of our living—then we are no longer encased in the armor of our own ego, utterly consumed by our own cares, utterly unbound by the bond which joins each man to his neighbor and all men to God" (202).

More than that, when compassion becomes our spirituality, God's waiting and God's pain ceases. God's compassion, which waits for people to show compassion, is now let loose. And God's prayer—which is itself a prayer for compassion—is heard. For God prays: "May it be My will that My compassion might overcome Mine anger and prevail over my justice, that I might deal with my children according to the attribute of compassion" (in D, 239).

Jesus' teaching of compassion as a way of life

It is evident from what has gone before that Jesus' teaching on compassion derives much if not all of its insight from the matrix of Jewish spirituality in which he was born, raised and nourished. His admonition in Luke (6.36) to "be compassionate as your Father is compassionate" is identical to Jewish admonitions we have just considered, with the slight alteration that was so characteristic of Jesus: namely his calling God "Father." We have already considered in the section above how, like the Jewish prophets before him, Jesus insisted on compassion's being an action of justice, a *mispat*, a deed of love and justice. "Happy the compassionate: they shall have compassion shown them" declares Jesus (Mt. 5.7). Compassion breeds compassion.

Two words are used in the Gospels in expressing Jesus' experience of compassion and his teaching about compassion. The first, *eleeo*, we have seen already. It is used by the sick and suffering who appeal to Jesus for relief from their pain. Examples of such instances are found when two blind men followed him shouting, "Take pity on us, Son of David" (Mt. 9.27); when the Canaanite woman implores for her daughter, saying, "Sir, Son of David, take pity on me. My daughter is tormented by a devil" (Mt. 15.22); when the father of the epileptic demoniac boy appeals to Jesus, saying: "But if you can do anything, have pity on us and help us" (Mk. 9.22); and when the ten lepers approached him crying: "Jesus! Master! Take pity on us" (Lk. 17.13). And other instances as well (Mt. 17.15; Mt. 18.33; 20.30–34; Mk. 5.19; 10.47; Lk. 18.38).

The second word used in the Gospels apropos of Jesus' compassion is the Greek word *splanchnizomai*, which means literally "to be moved in one's bowels." We have seen this understanding of the experience of compassion to be a basic Jewish grasp of the experience. This is the word used to express how Jesus responded to these cries for mercy and compassion and so we are told time and time again that Jesus was "moved in his bowels—i.e. that he had pity and compassion." [34] Some examples of Jesus' being moved to compassion are the following: He was preaching in the towns "and when he saw the crowds he felt sorry for them because they were harassed and dejected, like sheep without a shepherd" (Mt. 9.36). He multiplied the loaves and fishes after the following incident: "But Jesus called his disciples to him and said, 'I feel sorry for all these people; they have been with me for three days and have nothing to eat.'" (Mt. 15.32) When two blind men approached him we are told: "Jesus felt pity for them and touched their eyes, and immediately their sight returned and they followed him" (Mt. 20.34). When a leper asked to be cured we are told that Jesus, "feeling sorry for him, streched out his hand and touched him" and he was cured (Mk. 1.40). When he saw the widow Nain grieving over her son's death, he "saw her and felt sorry for her. 'Do not cry' he said" and he commanded him to get up which he did (Lk. 7.13ff). All these examples of Jesus being moved in his bowels to compassion—as well as others not listed here (eg., Mt. 14.14; 18.27; Mk. 6.34; 8.2; Lk.10.33; 15.20)—have two characteristics about them: First they result in his acting to relieve the pain of others. And secondly, it is the pain of others, very often expressed as such—"Have mercy on me"—for example, or by tears, that moves Jesus to his bowels in compassion.

It is evident that Jesus was a compassionate person and that people approached him for exactly that purpose, because they were seeking compassion. The Gospel writers identified this compassion of Jesus with its being a divine attribute in him as is clear in the restoring of the son of the widow of Nain to life: There, for the first time in Luke's Gospel, Jesus is called "Lord." The sentence reads: "When the Lord saw her he felt compassion for her." (Lk. 7:13) This title of "Lord" has been strictly reserved to Yahweh up to this time. Thus Jesus becomes the Son of the Compassionate One for Christians. Jesus is compassion incarnate, compassion made flesh and historical. Jesus becomes the Son of God, the Son of the Compassionate One.

Jesus urges those who believe in him and his Father to become compassionate themselves. This is evident in his parable of the good Samaritan (Lk. 10.29-37), which marries compassion with active relief of others' pain; his parable of the prodigal son (Lk. 15. 11–32), which marries compassion with celebration; and in the parable of the unforgiving debtor (Mt. 18. 23–35), which links compassion to pardon and forgiveness.

Moreover, as we shall see below, compassion is meant to be a way of life, a way of thinking in the Lord, for Jesus and his followers. His Sermon on the Mount and his beatitudes become the culmination of his teaching on compassion and his teaching on how to live. And this is how the first Christians understood his teaching of "the way"—that it be a way of walking in justice and compassion. In Galatians (5.13–25) Paul identifies "to walk in the spirit" (v. 25) with "by means of love serve one another" (v. 13). [35] Spirit is contrasted to flesh in Paul *not* as Greek asceticism plus Irish Jansenism has interpreted it, namely as non-material vs. sensual, but as a kind of walking that only lacks the attribute of divine compassion. "'To be carnal' is the same as 'to walk according to the man' *(kata anthropos peripatein)*." (M, 225) Carnality is the opposite of the "Spirit of God"—it is the jealous and competitive spirit of the world, (1 Cor. 2.12, 3.3) i.e. a spirit lacking in compassion. In John's Gospel and letters, as we have seen, there is this same stress on compassion as the heart of Jesus' personhood and teaching. When Jesus says in John 17: "This is eternal life: to know the Father" he is employing a technical term for doing justice just as the prophets understood it. "The meaning of 'to know Yahweh' is thus all the more clear, almost like a technical term: to have compassion for the needy and to do justice for them." (M, 48)

And so we see that, in the Biblical view of things, both from the Hebrew Bible and the New Testament which owes so much of its teaching of compassion to the Hebrew Bible, knowledge of God is very different from "acts of religion." (M, 47) Knowledge of the compassionate God is concerned first of all with the *imitatio dei* which is walking in the way of the Compassionate One. Jesus tried to emphasize this basic Jewish teaching and became, in the eyes of his followers, an incarnation of this way. An incarnation of Compassion. Have his followers followed that way? Might they?

COMPASSION IS NOT A MORAL COMMANDMENT BUT A FLOW AND OVERFLOW OF THE FULLEST HUMAN AND DIVINE ENERGIES

Compassion is not the eleventh commandment. Why not? Because it is, as we have seen, a spirituality and a way of living and walking through life. It is the way we treat all there is in life—our selves, our bodies, our imaginations and dreams, our neighbors, our enemies, our air, our water, our earth, our animals, our death, our space and our time. Compassion is a spirituality as if creation mattered. It is treating all creation as holy and as divine. . . which is what it is.

Those prone to building ethical systems or to moralizing will not be at home with the way of living called compassion. For compassion is not an ethical system. It is, as we have just seen, the fullest experience of God that is humanly possible. While it includes ethics, as all true spirituality must, it blossoms and balloons to something greater than ethics—to celebration of life and relief, where possible, of others' pain. Compassion is the breakthrough between God and humans. It is humans' becoming divine and recovering and remembering their divine origins as "images and likenesses" of God. When the Creator made us, God "breathed a portion of His breath into us. Each of us has a share in that breath. Each of us is a 'portion of the divine from on high.' Every soul is joined to every other soul by its origin in the Creator of all souls." [36] It is the "truth of all truths," Rabbi Dressner declares, "that every man is our brother, that we are all children of one Father, all sheep of one Shepherd, all creations of one Creator, all parts of one infinite, gracious spirit that pervades and sustains all of mankind." And he goes further in his grasp of what is at stake in compassion. "We are not only brothers under one Father, but all the very same brother, all the very same man, all part of one universal man" (D202f.). Compassion then becomes the "love of man for his fellow man, which is God's love for all men" (194f.).

The breakthrough in compassion is the break from dualistic and separatist thinking and acting. This separation is manifest at every level of existence, including that of human as distinct from divine existence. Compassion heals this wound, for it refuses to separate love of God from love of neighbor and experiences both at once. According to Matthew (22.37–40) Jesus taught exactly this: That the "law and the prophets" could be summarized in two great commandments, love of God and love of neighbor. By simply operating out of the Hebrew sources that Jesus himself knew so well, Rabbi Dressner sheds light on this New Testament teaching of compassion. He says:

> The possibility of fulfilling the commandment, *Love thy neighbor as thyself,* is only understood when we read the next phrase which follows it in the Bible, *I am the Lord.* Thus God tells us, *Thou shalt love thy neighbor as thyself* because *I am the Lord.* That is to say, because your self and his are bound up in Me; because you are not really distinct and competing beings, but together share in the one existence; because ultimately you are no 'self' and he no 'neighbor,' but one in source and destiny. Because I love you both, you shall love Me in him as yourself. (D, 201)

Matthew's Gospel quotes Jesus as summarizing the law and the prophets when he says, "Whatever you want people to do to you, do this to them" (7.12). Miranda observes that Matthew "takes it for granted that the God of Israel is loved in the love of neighbor" (70). And Paul reduces these two commandments to just one: "The whole of the law is summarized in a single command: 'Love your neighbor as yourself' " (Gal. 5.14). For Paul, as for John, love of neighbor is the name for love of God (1 Cor. 8.1–3). Compassion is one energy, divine and human. "Love one another, as I have loved you so that you might love one another," Jesus is cited as saying in John's Gospel (13.34). It is our works of compassion and love of neighbor that will constitute the dwelling of God among us—"if we love one another, God dwells in us." (1 Jn. 4.12) It also constitutes the presence of Christ after his going away. Kitamori comments that the two commandments that Jesus spoke of are in fact one as if one target were placed on another and a person were to shoot both targets with just one arrow. He "cannot help thinking that love of God and love of neighbor are two yet one, at the same time. . . . Because God is immanent in our neighbor, love of neighbor becomes love of God. Similarly, because the pain of God is immanent in the pain of reality, service for the pain of reality can become service for the pain of God" (99).

There is still another way in which morality and compassion as spirituality must be distinguished, and this concerns that tradition in spirituality regarding the "quest for perfection." This tradition bases its language ostensibly on Mt. 5.48, where Jesus is reported to say: "Be you perfect as your heavenly Father is perfect." However, the word often translated as "perfect" "does not have here the later Greek meaning of being 'totally free of imperfections' " and above all it "does not refer to moral perfection." [37] Instead, to be perfect is to be about truth and sincerity and being a "true" person. For this reason W.F. Albright translates the passage: "Be true, just as your heavenly Father is true." What is evident is that this line is the final summary of Matthew's entire chapter on the Beatitudes and the parallel saying in Luke also occurs in the context of his Beatitudes. Luke says: "Be you compassionate as your heavenly Father is compassionate." (Lk. 6.36) Both Matthew and Luke precede this injunction with the admonition to "love your enemies." Thus it can be said with certitude that the Biblical meaning of spiritual perfection is to be compassionate. It does not mean to attain some kind of static state of moral purity and perfection. Indeed, this is the conclusion Albright comes to when he cites a rabbinic commentary from the first-century A.D. which says: "Be like him. As he is gracious and merciful, so be you gracious and merciful." Jesus is recalling in down-to-earth terms (including love of enemies) this basic Jewish commandment.

Compassion, then, becomes the fullest experience of the spiritual life. It and it alone deserves to be called transcendence and even contemplation. For in relieving the lot of the pained we are truly 'contemplating,' i.e., gazing on God and working with God. "When you do it to one of these little ones, you do it to me" (Mt. 25.40) said Jesus so simply. Compassion is a flow in our walking in justice and even an overflow. It takes us far beyond imperatives. It takes us to where Jesus promised it would take us: "That all might be one, Father, even as I am one in you and you are one in me" (Jn. 17.21). The oneness indicated is not a oneness of mind alone but of action and of deep feeling and of celebration. A oneness of compassion.

While it is important not to reduce spirituality and a spirituality of compassion to mere moral norms and principles, it is also important to emphasize the integration of morality and spirituality. For in the fully developed individual and in a truly spirit-filled society, morality will become a way of living or a spirituality. When will this happen? It happens when compassion truly takes over. Then morality (justice-making) and spirituality (a way of living lives of justice and of celebration of justice) become one.

COMPASSION IS NOT ALTRUISM, BUT SELF-LOVE AND OTHER-LOVE AT ONE

Altruism has come to mean in common usage the love of another at the expense of oneself. Instead of loving others *as* we love ourselves, the degenerated use of the term "altruism" implies that we love others *instead of* loving ourselves. If this be the operative meaning of altruism today, then compassion is surely not altruistic. For the entire insight upon which compassion is based is that the other is *not* other; and that I am *not* I. In other words, in loving others I am loving myself and indeed involved in my own best and biggest and fullest self-interest. It is my pleasure to be involved in the relief of the pain of others, a pain which is also my pain and is also God's pain. Altruism as it is commonly understood presumes dualisms, separateness and ego differences that the compassionate person is aware are not fundamental energies at all.

Today an even more pressing need exists for recognizing how compassion is to everyone's own best interest and that is the issue of the survival of our common global village. If compassion is the best and perhaps only route to common survival, if it is true, as William Eckhardt maintains that "the world is dying from lack of compassion," (p. 1), then compassion is not altruism in the sense of loving others who are different from ourselves. It *is* loving ourselves while we love others. It is loving the possibilities of love and survival. It is one love that permeates all.

SUMMARY

To say that compassion is the fullest experience of the spiritual life seems an observation foreign to the mainstream of Christian spirituality which has for so long taught us to seek "the quest for perfection" rather than the quest for compassion. Everything depends on what one means by 'perfection' in this instance. It is clear where much Christian spirituality got its meaning of perfection—from hellenistic and gnostic definitions of perfection and not from the Bible. For this entire chapter, relying as it does on Biblical interpretation, has demonstrated that perfection for the Jews meant to "be perfect as your heavenly Father is perfect"—which in turn meant compassionate. For compassion is the divine attribute that we are instructed to pursue with all diligence and energy. Alongside of the saying to "be perfect as your heavenly Father is perfect," Jesus says: "Be compassionate as your Father is compassionate." Spiritual perfection means compassion and nothing less and nothing else.

Might one even say that, given the Biblical teaching on the Godhead as compassionate, that Jesus is not so much compassionate because he is divine as he is divine because he is compassionate? And did he, whom Christians believe is the incarnation of compassion, the Son of the Compassionate One, not teach others that they too were to be sons and daughters of Compassion? Sons and daughters of God? And therefore divine because they are compassionate?

We have seen that compassion without joy and celebration, without action and public justice-making, without ideas and ideals, without passion and caring, without a consciousness or a way of living, without cosmic and divine awareness and interaction, is not compassion at all. It is a co-optation of compassion. It is a demonic substitute for compassion. It is death-dealing, not lifegiving. All these elements of compassion are themselves interconnected, and to fail in one of these is to threaten compassion altogether for each energy depends on the others, much like spokes on a wheel. (See Figure A)

These Biblical insights into the meaning of compassion will continue to flow through the remaining chapters of this book. What might be attempted here is a summary "definition" of compassion. Compassion may be a passionate way of living born of an awareness of the interconnectedness of all creatures by reason of their common Creator. To be compassionate is to incorporate one's own fullest energies with cosmic ones into the twin tasks of 1) relieving the pain of fellow creatures by way of justice-making, and 2) celebrating the existence, time and space that all creatures share as a gift from the only One who is fully Compassion. Compassion is our kinship with the universe and the universe's Maker; it is the action we take because of that kinship. No wonder Meister Eckhart, who so outshines the popular but sentimental spirituality of Thomas à Kempis, could declare as he did: "You may call God love; you may call God goodness; but the best name for God is Compassion."

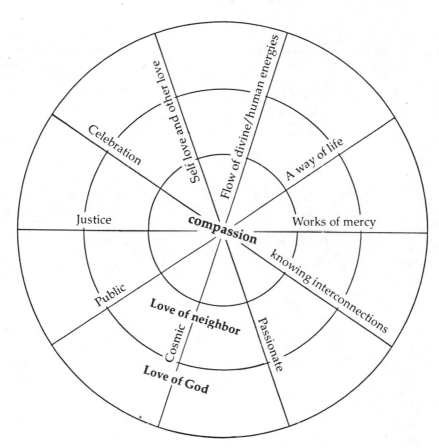

FIGURE A. All elements of compassion are interconnected like spokes on a wheel.

2

SEXUALITY AND COMPASSION:

FROM CLIMBING JACOB'S LADDER TO DANCING SARAH'S CIRCLE

We are dancing Sarah's circle,
We are dancing Sarah's circle,
We are dancing Sarah's circle,
sisters, brothers all.

Every ring gets fuller, fuller
Every ring gets fuller, fuller
Every ring gets fuller, fuller
sisters, brothers all.

Instead of a quest for compassion Christian spirituality has given us a quest for perfection and Western society has left us a quest for success. What price have we paid for these compulsive quests? "The almost total erosion of the interpersonal from the public sector of our life," responds ethician Beverly Harrison. Harrison urges that, if we are "to mobilize ourselves to do anything serious about it, we had better look again to see what the devastating strains between male and female in this society are *really* about." [1] The exile of compassion has left us with a sexually one-sided spirituality in which the prevailing patriarchal presumptions exclude nurturing, caring and earthiness. In such a situation men and their institutions become "dangerous to children and other living things, themselves included," [2] and women, insofar as they conform to this erosion of the interpersonal, become their own worst victims. In this chapter I want to explore what devastating sexual strains are "really about" in the history of Western spirituality. To do this I will analyze two contrasting symbols for the spiritual experience: That of climbing Jacob's ladder and that of dancing Sarah's circle.

CLIMBING JACOB'S LADDER

A major cause for compassion's having played so much smaller a role in Christian spirituality than it did in Jesus' teaching and spirituality is that Jacob's ladder has played so powerful a role. There is no theme in all of male-dominated mystical teaching in Western Christianity that is more recurrent than that of climbing Jacob's ladder. As one scholar has put it: "The theme of the ladder is constant, indeed capital, in the spiritual life and in the history of spirituality." [3] He should have said "in *my* understanding of the spiritual life and in the history of *western* spirituality." In the *Dictionnaire de Spiritualite*, an encyclopedia of numerous volumes dedicated to Western Spirituality, the entry under "spiritual ladder" comprises twenty-four full columns and includes an apology from the author for the treatment being only partial.

The Jewish tradition

Why this emphasis on ladder-climbing as spiritual progress? What does Jacob's dream have to do with spiritual growth? First, let us read the story on which spiritual writers have projected so much of their images and energies. Jacob's dream is recorded in the twenty-eighth chapter of Genesis:

> Jacob left Beersheba and set out for Haran. When he had reached a certain place he passed the night there, since the sun had set. Taking one of the stones to be found at that place, he made it his pillow and lay down where he was. He had a dream: a ladder was there, standing on the ground with its top reaching to heaven; and there were angels of God go-

ing up it and coming down. And Yahweh was there, standing over him, saying, 'I am Yahweh, the God of Abraham your father, and the God of Isaac. I will give to you and your descendents the land on which you are lying. Your descendents shall be like the specks of dust on the ground; you shall spread to the west and the east, to the north and south, and all the tribes of the earth shall bless themselves by you and your descendents. Be sure that I am with you; I will keep you safe wherever you go; I have done all that I have promised you.' Then Jacob awoke from his sleep and said, 'Truly, Yahweh is in this place and I never knew it!' He was afraid and said, 'How awe-inspiring this place is! This is nothing less than a house of God; this is the gate of heaven!' Rising early in the morning, Jacob took the stone he had used for his pillow, and set it up as a monument, pouring oil over the top of it. He named the place Bethel, but before that the town was called Luz. (Gen. 28. 10–19)

It does not take a degree in Hebraic studies to grasp the meanings of this passage about Jacob's dream. It is a promise from his God that Jacob will have progeny that will be numerous and will spread themselves in every direction; that safety understood as a return to the land is part of the promise; that the dream is so transcendent to Jacob that he feels he has slept in a holy place with a rock for a pillow and so he memorializes the place by the pouring of oil and the naming of Beth El meaning "house of God." This is the solid and evident interpretation of Jacob's dream and this is how the Jewish people have interpreted it for centuries. For example, the following Jewish commentary:

Jacob's precipitate flight from Beer-Sheba found him at sunset at a place in which he experienced a dream theophany. He saw angels going up and down a stairway which spanned heaven and earth. He then heard the Lord reiterate the promises of the land and numerous progeny that He had made to Abraham and Isaac. His offspring would be a source of blessing to the whole earth; he would enjoy divine protection wherever he would be, and would return one day to the land from which he was fleeing. Jacob awoke from his sleep, startled to discover the presence of God in that place, which he thereupon dedicated as a sacred site, renaming it Beth-El.[4]

Examples of the ladder in Christian mysticism

Male Christian mystics, late on the scene since the Jews had Jacob's dream many centuries before the Christians considered it, did something totally other with this progeny-oriented, land-oriented, close-to-the-earth dream. They used it as symbol of fleeing the earth in order to experience a transcendent, i.e., up-like God. They interpreted it as an upward climb to God and away from the earth. Thus Pseudo-Alcuin writes, "The superior part of us seeks the heavens but the inferior remains clinging to the earth."[5] Alan of Lille writes, "We pass from earth to heaven by this ladder" (in D 5, 82). And Gregory of Nyssa writes that:

> It was the virtuous life which was shown to the Patriarch under the figure of the ladder, in order that he himself might learn and also impart to his descendents, that one can ascend to God only if one always looks upwards and has a ceaseless desire for the things above ... Jacob saw God enthroned upon a ladder. To participate in the Beatitudes is nothing more than to participate in the Deity, to whom the Lord leads us up by means of what has been said.[6]

Gregory in this same passage invents at least nine phrases for "ascent" and insists that we "climb up to God's majesty". Prayer for Gregory is sprouting wings that will leave behind all that is material and corporeal. "I leave the whole earth beneath me, cross the whole intervening ocean of air, reach the beauty of the ether and ascend to the stars and behold their wonderful order!"[7]

It has been said that "Gregory's great and ever-recurrent theme is fellowship with God according to the scheme of ascent" (N, 432). And so it is. Not only does he interpret Jacob's dream in this manner but he does the same thing to the life of Moses and to the beatitudes of Jesus which according to him were given from a mountaintop.

> Those who wish to ascend a stair raise themselves, when they have mounted the first step, from that to the next, this in turn to the next. And in this way he who ascends finally arrives, by always raising himself from the step on which he is to the next one, at the top step. Why do I begin with this introduction? It seems to me that the Beatitudes are arranged as the rungs of a ladder, and this makes the successive ascent easy of contemplation.[8]

His commentary on the *Song of Songs* is said to "swarm with expressions for the soul's ascent to God" (p. 433 n. 6) and in his commentary on the Psalms he says that the five books of the Psalter represent five stages *up* to the Divine Life. Augustine too insists that upness is divine and down-ness is the demonic. In fairness to some other spiritual traditions, especially that of Thomas Aquinas and Meister Eckhart, both Dominican, it should be noted that they did *not* buy into the mentality of "degrees of contemplation signified by the ladder." [9] Eckhart says "down is up and up is down" which, obviously, destroys ladder-thinking. This less vertical spirituality claimed few adherents, however, in Christian spiritual history.

It is important to remember that while Christian spirituality encyclopedias give over 24 columns to the "spiritual ladder," Jewish ones do not even have a single entry under a ladder title. This, despite the fact that Jacob was a Jew and the Jews possessed his dream a thousand years before Christians reflected on it. Another dimension to this rank projection and eisegesis on Jacob's dream is the role of compassion in this upwardly mobile prayer life. In fact, contemplation is won *at the expense* of compassion in such a schema. Thus Pseudo-Bernard confesses that "we climb to God by contemplation and descend to neighbor by compassion." [10] Thus compassion is descent; it is also an afterthought, a luxury that one can afford only after a very long life-time of contemplative ascending. Compassion is thus put in competition with ascending or contemplation. Richard of Saint Laureant, writing in the thirteenth century, seconds this notion. Says he: "The summit of the ascent is the contemplation of God; the descent is compassion and pity toward men. By this ladder, we go from earth to sky".[11] Looking at the diagram (figure A) of this symbol for the spiritual life, one can see how the passage to God and eventually to neighbor (presuming one

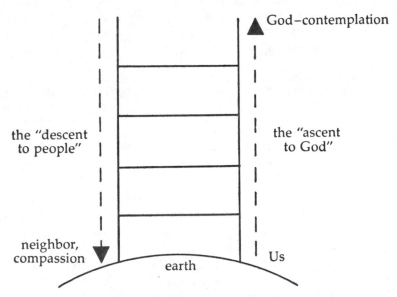

FIGURE A. The Climbing of Jacob's Ladder is unfortunately *the* dominant mystical symbol in Christian mysticism.

lives long enough) is like a very long game of pachisi with the descent-to-neighbor called compassion a very late experience in the game indeed.

Where did Christian mystics get this "up" oriented motif in their vision of the spiritual journey? It is derived from hellenistic and not biblical sources. It is, for example, the dynamic of Plato's ways of conceiving of our experience of reality, and the upward journey is also a journey into abstractions, as Boman points out. "Plato starts from the individual concrete thing, always thinking more generally, more abstractly, and more mentally, and *mounting ever higher* until he sees the prototypes of all appearances, the Ideas." [12] The Greeks looked *up* because they were eye-oriented and architecture was their paradigm for all reality. You build buildings from the ground *upward*. Perfection is upward. There can be no question that this drive upwards in the name of spirituality is a drive away from body, earth, matter, mother, the sensual. We will consider this more in Chapter Five, but it is of such great importance in spirituality that I have written an entire book about it, namely *Whee! We, wee All the Way Home: A Guide to the New Sensual Spirituality*.

In contrast, for the Jewish mind, which considered hearing to be the most important sense and music the paradigm of reality, a spiritual person grows ever more sensitive to those *around* one. God is not spatially up but in one's midst. "And I will know that I am the Lord their God, who brought them forth out of the land of Egypt that I might dwell among them" (Ex. 29.45f.). Amongness, not upness, is the dynamic of the spiritual journey. Divine Transcendence is not spatial but temporal for the Jew. The question is not so much *where* God is as *when* will the people allow God to be among them? Nor is Jewish spirituality involved in flights from the body or the earth or sensuality. Jewish spirituality is squarely in the midst of the earthiness of ourselves. It is not afraid of what appear to be the "imperfections" of the material and created universe. Adrienne Rich advises:

Let us return to imperfection's school.
No longer wandering after Plato's ghost.[13]

SOME CONSEQUENCES OF JACOB'S LADDER

Worship as worshup

What are the consequences of this dominant motif of ladder-climbing as contemplation of God? One is that worship has become worsh*up* in the West. In Roman Catholicism, up until Vatican II, each rung on the ladder represented a different form of worship: there was a low Mass, a High Mass, a Solemn High Mass, a Pontifical Solemn High Mass, etc., and each rung cost you a bit more as you rose up the ladder. Vatican II, by eliminating these rung-like degrees of worship, did a radical thing, for it took Liturgy off the ladder dominated mystical schema that had so long influenced it. I used to think that only Roman Catholics were born into worsh*up* attitudes until recently when I was invited to preach in several Protestant pulpits around our country. In climbing up, up, up to the awesome heights that some of those pulpits demanded, looking down, down, down on the people of God, I truly felt fortunate to get away without a nosebleed. It dawned on me how thoroughly both Protestants and Catholics have been committed to the up-ward spiritual motif of our ancestors. Worship as worsh*up*. Our urging of people to look up to worsh*up*; to look up and shut up. To look up and stay down. How powerful are our symbols—and how worn and wrong. For Jacob's dream, as we have seen, was about no such energy whatsoever.

Pedestal pieties

Still another consequence of the symbol of Jacob's ladder in Christian spirituality is that of pedestal piety. Worship as worsh*up* enforces and reinforces a pedestal piety wherein people are instructed to look *up* to venerate heroes, saints, success and upness. Those who are the furthest down the ladder, for example, women, are very often elevated the highest as a sort of spiritualized compensation for what they are missing. Psychologist Karen Horney warns of what is truly at stake behind this pedestal piety toward women. "Men who wish secretly to hurt and spurn women may in their conscious thought put them on a high pedestal." [14] In fact, all forms of pedestal piety rob persons of their own responsibility to create dynamics of equality for themselves and others. Pedestals enslave those they pretend to honor and they divert energies upward where they are easily scattered and lost that should be invested inward and outward. In fact, one does not honor those who went before by elevating them but by, if anything, standing on their shoulders and working and living where they left off. What is assured, for example, by putting saints on pious pedestals is that the true conflicts and courage of their lives will never really interact with our own. Pedestal pietisms make abstractions of all who are placed thereon. And, what is worse, of those who internalize such kind of worship.

Psychologist Karen Horney points out an even more dangerous dimension lurking behind pedestal pieties. What is really being encouraged is masochism, for the masochist despises his own weakness and "adores" the strengths of others, feeding on them, and all the time resenting their strength and becoming more and more hostile. And from this masochism, sadism is born (257, 164).

Justice as judgment, mercy as pity

Still another consequence of the ladder symbolism in the West has been the separation of compassion or mercy from justice. Mercy came to mean a buffer between God and the poorest of the poor at the bottom of the ladder. Why was this so? Because, as the ladder-top people became the ones to define justice more and more for us, then the God of justice was turned into a God of Judgment. If God is a Judge, reigning on high (at the top of the ladder) and passing down stern judgments especially to those most distant from the top, namely the poorest and weakest in a culture, then the "little ones" need a buffer between God and them. And mercy became that buffer.

However, and this is where Biblical thinking is so important, God is *not* judge but the "Savior from oppression" for the little ones or *anawim*. The Christian empire distorted the Jewish words for justice, namely *saphat* and *mispat*, translating them as "judgment," when in fact they meant "justice." Jose Miranda says that "the true meaning of *saphat* is not 'to judge' but rather 'to do justice to the weak and oppressed' " (M, 113). Mercy, then, does not have to enter between the divine Judge and the people; for God, the justice-maker, is already among the people, if you will, at the foot of the ladder. Mercy (*mispat; hesed*) and compassion *mean* justice. Mercy is not a tempering of judgment but a bringing about of justice. Thus the Psalmist sings: "Do justice to the orphan and the oppressed, so that earthborn man may strike fear no longer" (Ps. 10). This is the meaning of mercy, to do justice.

The Dutch theologian Father Schillebeeckx has declared that "Transcendence is no longer up. It is the future." We celebrate the end of up-spirituality, of climbing, of worship, of pedestal piety, of God as Judge instead of God as justice, of mercy as buffer instead of compassion as justice-making. What will the future be? What new symbol being born is truer both to our spiritual origins and to the demands the future makes of us?

DANCING SARAH'S CIRCLE

I believe that a far richer and more scripturally grounded symbol for our spirituality is that of dancing Sarah's circle. "Dancing Sarah's circle," people ask, "where is that in the Scriptures?" Let us look at what the Scriptures tell us of Sarah. Sarah was ninety years old and Abraham was one hundred when she heard from a visitor that she would bear a child.

> Now Abraham and Sarah were old, well on in years, and Sarah had ceased to have her monthly periods. So Sarah laughed to herself, thinking, 'Now that I am past the age of child-bearing, and my husband is an old man, is pleasure to come my way again?' But Yahweh asked Abraham, 'Why did Sarah laugh and say, "Am I really going to have a child now that I am old?" Is anything too wonderful for Yahweh? At the same time next year I shall visit you again and Sarah will have a son.' 'I did not laugh' Sarah said, lying because she was afraid. But he replied, 'Oh yes, you did laugh.' (Gen. 18. 11–15)

And the surprise event happened.

> Yahweh dealt kindly with Sarah as he had said, and did what he had promised her. So Sarah conceived and bore a son to Abraham in his old age, at the time God had promised. Abraham named the son born to him Isaac, the son to whom Sarah had given birth . . . Then Sarah said, 'God has given me cause to laugh; all those who hear of it will laugh with me.' She added, 'Who would have told Abraham that Sarah would nurse children! Yet I have borne him a child in his old age.' (Gen. 21. 1-4, 6-8)

The name Isaac, given to Sarah's surprise son, means "God has smiled, God has been kind."

Thus a spirituality of Dancing Sarah's circle is one of laughter and joy. Sarah was able to be surprised, filled with unexpected wonder, and to laugh. This already sharply distinguishes her symbol from that of male interpretations of Jacob's dream, since as you may have observed, there is little laughter and joy among those who climb ladders. Ladder-climbing is ever so serious. Ego's are so much involved. A second insight from Sarah's story is that the cause of her laughter is pregnancy. She is a symbol of birthing, creating and fruitfulness—her laughter stemmed from the fact that God's imagination for creativity is so much greater than the human imagination. She laughed because human wisdom said pregnancy was impossible; but divine wisdom said nothing is impossible. Sarah, then, like Mary, the mother of Jesus, was to turn the tables on the strict and serious knowledge that people presume they possess about exactly when and where the boundaries to birth are to be found.

CLIMBING JACOB'S LADDER CONTRASTED TO DANCING SARAH'S CIRCLE

Sarah then is a symbol of laughter and creativity. One might say, of Shalom. But the contrasts between Dancing Sarah's Circle and Climbing Jacob's Ladder is even more telling than that. They can be diagramed as follows:

Climbing Jacob's Ladder	*Dancing Sarah's Circle*
a. up/down	a. in/out
b. Flat Earth	b. Global village
c. Climbing	c. Dancing, celebrating
d. Sisyphian	d. Satisfying
e. Competition	e. Shared ecstasies
f. Restrictive, elitist: Survival of the fittest	f. Welcoming, non-elitist: Survival of all
g. Hierarchical	g. Democratic
h. violent	h. strong and gentle
i. sky-oriented	i. earth-oriented
j. ruthlessly independent	j. Interdependent
k. Jealous and judgment-oriented	k. pride-producing and non-judgmental
l. Abstract, distant-making	l. Nurturing and sensual
m. linear, ladder-like	m. curved, circle-like
n. theistic (immanent or transcendent)	n. panentheistic (transparent)
o. love of neighbor is separate from love of what is at the top	o. love of neighbor *is* love of God

Up/Down, Flat Earth; In/Out, Global Village

The climbing of Jacob's Ladder presumes an up/down way of looking at life and the universe as well as looking at God and neighbor. It accounts for the numerous spiritual thermometer tests that control-oriented spiritual systems have inculcated in their disciples over the years. Are you in the first stage? the second? the third? Even Teresa of Avila's non ladder-like pictures of rooms in a mansion became rungs on a ladder for the ladder-oriented. But the biggest objection to up/down spirituality is that it no longer (if it ever did) makes any sense. For up/down presumes a flat surface, a flat earth and flat heavens. One doesn't put a ladder on a ball. Which is, in fact, the kind of earth and universe we inhabit. Engineer Buckminster Fuller rightly states that "anyone who is still using the words 'up and down' is 500 years out of date." The only group he knows that has adjusted their language and therefore their consciousness accordingly is, he insists, "airplane pilots. When they radio to the control tower they do not say 'now I am flying up and now I am flying down.' They say 'Now I am flying in and now I am flying out.' "

Fuller is absolutely correct. In and out and not up and down are the basic dynamic of our curved earth and curved universe. And, I insist, of our spiritual worlds as much as of our worlds of physics, for the Creator of one is the Creator of the other. The proper dynamic of our spiritual lives is in/out and not up/down. (See Figure B.) In my *Musical, Mystical Bear,* I call the In experience Mysticism, meaning our taking in of the beauties, joys, pleasures of living; and I call the Out experience Prophecy, meaning our going out to re-shape society and history to better mirror the beauty we have received. Would that spiritual persons would enter so fully into Sarah's Dance (in which one is

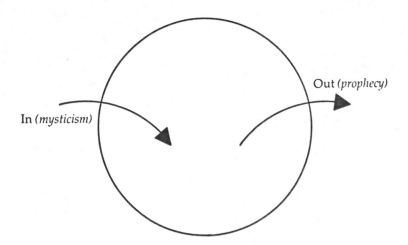

FIGURE B. In-Out (not Up-Down) constitutes the proper dynamic of our physical *and* spiritual lives.

either in or out but not up or down) so that, in the future, Fuller could speak at least about airplane pilots *and* religious believers. It is evident that only a Sarah Dance dynamic is adequate to the energies demanded of a Global Village spirituality.

Climbing, Sisyphusian: Dancing, Satisfying

There is a difference between climbing and dancing. Both take exertion and effort but ladder-climbing implies a Sisyphian experience. There is something intrinsically frustrating about it as was the case with Sisyphus, who was condemned to roll a stone up a hill, and when he arrived near the top the stone always returned to the bottom. In a ladder-climbing dynamic there is this sense of never having arrived. There always seems to loom a new rung or even a new ladder when one appears to have made it all the way up. In contrast, folk dancing is a satisfying exertion. It is satisfying because one never has to leave the earth. Folk dances are earth dances that remind us of our relation to the earth rather than compel us to escape the earth for sky. In folk dancing, a group lets go together. And that, for some mysterious reason, satisfies. It demands much on the part of each individual, but it refreshes instead of enervates.

Another contrast between climbing and dancing is the transformations of person that can happen in the latter activity and that I have never really seen transpire in the climbing dynamic. Once when I was involved in folk dancing with college students on a retreat, the folk dance caller taught us to dance a minuet. I will never forget the astounding transformation of energies that took place when college-aged young men, wearing thick mountain boots, danced a minuet. One can only speculate at what favorable results one might obtain should heads of the USSR, USA, GM and ITT be invited to dance minuets on a regular basis.

Competition: Shared Ecstasies

Competition is built into ladder-climbing. For one thing, only a few can be on the ladder at a time—in fact, if too many crowd on, the entire edifice will fall. Especially is this so near the top—a ladder is very sensitive to being top heavy. And "the bigger they are, the harder they fall," meaning that the higher up one is the more dangerous is the fall. On a ladder one studies one's competition and knows well exactly who is on the rung above and who is pushing from below. Competition and combat are intrinsic to ladder climbing.

In contrast, circle dancing is not about competition at all but about sharing ecstasies. There is always room for another person in a circle and in fact the fun of all is increased, not threatened, by the arrival of a new dancer. Should the circle get too large and unwieldly, then it is a simple matter to break into smaller rings or circles. There are no winners or losers in such a schema—only dancers with the dance in common.

Restrictive, elitist: welcoming, non-elitist

The restrictive character of the ladder (limited as it is to a few survivors or winners) makes for an automatic elitism. The ladder implies survival of the fittest and is proud of it. A circle, on the other hand, can welcome those who in some category of living may not be so fit. The handicapped, for instance, or the aged or the so-called mentally retarded, who in turn are so often emotionally advanced. I recall once being part of a folk dance evening in which the person next to me a good deal of the night was a spastic. He fell often but it was a simple matter for myself holding one of his hands and the person on his other hand to pick him up and keep him very much in the dance. He told me that evening that the day was "the happiest of my life." You may have observed, as I have, that there is little room for handicapped on a ladder that demands that all be ladder-climbers in a game of survival of the fittest. The ladder motif, then, is restrictive and the Circle motif is welcoming and compassionate. So non-elitest is folk spirituality that, as Erich Fromm comments about folk art in modern culture,[15] we don't even have a word for it! Sarah Circle may be that word, however.

Hierarchical, violent: democratic, strong and gentle

The ladder is so full of insecurity that, once persons ascend on high, they are intent on preserving their perches. How is this best achieved? By sacralizing the upness and the rungs of the ladder. The proper name for sacralizing of the ladder is "hierarchy." This word does not come from the word higher but from the word for sacred. Upness is sacred in a hierarchy and becomes the norm for other peoples' acting and interacting. The sacred rungs of the ladder then become untouchable and divinized much like the gods on Mount Olympus who, whatever their sins, remain the gods. Competence and accountability count for nothing when hierarchy is invoked. E.F.

Schumacher comments on how intrinsically violent such upness is, for when you are high up, say in a skyscraper's top floors, those below look very tiny indeed. It is thus very easy to rationalize one's decisions that lead to violence since one never sees the individuals below face to face.

In contrast, a circle dance is intrinsically democratic and non-violent. It is non-violent for two reasons. The first is that, when you are eye to eye as you are when all are on the earth, you can see tears in your neighbor's eyes; and if you have any sense of shared humanity at all, you do not wish to be the cause of those tears. But the second reason why eye-to-eye circle energies are intrinsically gentle is even more compelling: when you are eye to eye what you do to another, that person can do back to you. There is a built-in equalizer in such a situation that does not obtain when persons deal from on high. One might even suggest that if the Creator had intended us to worsh*up* she would have made us with eyes in the top of our heads! Since she did not, it might be a reasonable assumption to conclude that the energy of looking another person in the eye and being looked into, therefore the in/out energy of looking at another, was intended for a significant purpose by the Creator of each of us. Our ears too are evidently not created to hear upwards but in, out and around.

Ruthlessly independent, jealous: interdependent, pride-producing

Another contrast between climbing Jacob's ladder and dancing Sarah's circle is that the first one demands a ruthless independence. Rugged individualism is its basic spirit for survival. Too much care, concern or empathy could only make one tumble. In Sarah's circle, on the other hand, a mutual interdependence is the basic requirement. Now interdependence is not dependence: there are heavy demands made on each and every dancer in the circle but in fact people are too busy making their unique contribution to stand about judging or growing jealous of the contribution of others—an observation that I cannot make of ladder-climbing situations, wherein gossip and envy so often rule. But the fullness of self-exertion in the dance is not measured by others' self-exertion. Rather, a true interdependence is the reigning energy.

When one is climbing a ladder one's hands are occupied with one's own precarious survival and cannot readily be extended to assist others without putting one's climb and even one's life—if one is high enough up on the ladder—into jeopardy. In contrast, when one dances a circular dance one's hands are freed to extend to others in assistance and in celebration. They are also freed to ask for and receive assistance. Perhaps the time has come to celebrate Interdependence Day instead of Independence Day.

Abstract, distant-making: nurturing, sensual

Still another contrast is that ladder-climbing is profoundly abstract. The purpose is to get away from what binds us all, namely the earth, and up to what might set us off from others. It creates distances instead of nearnesses; separates instead of unites. The air gets more rarified as one climbs higher and higher to one's ivory or marble towers. In contrast, the dancing of a circle together implies physical nearness, common smells and exchanges of sweat and smiles, hands meeting hands, all meeting a common earth. It is a nurturing rather than an abstractionist dynamic. Being nurturing, it must needs be sensual. Of the earth, earthy. For it is body and earth that we all share in common—if not in this life then immediately thereafter.

Being nurturing, it is also motherly. In this regard the challenge that feminist thinkers like Adrienne Rich put to men is of profound importance. She urges men to learn mothering, especially of one another and in this way women would be freed to do more than mother men. Rich is alarmed by the way our culture "suppresses the nurturant qualities in men, in children, and in societal institutions." Erica Jong says that for Adrienne Rich "femininism *means* empathy" (sic) and for herself, the feminine means "the nurturant qualities in all people—whatever their sex." [16] Empathy and nurturing—elements of feminism, elements of compassion, elements of earthiness.

Linear, ladder-like: curved, circle-like

There is a big difference between a ladder which is straight and linear and a circle which is rounded, curved and circle-like. One of the biggest contrasts is that the former is artificial—the idea of straightness is not an idea found in nature but only in an abstraction of Euclidean geometry. On a small scale it is useful to our goings-on in our every-day lives, but as a matter of fact it is not harmonious with the way the universe is built. Buckminster Fuller comments that "Physics has found no straight lines, it's found only waves. I find human beings talking about planes and straight lines and so forth that just do not exist." [17] A ladder, then, is an illusion insofar as it is linear.

In contrast, the rounded, the curved and the circular do indeed correspond to the energies of our universe which is curved and to our earth which is rounded. Thus a circle is intrinsically harmonious with the cosmos (witness the therapeutic power of mandala-drawing) and does not conflict with curved energies as ladders do. St. Augustine said that "to be curved is to be sinful," but we know today that to be curved is to be at one with the universe. It is now clear that the Creator of this universe was biased in favor of the curved.

How important it is that Sarah's circle be an open one and not a closed one. The closed circle suggests a return to the womb in an act of withdrawal and search for ultimate security. It is narcissistic and suggests flight from the world. An open circle, in contrast, seeks to make contact with the energies of our origins but is not content to stay there. It moves on into greater and greater circular or spiral energies.

Theistic (immanent or transcendent): panentheistic (transparent)

Jacob's ladder presumes a distance between us and God. This presumption should not be taken for granted by religious believers, based as it is on philosophical categories of subject/object, I/God, you/me, us/God. In fact, while God is not adequately represented by total immanence (that way lies pantheism or the conviction that everything is God and God is everything—an affront to the transcendence and absence of God), still God is wholly present where we are and not up, up and away from us. The classical term for this omnipresence of God wherein God is in all and all is in God is panentheism. The most appropriate symbol or picture of this divine omnipresence is that of a circle of water with fish in it (Figure C). We are the fish; God is the water. We breathe God in and out all day long. We are in God and God is in us. Such a world-view corresponds to Jesus' saying that where "two or three are gathered together in my name, there am I in the midst of them". Not only does God dwell in us but we dwell in God. We do not have to look up to find God. We need simply to wake up to the truth that God has been here all along and very likely our consciousness was blocked up and lacked the simplicity of waking and seeing. The circular dynamic of Sarah's circle corresponds to the in/out energies of panentheism, while the ladder motif of Jacob's ladder corresponds to the God-distinct-from-us motif of theism. The way of Sarah's dance is a simpler, less enervating route. To enter fully into it we need not climb up and up, merely wake fuller and fuller to what is already present and pulsating in our midst.

In theism, separatism is given religious sanction. Dualism is unrepentant. Apartness is raised to the level of a religious presupposition. In panentheism, energies are not presumed to be *apart* but rather *a*

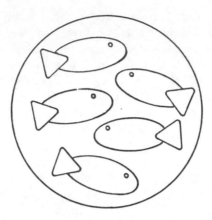

FIGURE C. Panentheism – the proper relationship of us to God – wherein God is an ocean and creatures are the fishes, breathing God in and out daily.

part of one another. Ivory tower existence is seen as a lie, for if God is fully among us, why are we not fully among one another?

Thorleif Boman observes that "the concepts immanence and transcendence are oriented to space and thus are formed by the Greek mind" (190, n2). The Jewish mind thinks of time and eternity instead of space. Boman introduces a new, more Biblical, category for the presence of God. He calls it "the transparence of God." In such a relationship, "God is not only above the world and in the world, but he is also through the world." Thus Paul can speak of "one God who is Father of all, over all, through all and within all" (Eph. 4.6).

Love of neighbor is separate from divine love: love of neighbor is love of God

In the ladder symbolism, as we saw in reading what Jacob's-ladder mystics had to say about the experience, we learn that love of neighbor is an after-thought, a "descent," an act of philanthropy or charitable giving to neighbor of left-overs. In Sarah's circle, God is not separate from the human dancing. God is found there, where neighbor suffers or is in need or celebrates. Justice is not separate from love nor is either separate from our love of God. God is in creation and in neighbor as brother or sister or not at all.

It is clear from this brief consideration of the different energies of climbing Jacob's Ladder and Dancing Sarah's Circle that we are dealing here with two irreconcileable symbols. We cannot have it both ways. A person with one foot on a ladder and another in a circle dance will succeed at neither. Both dynamics demand the whole of us in so far as we see that whole. Neither an individual nor a society can be, in its basic energies, both ladder-climbing and circle-dancing simultaneously. We must make a decision for one or the other. It is clear which our society and even our religious terminology has chosen for us for the most part. One-Up-Man-ship might be called the name of the uppity, ladder-climbing game. But there are alternatives.

EXAMPLES OF SARAH'S CIRCLE DYNAMICS

Sarah's circle symbolizes a dynamic that has been among us for a long time though we had never named it as such. It is present, for example, wherever eating with others is of importance. After all, when we invite someone over for dinner, we do not climb a ladder and drop crumbs on them, much less pour drinks from that height. We talk of "sitting *around* the table"—even when the table is oblong, for sitting and eating together is a Sarah's circle experience. It is sensual and earthy, all are eye-to-eye; it is inter-dependent ("please pass me the jam") and yet not dependent; it is shared fun, shared conversation and shared ecstasy (provided the cook is adequate to the occasion). Wherever there is true conviviality (Illich's phrase) as in dining together, there is Sarah's circle in action.

Circle dancing

Another example of Sarah's circle already in our midst ("the reign of God is among you" said Jesus) is folk dancing. In folk dancing barriers of age, sex and professionalism are broken through. Eight year olds and eighty year olds and all ages in between can enjoy themselves equally at a folk dance—indeed, at the same folk dance. Competition between male and female, young and old, expert and amateur is broken through. Even cultural differences thaw in the warmth of folk dancing. And yet exertion and physical weariness is one of the healthy results of everyone's personal and inter-dependent efforts. I have experienced transformations of egos and spirits in persons taught to change the militant words of "We are Climbing Jacob's ladder" to "We are dancing Sarah's Circle." Joining hands and weaving about a chapel, church or room as a curved line in motion, as a spiral or circle, is truly a spiritual conversion for many who have never before been invited to put their bodies into worship. (In worsh*up* bodies are usually instructed whether verbally or non-verbally to stay behind). The traditional hymn to climbing Jacob's ladder that Protestant children sing from a very early age goes as follows:

We are climbing Jacob's ladder/We are climbing Jacob's ladder/
We are climbing Jacob's ladder/Soldiers of the Cross.

Every round gets higher, higher/Every round gets higher, higher/
Every round gets higher, higher/Soldiers of the Cross.

Notice with what violence these verses—and each subsequent verse also—ends. The music to this hymn is catchy and very danceable and to simply alter the words in the following fashion while keeping the memorable music intact is a powerful undoing or conversion for those raised on too violent and ladder-like a liturgical song.

We are dancing Sarah's Circle/We are dancing Sarah's circle/
We are dancing Sarah's Circle/sisters, brothers, all.

Every ring gets fuller, fuller/Every ring gets fuller, fuller
Every ring gets fuller, fuller/Sisters, brothers, all.

We are dancing Sarah's circle/We are dancing Sarah's circle/
We are dancing Sarah's circle/sisters, brothers, all.[18]

Rap groups

Another example of Sarah's Circle dynamics in our midst already is that of rap groups, especially those where persons in pain get together to share their weaknesses and thereby derive strength. Alcoholics Anonymous would be an example of such a dynamic, as would many forms of shared conversations. Some of these operating today at a truly healing level would be women's consciousness groups, prayer groups, groups of prisoners, of drug addicts, of relatives of drug addicts, or gay persons, male liberation groups, etc. The telling of personal stories that is common to each of these groups presumes a fall from the ladder. The groups work from an admission of powerlessness and from this stage of shared truth and humility a bonding is built that for many comprises a discovery of re-birth, ecstasy and compassion. There is little or no hierarchy in such groups: Leadership is generally rotated if it is needed at all. The following example shows how one alcholic explained his experiences in Alcoholics Anonymous:

We couldn't get rid of alcohol unless we made other sacrifices. Big-shotism and phony thinking had to go. We had to toss self-justification, self-pity, resentment right out the window.

We had to quit the crazy contest for personal prestige and big bank balances. We had to take personal responsibility for our sorry state and quit blaming others for it. . . . We have abandoned do-goodism, and paternalism. We refuse charitable money and prefer to pay our own way.

In the way of AA we see the themes of Sarah's Circle in evidence: interdependence without dependence, democracy, non-elitism, self-responsibility, leaving the ladder of prestige and compulsive money-making, looking others in the eye in place of self-pity, action and letting others hit bottom rather than sentimentalism, living a day at a time in place of striving up a pre-ordained ladder. This sense of time leaves one closer to the earth, more vulnerable to dancing Sarah's circle any day a dance is called.

William Eckhardt, in his study on alcoholics who joined AA found that "every individual case" of the twelve persons studied before then after joining AA passed from being "highly egoistic" during the pre-alcoholic and alcoholic periods of their life to being highly "altruistic" or compassionate. This amazing accomplishment seemed to come about, Eckhardt comments, because AA provided service without compensation on the one hand and accepted frustration without retaliation on the other.[19]

A similar theme is struck in other rap-like groups, for example in a male liberation group operating out of Chicago called Chicago Men's Gathering. In their Declaration of Principles drafted for discussion in April, 1973, they state what is clearly a Sarah's circle dynamic:

To achieve our goals, we have come together in a non-hierarchical, non-elective community, devoted to fostering the development of a new male identity. The heart of our community is the rap groups, each consisting of eight to ten men who come together once a week. In these groups we share our thoughts, feelings and experiences, nurture and support each other, gain new insight into how the traditional masculine role is a source of our pain and anxiety, and develop and grow in a variety of new, positive directions.

The Declaration goes on to declare that "men are capable of being warm, loving, open, sensitive and cooperative human beings" who are capable of "loving, nurturing, and supporting other men as well as caring for and nurturing children." They support "the right of men to be homemakers" and they reject the "success ethic." Finally,

We deplore the rigid and destructive traditional masculine role which demands of us that we be tough, aggressive and competitive, that we suppress our emotions and become in-

sensitive to the feelings of others, and that we 'prove our
manhood' by dominating and intimidating others, sometimes
through violence. We are committed to freeing men from the
destructive impact of this stereotyped role!

The emphasis on nurturing, on eye-to-eye democracy, on feeling, on
rejection of ladder-mentalities at a sexual level and at a financial level,
all give evidence of the Sarah Circle energies of such groups. Liberation groups that come together to share their pain and thus build
bonding and who strive for mutual enpowerment are already practicing a Sarah-Circle dynamic.

Jesus on Sarah's circle

Jesus continually operated from the vantage point of Sarah's
Circle. How else can one interpret his saying, "the first shall be last
and the last first"? For it is precisely in a circle that the first are last;
the last are first; and, what is more to the point, no one knows who is
first, who is last, and above all, no one cares. Indeed, when he was
pressured by his disciples to name their proper place at table he utterly rejected the notion of ladder climbing (Lk. 14. 7–11). His supper
times with his disciples were clearly a Sarah circle kind of intimacy
and his Last Supper rings especially true to this dynamic. The rich
man at the ladder's top whom Jesus describes as dropping crumbs
from the table top on to Lazarus was one who would pay the punishment
of Gehenna's fire. (Lk. 16.19–31)

The sacrament of washing of the feet that meant so much to Jesus
the night before he died is a patent example of a Sarah circle dynamic.
What is more eye to eye, more a matter of nearness to the earth and
more distant from ladder climbing than to wash another's feet? Christians really ought to revive this sacrament for more than once-a-year
ceremonial reenactments. If parents washed children's feet, children
parent's, if leaders washed the folks' feet and the folks' washed the
leaders', if lovers washed one another's feet, our world would be a
gentler place in which to dwell. Those who take their sacralized and
hierarchized positions on the ladder too seriously should meditate on
how Jesus both washed his disciples' feet *and* had his feet washed
with ointment by a woman willing to dry them with her long hair. All
of Sarah's circle dynamic is as much receiving as giving. There lies the
clue to its healthy, com-passionate (passion-with) energies. Some
people can only "love" by giving—this is not love: its right name is
control; while others seem only to receive—which is another kind of
control. Jesus was not such a control-oriented individual.

Another example of Sarah-Circle in Jesus' consciousness occurs in the context of his healing the suffering ones and his feeding the hungry (Mt. 15. 29–39). We read:

> Jesus called his disciples and said to them: 'I feel compassion [i.e. my bowels are turning within me, *splanchnizomai*] towards all these people; they have been with me now for three days and have nothing to eat. I do not want to send them away unfed; they might faint on the way.' . . . So *he ordered the people to sit down on the ground;* then he took the seven loaves and the fishes, and after giving thanks to God he broke them and gave to the disciples, and the disciples gave to the people. . . .

Notice that Jesus requires for this Sarah-circle eating occasion, which parallels in many respects a Eucharistic experience, the sitting down on the ground. Earthiness, being close to the earth and therefore eye-to-eye, lies at the core of Jesus' spiritual consciousness.

Churches and Sarah's circle

Churches today are dealing with the passage from climbing Jacob's ladder to the dancing of Sarah's circle. This movement is demonstrated, for example, in the emergence of team ministries. Previously, ministries of rugged individualism dominated. So deep is the personal and sexual commitment to the ministries of rugged individualism that for many persons once trained in that kind of work, to pass to true team ministry is traumatic and a metanoia-like experience. Team ministry requires true democracy whereby individual talents are recognized and encouraged; it is eye-to-eye, it is inter-dependent and it is non-hierarchical. I once presented these two symbols, Jacob's ladder and Sarah's circle, to a minister, and she exclaimed that this made sense of her experience at work. She worked in a downtown ecclesial office where, she said, the church workers occupied two floors. On the one floor, her floor, the group worked as a team; on the other floor, they worked still in a ladder model. When the two groups got together to work there was "utter breakdown in communication." They no longer shared a common language. That is how different dancing Sarah's circle is from climbing Jacob's ladder.

Another example of Church responding to Sarah's circle is the Declaration of Vatican II that church means primarily the "People of God." To define church as people or as folks is a far cry from defining it as hierarchy. It is a Sarah's cry, not a cry from the ladder top. The implications of this radical statement by bishops themselves are still being born and worked out. One example among others is the ordination of women and of married persons, male and female, as well as of gay persons. All these issues are issues of Sarah's circle vs. Jacob's ladder if for no other reason because a circle must be small in size since eye-contact and dancing presumes a manageable number of folks in any one ring. As the ladder has developed in Roman Catholic sacerdotal ordination, however, nothing is clearer than the fact that ordained persons are a uniquely tiny and elitest minority (male, celibate, seven to ten year theology students) and thus the exclusion of others to church leadership means that giant-sized worship services are inevitable. I recall meeting a young and energetic priest this past year in Texas who with one other priest is the 'pastor' to a parish of 1500 families! Such giantism is intrinsically violent to all concerned and there is no way such an individual will survive it as a gentle person. Much less will the thousands of individuals in the parish eager for spiritual sharing and celebrating learn about either. E.F. Schumacher's principle that small is necessary for human gentleness applies to ecclesial life as much as to other forms of planetary gatherings.

Still another example of Sarah's circle replacing Jacob's ladder in church circles is that major concession from Vatican II, the vernacular in the liturgy. As long as worship is in a tongue that only a few initiates understand, then the ladder is maintained intact and with it the energy of worsh*up*. In this regard it is worth reflecting on whether Protestantism, rightly proud of its commitment to vernacular, has not at times substituted theological jargon for the Latin so that what appears to be the speech of the folks is in fact a language restricted to those who have academic perches on the ladder. Theologians who cannot translate their language to the language of the folks may well be serving their own interests on the ladder more than the interests of the People of God. There is a subtle struggle here between anti-academic and anti-Latin and anti-intellectualism. I have never known a true intellectual — as opposed to an academic achiever — who could not speak the language of the people and with the people. Especially, the language of shared pain which is so universal a dialect for anyone still close enough to the earth to hear its cries and whispers. One has to ask whether the ladder, in its compulsion to escape the earth, is also escaping the common pain of earth people and earth creatures, and if it is for this reason that ladder people insist on wrapping themselves in their own private and monopolistic languages which only their grand ghettos of ivory-tower professionalism can understand.

Further examples of Sarah's Circle replacing Jacob's ladder in theology today include the passage from the excessively "high" Christologies which put Jesus Christ pedestal-like on so lofty a ladder that only lip service was paid to his being a human person. No one could identify with such docetistic images of Jesus, nor should one have to. For not only did Jesus walk the earth barefoot and live, eat, celebrate and suffer like all human persons, but his death on a cross might well have been meant to be the death of ladder consciousness. Did not the ladder die on Calvary? Was the crucifixion not the last erection of the patriarchal powers so that a new reign of God's presence would begin? Today's emphasis in Christology on resisting christolotries wherever they are found and to emphasizing the humanity of Jesus is a sure stage of passing from Jacob's ladder to Sarah's circle.

A renewal of creation-centered spirituality wherein a genuine role is recovered for God the Creator (or Father) and God the Spirit, in other words, a renewal of Trinitarian theology, is a healthy antidote to temptations to christolatry. Such a Trinitarian theology is basically a Sarah-circle dynamic, for a trinity implies a circle. Liberation theology is obviously a recovery of the sense of God's nearness to the poor of the earth who are not engaged in ladder-climbing. Its thrust is not to get everyone on the ladder but to redesign the very fabric and model of how society wants to live. And feminist spirituality as explicated by Mary Daly and Rosemary Reuther, for example, leads us off the ladder and into the circle.

Still another similar movement is that in sacramental theology from the dispensing-of-sacraments motif to the celebration motif. An example of this movement at the daily level is communion in one's hands, the taking of divine energy into one's own hands and the consequent democratic implications of this experience. It is worth commenting that one concerned American Cardinal suggested, just prior to the American bishops' voting to allow communion in the hand, that such a practice would lead to "devil worship." Apparently he sensed the depth of the symbolic change that was implied in the movement from the ladder to the circle. From Sacrament as an anointed one's power to sacrament as celebration.

Society and Sarah's circle

Other examples of Sarah's circle already at work in our midst are cooperatives such as food or clothing or housing. All such co-ops promote Sarah's circle in their dynamic. Their energy is wasted and they are ruined when the ladder invades them. This happened with a woman I met who explained how much she loved working in a co-op food venture in California. She could get her work done in four hours each day and have the remainder of the day for important activities such as making friends, studying nature and books, making music, etc. Then the co-op decided to start paying wages by the hour and the entire enterprise changed drastically. She noticed how it now took everyone eight hours to do the same tasks it previously took four hours to accomplish. She left the 'co-op'—now a ladder—as a result.

Another example of Sarah's circle in society is the interest in solar, wind and water energy systems. These systems are intrinsically decentralized and therefore non-hierarchical. The idea that anyone might have solar taps on their roof to take in energy from the sun that belongs equally to all who inhabit the earth scares those who make their very hefty livings by parceling out energy down to the people from the lofty ladders of oil companies. I have often maintained that if Esso could claim ownership of the sun we would have had solar energy years ago. But it can't—and there lies good news for all Sarah-circle people in the future! There also lies the roots of the powerful forces lined up to prevent basic monies for research and development of what would be a non-ladder energy source.

Another example of Sarah circle dynamic would be parents who insist on natural childbirth wherein their child will be welcomed eye to eye by a circle of fully conscious and celebrating, wonder-struck family. It includes para-medics and para-priests; gay people and third world people at home and abroad. It includes anyone or any group that is angry enough at the injustice they have experienced to be able to understand the words of Chairman Mao when he declared that there must be no luxuries for some until there are basics for all. Such a declaration presumes we know what basics are. Perhaps we need a large national and/or international jamboree to determine what basics are and what luxuries are. I suspect, however, that work, education, health care, food, shelter, creative recreation might make a good starting list for what are basic. Luxury living makes sense only on a ladder. In a circle all are too close—and to fun-filled—to have to depend on luxury items and goods for their pseudo-ecstasies.

MYSTICAL SYMBOL AS A LEGITIMIZATION OF SECULAR VIOLENCE

The stakes in playing the symbol game are very dear indeed. I would like to propose that, for all its hoopla about being a secularized culture and a secularized city, our modern society runs on the basic dynamic of a mystical symbol, that of climbing Jacob's ladder. Indeed, it is precisely this ladder, invoked so piously by religious persons, that legitimizes and reinforces some of the most obvious violence in our society.

Wealth, poverty and Sarah's circle

For example, the violence between the haves and have-nots. If you draw a diagram of the distribution of money in our society (Figure D) you find that the persons at the top of the ladder, though numerically the same as the persons at the bottom of the ladder, divide among themselves over 49% of the wealth. The persons at the bottom divide 3.1% of the wealth. Indeed, the top 1% divide among themselves more than 100% more than the bottom 20% of human beings! The difference between top and bottom continues to grow greater.

What does this mean, practically speaking? That the top 20% have a lot of money in the bank or in stocks or in bonds? Yes. But much more than that. It also means that those at the top are the ones who dictate to the rest of us the sentimentalized fare we get on television for they comprise the media boards after all; the way money is or is not spent on research, eg., regarding solar energy as referred to earlier; what laws are passed and not passed; the courses that are and are not

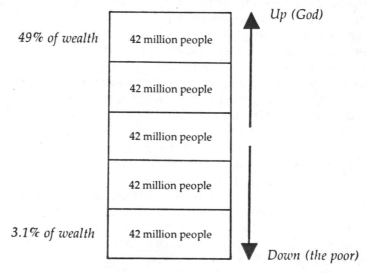

FIGURE D. The mystical symbol of climbing Jacob's ladder legitimizes the economic violence between haves and have-nots because it tells people to worship.

taught in our giant universities (one study in Chicago found that 95% of the members of the boards of trustees of six major universities in that city were on boards of other schools as well), etc. etc. What is at stake in keeping the ladder erect is keeping everyone in their place so that the ladder does not tumble. And, above all, that it not turn into a circle of people dancing a dance together. Subversive activity, that, for those who worship ladders and want others to worsh*up*.

As long as religious people continue to worsh*up*, the ladder is never questioned. If, however, people with faith started looking *around* and maybe even leaving the ladder for a more joyful dance (figure E), then a revolution (from the word "to turn around") of a non-violent kind may well be in the offing. This is what happened with St. Francis of Assisi. Trained by his upper class and highly successful father to enter into well-established merchant business of fine silks, he said, No Thank You. It was a violent conversion and confrontation with his father who, in fact, put him in a prison for his disobedience. Francis held to his insistence to dance off the ladder, however, and in doing so identified with the poor at the ladder's bottom and started a Sarah-Circle energy of living.

Another example, closer to home, is Martin Luther King, Jr. He, too, might have inherited a fine position in his father's well established church. Well educated, Martin Luther King, Jr., had a fine future ahead of him. Then, he, too, looked around, left the ladder dynamic and danced off with the people at the bottom, dying as we all know while marching with garbage collectors of Memphis.

These two examples of middle-class persons who learned *to cease worshupping* demonstrate the tremendous power and potential those in the middle of the ladder possess for good or for bad. Those at the top are usually too preoccupied making sure they stay there, and those at the bottom are usually too busy surviving to be able to choose to leave the ladder for another vision. It is those in the middle who are called to wake up and dance off. To "shake the dust from their ladder feet" and learn to love the dust of the earth in Sarah's dance.

The ultimate expression of ladder consciousness in our culture, as far as money and institutions are concerned, is the skyscraper. A skyscraper is itself a symbol; it is a projection of our insides. A culture that worships up-ness considers skyscrapers to be the ultimate in accomplishment. They dominate the skylines of our cities no matter how cruel and inhuman and out-of-work-and-play our people, neighborhoods and especially our minority youth find themselves. Skyscrapers are a symbol, an offering to our sky gods, our ladder gods. Have you ever noticed how many skyscrapers are insurance buildings? In the city near where I live, Chicago, all the major skyscrapers are insurance

FIGURE E. True non-violent revolution happens when those in the middle quit their worsh*up* and look *around*, thus hearing the poor, and dance off the ladder as in the case of Francis of Assisi and Martin Luther King, Jr.

companies. Sears Towers, the largest skyscrapers in the world, Prudential Building, John Hancock building. Why does so much of skyscraper worsh*up* involve insurance companies? Because, in a Jacob's ladder society and economy, insecurity is, as they say, the name of the game. With so much rugged individualism and so much competition and so many heights to scale, it is clear that the best investment of all would be in some insurance. Anyone might tumble at any time. Thus, insurance is the name of the game in a ladder-dominated society.

The spiritual conversion of believers from climbing Jacob's ladder to dancing Sarah's circle is the beginning of the end for the skyscraper worsh*up* dynamics of our ladder culture. By it we pull the rug out from under the ladders we worship and convert them to more celebrative purposes.

Sado-masochism and Sarah's circle

There is still one more energy which needs to be named and recognized for what it is in the ladder society. It is painful even to talk about but it must be exorcised. It is the twin energies of power-over and power-under. Its proper names are sadism and masochism. These are the basic sexual-political energies that are rained down upon people from the impressive heights of our ladder tops. I have felt them at work, as I am sure you have in every one of our ladder-oriented institutions, be they military or government, church or family, education or business, media or self. Only people can break through this sadism and masochism. Only they can change this power-over, power-under cycle to power-with, or compassion.

Both masochism and sadism are about power as control: "The way the masochistic person exerts control is by his very suffering and help-lessness" points out Karen Horney (268), and it is evident enough that sadism is a way of treating others as objects of control. Sadism also "kills joy" according to Horney, and is at root an act of self-contempt growing out of masochism. "The more he despises others the less is he aware of his self-contempt" (204). Sadism and masochism are far more common than we might suspect, because the sexual expression of them is in fact "comparatively rare," according to Horney, and because "when they are present they are merely one expression of a general attitude toward others." What is at the core of sadomasochistic power is destructiveness of a "desperate individual who seeks restitution for a life that has defeated him" (216). There is passion over and passion under but no passion with or compassion.

It is a sad but true story that an unusually high percentage of persons at the top of our ladders, passing on culture's values to the rest of us through their institutions of media, courts, legislatures, etc. are sadomasochistic in their recreation no less than in their work. Dr. Sam Janus, clinical assistant professor of psychiatry at New York Medical College, has published a seven-year study of "high class" call girls and prostitutes. A majority of the customers of the $100 per hour prostitutes were politicians or top executives. Seeking reaffirmation of their power and youth—apparently the ladder does not satisfy all one's needs— these persons need to dominate a woman in order to make her do what they want. Top level politicians spend as much as $10,000 a year on prostitutes who are paid to dupe them into believing that they are proving their masculinity through their sexual performance. Much of this money, or course, comes from the grass roots people whose taxes pay for public funds. What do they get for their—our—money?

Many of the men in positions of power, such as politicians, want kinky sex like bondage, flagellation, etc. Some of the men who like sadomasochistic practices, such as being whipped, told the prostitutes they feel that being hurt is atonement for their compulsive sexual needs. One prostitute told of a former high-placed politician in the executive branch of the federal government who could have sex only after his arms and legs were tightly bound while he was lying supine with arms outstretched in the form of a cross.[21]

What is the conclusion of this study of the sexual habits of those who habitate our lofty ladders, begging us too to worshup? Says Dr. Janus: "We concluded that for many politicians and executives the power drive and sex drive become so closely linked that they become one and the same." In other words, climbing Jacob's ladder makes as much sexual sense as it does spiritual or political sense. It is violent to self and others, no matter how one looks at it. In passing over to a new energy, which I have named Sarah's circle, the new spirituality would do these men and women a giant favor indeed even if initially they would not recognize it as such.

SUMMARY

As long as the West remains dependent on the ladder symbol there will be more violence, more sadism and masochism in the name of all of our numerous gods—and the exile of compassion will continue. Phallicism, the worship of up-ness, remains America's dominant religion. The great locker room in the sky urges men on and dictates how "their women" will be treated. But heaven is not so distant, nor so up. It is, as Jesus tried and tried and tried to teach, "in our midst." It is where people can learn to love as brothers and sisters, eye-to-eye, dancing Sarah's circle and relieving one another's pain. It is wherever compassion is practiced. When theologian Edward Schillebeeckx speaks of transcendence as "no longer being up but the future" he is correct. Now, however, we can begin to name that future. It is Sarah's Circle. Transcendence is Sarah's circle and Sarah's circle is transcendence. Therein lies salvation for a global village and the holy people who inhabit it—which is all of us.

A contemporary American poet living and working amidst earth people in Appalachia has written a poem that captures many of the symbols I have spoken about in this chapter. While his images apply directly to church workers, indirectly they apply to us all, no matter what contribution we make or wish we made to society.

Concerning the why and how and what and who of ministry,
one image keeps surfacing:
A table that is round.

It will take some sawing
to be roundtabled,
some redefining
and redesigning

Such redoing and rebirthing
of narrowlong Churching
can painful be
for people and tables

But so was the cross,
a painful too table
of giving and yes

And from such death comes life,
from such dying comes rising,
in search of roundtabling
And what would roundtable Churching mean?

It would mean no diasing
   and throning,
for but one King is there,
and He was a footwasher,
at table no less . . .

For at the narrowlong tables,
servant and mirror
became picture framed
and centers of attention

And crosses became but gilded ornaments
on bare stone walls
in buildings used but once a week only

But the times and the tables
are changing and rearranging

And what of narrowlong tableministers,
when they confront
a roundtable people,
after years of working up the table
(as in 'up the ladder')
to finally sit at its head,
only to discover
that the table has turned around???

Continued rarified air
will only isolate
for there are no people there,
only roles

They must be loved into roundness,
where *apart* is spelled *a part*
and the call is to the gathering

For God has called a People,
not 'them and us'

'Them and us'
are unable
to gather around,
for at a roundtable,
there are no sides

And ALL are invited
to wholeness and to food . . .
Roundtabling means
no preferred seating,
no first and last,
no better, and no corners
for 'the least of these'

Roundtabling means
being with,
a part of,
together, and one

It means
room for the Spirit
and gifts
and disturbing profound peace for all . . .

And it is we in the present
who are mixing and kneading
the dough for the future.

We can no longer prepare for the past. . . .[22]

3

PSYCHOLOGY AND COMPASSION:

FROM A PSYCHOLOGY OF CONTROL (COMPETITION, COMPULSION AND DUALISM) TO A PSYCHOLOGY OF CELEBRATION (LETTING BE, LETTING GO AND LETTING DIALECTIC HAPPEN)

> *Compassion is the ultimate and most meaningful embodiment of emotional maturity. It is through compassion that a person achieves the highest peak and deepest reach in his or her search for self-fulfillment.*
>
> —*Arthur Jersild*[1]

Poet Chuck Lathrop has urged that we cease preparing ourselves for the past. What might the future, psychologically speaking, be about? One psychologist has named compassion as the fullest experience of personal maturity. Arthur Jersild writes: "Compassion is the ultimate and most meaningful embodiment of emotional maturity. It is through compassion that a person achieves the highest peak and deepest reach in his search for self-fulfillment." Having considered in the previous chapter the move from a basic mystical-sexual-cultural symbol of climbing Jacob's ladder to the more compassionate one of Dancing Sarah's circle, we can now explore some of the psychological ramifications of this journey. For if we are talking about a deep change in symbols, we are talking about a deep psychological transformation as well. Reserving a later chapter for some of the social obstacles, in this chapter we will consider the following psychological obstacles to compassion: Competition, Compulsion, and Dualism. In dealing with this unholy trinity I will first interact with psychologist Karen Horney as regards competition; with psychologist William Eckhardt as regards compulsion; and with psychologist Robert Ornstein as regards dualism. To undo a ladder society's investment in competition, compulsion and dualism would mean to release psychic energies for compassion once again. It would be the beginning of the end of the psychological causes for the exile of compassion—a beginning of calling compassion and people capable of compassion home again.

COMPETITION VS. COMPASSION

Psychologist Karen Horney suggests that our quest for reassurance against anxiety is obtained in a quest for power, prestige and possession. We seek power to brace ourselves against helplessness and our resultant hostility is expressed in a tendency to dominate; we seek prestige to brace ourselves against humiliation and our resultant hostility is expressed in a tendency to humiliate; we seek possession to brace ourselves against destitution and our resultant hostility is expressed in a tendency to deprive others.[2] It is clear how advantageously the ladder motif matches these neurotic forms of hostility: domination, humiliation, and deprivation seem intrinsic to climbing Jacob's ladder. Horney offers an explanation why some people climb so fast, rise so furiously, and insist on preserving the ladder at all costs. The ladder serves their needs for personal survival and esteem. Unfortunately, when these needs are taken at the expense of others, others suffer the loss of their own needs, and more pain, not less pain, is the result. John Gardner once remarked that in all of the battles he had fought in Common Cause and elsewhere, he had never fought any tougher battles than with those who, being at the top of powerful ladders, were requested to relinquish some of their power. He says: "I'd been through some rough issues—race and poverty, but I never knew what real slugging was until I got into the ways people in power preserved their power."

To what extent, then, has a ladder-oriented culture so institutionalized competition that it almost creates of itself, much like a self-fulfilling prophecy would, a competitive personality who is forced to succeed in a competitive system? Competition invades such a society at every level of action, inter-action and self-awareness. This is Horney's starting point for her essay on "Neurotic Competitiveness." Competition, she says, is a "problem for everyone in our culture." For if:

> power, prestige and possession have to be acquired by the individual's own efforts he is compelled to enter into competitive struggle with others. From its economic center competition radiates into all other activities and permeates love, social relations and play. Therefore competition is a problem for everyone in our culture, and it is not at all surprising to find it an unfailing center of neurotic conflicts. (188)

This "unfailing center of neurotic conflicts" will also prove to be the unfailing obstacle to compassion. For the demonic power of competition is such that it so isolates the ego and defines it so narrowly in relation to striving with another ego that all hope of sharing something deeper than ego—whether that be joy or pain—is lost.

I use the word "demonic" in regard to competition very deliberately. For one aspect of what is demonic and not merely undesirable is the subtleness of the evil experienced therein. Demonic evil always comes clothed in righteous rationalizations, putting its best side forward (yes, the demonic does have a good side). So many persons object to criticizing competition by exclaiming: "But competition is good for people. It is natural and necessary for survival." It is the height—and depths—of cynicism to say that "competition is natural" and that "without competition nothing new would happen." Consider dogs at play. They strive *to play* more than to win. This is also the case with children, until they have been taught otherwise by aggressive parents. I do not deny that there is a good side to assertive as distinct from aggressive competition. Competition, for example, is a cure for laziness—though one should not rule out other, less tried cures, such as compassion as celebration. Competition can assist to "get the best out of people"—though one should not exclude other, less tried methods as well. As for competition being "normal," studies show that in fact, adults in our society are far more competitive than children,[3] and children are competitive in an assertive but not in an aggressive sense—

unless their parents force them into this very unnatural role. Thus, aggressive competition is taught by society and is not an inherited instinct.

How shall we distinguish the two kinds of competition — that which is sick, neurotic and aggressive from that which is at times useful, healthy and assertive? One way is by our gut feelings. Recently I listened to a parent, who was himself an all-state football player, tell me that his children would never play organized sports. Why? Because, precisely out of his love for sports, this parent attended numerous high school and grade school games in his city. He observed high school coaches screaming and slapping the players; he observed parents of grade school children yelling and berating their children for a dropped ball or a missed block. "I will play neighborhood sports and games with my children but I am determined they will not join organized athletics. It has become sick in our culture today," he went on.

I fear the truth of this painful observation. To what extent has the poison of the business called professional sport dripped down from the ladder top to infiltrate college, high school and even little league players at what was once a game? How much has this poison infested other areas of play, entertainment, work, living and business in our society?

Horney does not leave us to rely solely on our gut instincts to determine when competition is sick or healthy. She offers three criteria for testing the health of competition in our society. First, if measurement against others is a constant need and only one thing seems to matter: namely getting ahead of the other. Second, when ambition, even if repressed, drives one to be not only "better" than the other or others but "the best." The need to be "unique and exceptional" interferes then with the very ability to enjoy success. And third, when an implicit hostility is present in the competition such as when one declares, verbally or non-verbally, that "no one but I shall be beautiful, capable, successful." In this way competition is aimed at destroying the other rather than at creative construction of oneself and others.

It is characteristic of all neurotic competitiveness that one "fight(s) against feeling any gratitude." (196) Thankfulness is always lacking in such ego-oriented and war-torn mentalities such as competition breeds. The reason for this, Horney suggests, is that the neurotic feels humbled to have to give anyone else credit for anything. How prevalent is this neurotic competition in our ladder-oriented culture? According to Horney, it is "almost a cultural pattern." She wrote these words in 1937 and it would be difficult to argue that society has become *less* competitive in the past forty-two years.

> Hostility is inherent in every intense competition, since the victory of one of the competitors implies the defeat of the other. There is, in fact, so much destructive competition in an individualistic culture that as an isolated feature one hesitates to call it a neurotic characteristic. It is almost a cultural pattern. (192)

Compassion suffers miserably at the hands of competition, for compassion seeks our common likenesses—which in fact are joy and tragedy—and not our differences. Yet it is competition's task to make us different—winners and losers, ins and outs. In doing so competition demands violent and destructive energies which are not those of compassion which flow one into another. Competition isolates, separates and estranges. Compassion unites, makes one and embraces. Since thankfulness is lacking in all sick competition then too is all potential for celebration or Eucharist, which is merely the theological name for thanking. Here, more than in revised rituals or liturgical scholarship oriented at lost periods of ecclesial history, may lie the richest soil for turning over and planting a revitalized worshipping community. If we can move from competition to compassion we will have moved from dull and moralistic and ungrateful and legalistic worship (or is it worsh*up*?) to celebrative thanking.

The play between the sexes is deeply affected by the neurotic competition of our culture that results in destructive acting out. "In love relationships the neurotic's tendencies to defeat, subdue and humiliate the partner play an enormous role. Sexual relations become a means of either subduing and degrading the partner or of being subdued and degraded by him, a character which is certainly entirely alien to their nature." (197) Thus the art of love-making and relating between sexual partners becomes itself a battleground, a further carrier of poisoned competition. A vicious spiral is created here since it is precisely in a competitive and individualistic society that sexual intimacy is most needed as a great healer. And yet, it becomes one more weapon in the arsenal of competition (206).

If the energies of competition were kept among adults as adult games that would be one thing. But all evidence points to their poisoning the youth and young adults of a society as well. Competition is that kind of powerful energy force. Suicide rates among youth from 15 to 24 years old have doubled since 1960 in America, making suicide the second biggest killer of adolescents. According to one report, it is "the anguish of increased competition for grades, jobs and graduate school admission" that is the cause of this jump in suicide and of the need for more and more counseling on college campuses.[4]

Horney endorses a healthy ambition that should not be confused with neurotic competition. A person with such an ambition would be willing to enter into both failure and success and live with either. The sickly ambitious are in fact conformists, afraid to stand out from the crowd either by way of failure or success. Everyone the same. No risks to take. Nothing lost. "Needless to say, such an attitude brings with it a great impoverishment in life and a warping of potentialities. For, unless circumstances are unusually favorable, the attainment of happiness or any kind of achievement presupposes taking risks and making efforts." [5]

In an essay on "Culture and Neurosis" Horney presents a dilemma for a religious person caught in a competitive culture like ours.

> The first contradiction to be mentioned is that between competition and success on the one hand, and brotherly love and humility on the other. On the one hand everything is done to spur us toward success, which means that we must be not only assertive but aggressive, able to push others out of the way. On the other hand we are deeply imbued with Christian ideals which declare that it is selfish to want anything for ourselves, that we should be humble, turn the other cheek, be yielding. For this contradiction there are only two solutions within the normal range: to take one of these strivings seriously and discard the other; or to take both seriously with the result that the individual is seriously inhibited in both directions. [6]

As a theologian, I cannot agree with Horney's presentation of the Christian ideal as yielding by turning the other cheek. In chapter one we have seen how Christ was far more nuanced in his psychology, sociology and spirituality than that. He insisted that we love others as we love ourselves and that this love take the form of action. Above all, he insisted that we be "compassionate as our heavenly Father is compassionate." Here lies a healthier solution to the dilemma that Horney presents to us: that between an aggressive and sickly competitive society and what we might become. The proper cure to competition is compassion. But compassion is not so simplistic as turning the other cheek. It might mean at times taking whips and driving out moneylenders with anger and threats. It might mean converting a ladder to a circle. It might mean dancing with all the assertiveness and interdependence that that implies. One thing is certain: there will be no compassion as long as we continue to honor the god of competition. The two energies cannot be of equal value to us. You cannot worship two lords at once: that of separateness and hostility and that of togetherness and mutuality. I recall once polling a group of a thousand college professors, students and administrators. How many, I asked, in all the tens of thousands of years of American education represented in this room, had ever had a course called "Compassion?" No one raised a hand. How many have ever in all those years ever heard even one lecture on compassion? Three persons raised their hands. And now, how many have felt quite well schooled in the classroom and in extra-curricular activities in competition? With that question, one thousand hands went up.

It is clear which of these gods, competition or compassion, our culture has instructed us to worship. It is time for an exorcism. For there exists a better way. The way of shalom and Sarah's circle. A way called compassion.

COMPULSION VS. COMPASSION

Psychologist William Eckhardt, in his ground-breaking book entitled *Compassion: Toward a Science of Value*, suggests that competition, "far from being a function of nature . . . is a function of compulsion" (100). He feels that the opposite energy to compassion is properly named compulsion and that it is in instructing ourselves and others in compulsion that we drive out any hope for compassion and that we introduce the gods of competition. "It would seem that any increase in compulsion necessarily reduces the power of compassion in human affairs and, conversely, any increase in compassion necessarily reduces the power of compulsion in human affairs" (1).

Something rings true in Eckhardt's analysis. It is when I feel compulsive that I am a bad laugher, a bad listener, a bad celebrator. It is precisely the compulsively moral and the compulsively *up*right—there is that word again—and the compulsively successful who cannot celebrate, let go or identify with others' suffering. The inability to roll with the paradoxical dimensions of life seems to characterize the compulsive and to inhibit them. A culture that is compulsive knows no more about celebrating than it does about relieving the pain of its own pain-ridden people.

No one could deny that religion itself has often instructed persons in compulsion, and Eckhardt's empirical studies verify the fact that a high percentage of church-going persons are compulsive. Today we are recognizing how religious traditions that emphasized work as a sign of salvation and divine election have instructed us to be compulsive about work. In such a situation, those with good jobs in society become driven over-workers and over-achievers which is bad enough, for it eliminates their potential for celebration. (They never "have the time".) At the same time, however, others are immediately affected adversely by being excluded from work, either by unemployment or underemployment. Thus the sign of compulsive work becomes a sinful spiral that leads to destroying many in society. There is such a thing as compulsions even to religious practices including Liturgies, retreats, pieties, pedestal hero-worship, the quest for the perfect spiritual director, for community, etc. All such compulsions are inimical to compassion because they are compulsive. Worse than that, however, they truly deserve the name of demonic, for the apparent goodness of their activity covers up for the violence behind their compulsive drivenness. As Krister Stendahl warns, "most of the evil in this world is done by people who do it for good purposes. . . . Real evil in this world happens when Satan disguises himself as an angel of light (2 Cor. 11.14)." (KS, 105f.) This temptation to compulsion is one more reason why contemplation and solitude are so important an ingredient for compassion. We need to learn to let go even of our good intentions, our good works and attitudes and this kind of letting go is learned in solitude and cosmic contemplation. It has been my experience that behind these compulsions there generally lurks a fear of nature and a fear of things. How right Paoli is when he comments that "before we can talk about peace among nations and people, it is necessary to talk about peace between people and things." Things have become our enemies in industrial society, he laments. (p. 3)

Eckhardt offers an insight into the profound psychological difference that exists between creation or Biblical spirituality and sin-oriented spirituality when he indicates that compassion requires a "radical faith in human nature" (p. viii). He distinguishes compassionate philosophers from egoistic ones according to the following norms: the former "generally assumed that human nature was basically good and that the human mind was able to choose between good and evil" while the latter "generally assumed that human nature was basically evil and determined to be selfish." (10) Psychologically speaking, this faith in human nature is what distinguishes compassion from compulsion—but it is also what distinguishes creation-centered spirituality (which takes seriously the Genesis story that creation is "good" and humankind "very good") from a spirituality that begins with sin and builds up to redemption. Eckhardt is thus revealing one more reason why compassion has played so small a part in spirituality in the past centuries: creation centered spirituality has been forsaken for the sake of a redemption oriented one. With the revival today of creation spirituality, however, compassion has a future.[7]

For Eckhardt, compulsion is characterized by self-centeredness which ignores others' needs and feelings, whether expressed affectively, politically, religiously or cognitively. A drivenness and egoism which Eckhardt equates with gross immaturity dominate such a personality. In this stage of underdevelopment justice would be understood merely in terms of conformity to the status quo. Children, Eckhardt concedes, have a right to a stage of egocentric development from birth to around six years of age which is not, properly speaking, compulsion, however. Following this period there would ordinarily develop a "conformity" period from six to about twelve years of age; and finally, the emerging adult would grow into compassion. "Progress toward compassion would be expected during adolescence (roughly 12 to 18 years), and would be the norm for mature adulthood" (190). What would characterize this growth into compassion? A dialectic would emerge, what Eckhardt calls "the principle of coherence" between self and others, pain and joy, celebration and relief of suffering. Eckhardt writes:

> Compassion would be characterized by the reconciliation between self and others in the affective part of the personality, . . . between the individual and society in the ideological part of the personality, and between freedom and equality in the cognitive-moral part of the personality. At this mature level of development, the self would be treated as well as others, the individual would be valued as much as society, and justice would be defined in terms of these progressive equalities . . . In this manner the conflicts at the lower levels of development between egoism (self) and altruism (others), between freedom (capitalism) and equality (communism), and between freedom (existentialism) and reason (rationalism) would be resolved in a process of creative interchange by the principle of coherence. (191)

For Eckhardt, then, learning to live dialectically or both-and instead of dualistically, either-or, is a sign of psychological fullness. This principle will be developed below when we treat of dualism as an obstacle to compassion.

Eckhardt considers the human personality on a scale running from Compulsion (at its least mature end) to Compassion (at its most mature end) with Conformity representing the average level of human personality development. Compulsion would correspond to Piaget's egocentricity or to Freud's developmental use of the term Id; Conformity would be similar to the Superego of Freud; and Compassion would correspond to Freud's Ego, Piaget's reciprocity, Kant's categorical imperative and Scripture's Golden Rule. While I sense ladder-like dangers in offering these guidelines of Eckhardt's, I can also sense a usefulness to them provided that the user not imagine that an adult ever needs to or ought to reject his or her child or adolescent self in striving for fuller compassionhood. We dare not welcome the replacement of mystical-symbolic ladders of the spiritual life with psychological ladders of moral development if it is true that spiritual fullness takes place in circle terms, not linear ones. Furthermore, compassion, while it includes moral sensitivity and action, is so basic that it operates more at the level of spirituality than of morality, as we have discussed in Chapter One.

Given these reservations, there is much to be learned by further study of Eckhardt's detailed and critical analysis of compulsion vs. compassion. If our society, as he suggests, is even more fundamentally compulsive than it is competitive, then we have clearly named an enemy of compassion in calling forth the evil spirit called compulsiveness. To what extent do we succumb individually and collectively to this drivenness? To what extent, for example, do our laws, written or unwritten, compel us to act inhumanly, i.e., without making moral decisions? To what extent are we blinded to the cost we pay for ladder energies? To the cost others pay who are worse off than ourselves? To the lost energies of talents, gifts and possibilities for celebration that never get tapped or utilized?

Eckhardt further delineates the contrast between compulsive and compassionate value systems. Concerning consciousness, he maintains that compulsive personalities and societies will consider it their vocation to remain uncritical and to make the conscious unconscious, especially as regards inequality in the world. In contrast, compassion "virtually glorifies human consciousness" because without this awareness there can be no change of self, others or the world. Indeed, "without consciousness, there can be no human values" (256). Learning or discipline will be understood differently in each mode. The compulsive mode will involve absolute obedience exercised by means of "directive, punitive, and restrictive control exercised by authority figures." In contrast, a compassionate theory of learning or discipline assumes that individual freedom—which always includes others and not just oneself—"generates its own sense of social responsibility." In this setting the learner is encouraged as regards his coming to his or her own insights and is treated as an equal.

Compulsive freedom would limit freedom to "superior" individuals and groups who occupy the top of the ladder whether by their being self-made successes, or being divinely chosen, or being products of natural selection and the survival of the fittest. "Compulsive personalities seem to be primarily motivated by the will to power, the will to control and dominate the behavior of others, the will to be supermen or superior beings" (235). Compassionate freedom is freedom meant equally for all human beings. It must be carved out and made since it is not inherited as such. Compulsive justice looks more like judgments for it is always hierarchical in its ordering of human relations. Social movements toward equality will be suspect. Compassionate justice would mean a moving toward equality since all humans are equally human.

In a compulsive framework, love will tend toward "dominance-submission relations, tending toward sado-masochism" (258) while a compassionate understanding would perceive love as a free choice of equals who treat one another as ends in themselves. Under compulsion, mental health becomes defined as egoism. Prosperity is a sign of health and sex is a necessary evil. In contrast, under compassion, mental health means the healthy person considers others as well as herself or himself. Creativity is a sign of health and sex would be one example of creative interchange in general. Peace for a compulsive or non-critical ideology or person implies acceptance of the status quo, including all of its injustices. Thus a state of structural violence is allowed, indeed encouraged, to continue. In contrast, "compassion requires commitment to nonviolence as a means of achieving its values." (260) Peace in that context is something that needs to be won, fought for, and in fact is never fully achieved. Like justice, it is a verb and not a noun.

Power in a compulsive setting implies control, dominance and ruling of others and thus reinforces any basic inequalities already existing. Power in the compassionate context implies an equal distribution of power to all the people. This kind of power, namely an equally distributed one, will not corrupt.

Eckhardt, by his empirical studies and his critical analysis, has performed a powerful service to all interested in the psychology of compassion. His holistic approach—he refused to isolate self from society—is a refreshing one and indeed the only kind of psychological approach that is capable of assisting the path to compassion. Unfortunately, some priest psychologists and others have overlooked this all-important social dimension in studies on compassion and thus run the grave risk, when mixing their thoughts with the romance of monasticism, of sentimentalizing compassion. Perhaps compulsiveness is hostile to compassion in the long run because compulsiveness is so hostile toward self. It does not trust self or in Jesus' words "love oneself." Compulsion is aimed always outside oneself—to a rule or a norm or a Rulegiver or Authority figure. It lacks the moral ingredient of personal choice and decision-making. Like a TV dinner, it was made by some-one else. This someone or Something else is often so far outside that it is unconscious. From this unawareness comes the *drivenness* that marks all compulsion. It is, for all its conscious pronouncements of freedom, a cry of an utter lack of freedom. Compassion, to be com-passionate, must be conscious and aware, though always in touch with the dreams and unnameable, unspeakable, ineffable images that we only occasionally dare play with.

There is something about compulsiveness that blinds one to all but one direction and renders one dangerously single-minded. Like lemmings dashing to their death, compulsive persons or cultures hear only one cry, one call, one direction, one ideology. This exclusivity which is common to so much drivenness is so simplistic, so one-di-mensional and so cold to others' pain and joy that the possibility of compassion is thoroughly banished. It results in a fundamental lack of imagination that is easily threatened by creative persons.

It is here, perhaps, that Horney's understanding of competition and Eckhardt's grasp of compulsion come together: the person *driven* to power, *driven* to prestige and *driven* to possession sets about driving others. The ladder creates more ladders. No circles. No thanks. No laughter. No sensitivity to the pain of others. No celebration. A bleak world, this. With hardly a place or space for the gentle or the just or for an equal distribution of the gentle. Eckhardt concludes his study on Compassion in this way.

> Compassion is the truth that sets men (sic) free from the com-pulsion to destroy one another. Far from being an instinct over which we have little or no control, compulsion is deter-mined by material conditions of inequality, and these condi-tions and theories are made by human beings. Consequently, they can be changed by human beings. . . . (270)

DUALISM VS. COMPASSION

A third member of the demonic trinity that poisons us psycholog-ically in regard to our inherent capacities for compassion and unity and interdependence is called dualism. In many respects the spirit of dualism is inherent in the other members of this trinity we have been discussing—it is part of competition which is invariably an Us-versus-Them or I-versus-you strategem. It is part of compulsion which is so often an I-It strategem, me and my bottle, me and my goal, the corporation and its rising black lines, etc., etc. The members of this trinity are not isolated but interact in a kind of vortex and tornado-like funnel that carries us deeper and deeper to where the demonic lies and lies and lies. And maybe—as theologians Mary Daly (twentieth century) and Meister Eckhart (fourteenth century) insist—dualism is the ultimate alienation, the ultimate rending of the truth of ourselves, the ultimate sin. Or, as they say, dualism is the original sin . . . that is not all that original, alas!

Dualism: A sin of sins

What is this (un)original sin called dualism and how does it go about poisoning our spirits and our society? Dualism is a psychic perception, a way of seeing life in terms of Either/Or. Either male *or* female; either me *or* you; either up *or* down. I symbolize dualisms in the following manners—first as a simple, logical division (Figure A); next as two fishes swimming in opposite directions (Figure B). The astrological tradition employs this latter symbol, tellingly enough, to characterize the age of consciousness that began around 1 A.D. and that is to come to an end within twenty years. This Age of Fishes or of Pisces

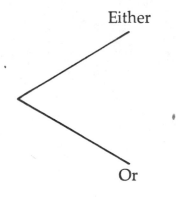

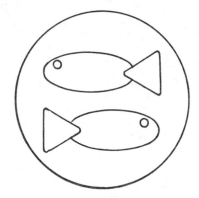

FIGURE A. Dualism teaches us to think Either/Or.

FIGURE B. In the Piscean Age, the basic symbol is two fishes swimming in opposite directions. Dualistic conciousness reigned supreme in this age, which is soon coming to an end.

is an age characterized by dualistic thinking, acting and symbolizing. We have, for example, considered in the previous chapter in discussing skyscrapers how our institutions are indeed symbols and how in fact they derive much of their power from the fact that they represent on the outside what in fact we worship on our insides. They are our insides coughed outside.

If there is some truth to the theory that a period of consciousness characterized by dualistic thinking is coming to a close,[8] then we ought to be able to begin to name the dualisms that are beginning to yield. Here, I invite the reader or readers to pause and to take the following seven-minute exercise: Brainstorm with self or your partner(s) for seven minutes about the following question, how many examples of dualisms can you name that you sense are coming to an end? I have already given some examples of what I mean: male/female; me/you; up/down. Now discover your own.

Examples of dualisms being questioned today

Here I would like to list some dualisms that groups I have brainstormed with have named. This is by no means a comprehensive listing, however, but in the serious games of symbol-making and symbol-naming, total and exhaustive comprehension is never necessary. Suggestion is more important to the imagination than exhaustive listing. For with suggestion one's imagination is triggered to make one's own list or to continue observing other possibilities. That is best for it is more democratic to trust one another's imaginations so. It is also more fun. And everyone learns more that way.

Old/Young
Fixed/mutable
in/out
urban/rural
yin/yang
handicapped/non-handicapped
strong/weak
black/white
churched/unchurched
conservative/liberal
static/fluid
light/dark
verbal/non-verbal
work/play
art/life
sane/insane
sated/hungry

college educated/life-educated
employed/non-employed
Christian/non-Christian
life/death
joy/pain
happiness/sadness
hopeful/desperate
creative/stifling
violence/non-violence
love/hate
doors/windows
heterosexual/homosexual
God/human
gay/straight
marxist/capitalist
potent/impotent
contextual/literal

atheism/theism
science/religion
rich/poor
rural/urban
literal/symbolic
mother/father
left/right
East/West
authority/power
formal/informal
push/pull
ugly/beautiful
sharing/keeping
open/closed
saint/sinner
warden/inmate
ordained/lay
complexity/simplicity
good/evil
work/leisure
night/day
natural/supernatural
God/devil
haves/have-nots
majority/minority
win/lose
being/having

body/soul
spiritual/sensual
male/female
clean/dirty
Catholic/Protestant
Christian/Jew
believer/non-believer
body/soul
first world/third world
war/peace
powerful/powerless
nation/state
blue collar/white collar
. teacher/student
parent/child
management/union
we/they
I/you
humans/animals
earth/heaven
future/now
past/present
urban/suburban
roles/person
be/do
religion/health

So much for a partial and suggestive listing of dualisms we live among and that just might be able to be altered.

But altered to what? The fact is that all these dualisms contain some truth—there *is* a difference between male/female, East/West, Third World/First World. But the question is: How much of a difference? Has an era of excessive dualistic consciousness left us thinking that the differences are more objective and less reconcilable than in fact they are? If so, what alternatives exist for us?

Dialectical Consciousness

The alternative to dualistic consciousness is dialectic. Now to persons raised in a dualistic culture and period of consciousness the word 'dialectic' is a foreign word. It is strange to those reared in a materialistic culture, for materialism by definition has a weighty investment in dualism. Buyer/seller, paid/not-paid, producer/consumer—where would materialism be without these dualisms so basic to its energies? While the term "dialectic" appears strange to us, it is in fact an every-day experience. Every time we laugh we are expressing the dialectical or paradoxical truth of our existence. In fact, so basic is laughter and the dialectical and paradoxical truth it expresses that surely there is no test of sanity that is more accurate than a sense of humor. The best test of self-love is the ability to laugh at oneself; of the love of another is the ability to laugh *at*—and not just with—another and to *be* laughed at by another. It is telling that neither competitive psyches nor compulsive ones have the time or space to laugh very much. Where humor is allowed in the ghettos of competition and compulsion, it is invariably laughter *down* on others. A sadistic, slapstick kind of humor.

Ernest Becker defines the human person as "a god who shits," an "angel who craps." [9] I hope that you laughed when you read Ernest Becker's definition of me, your author. And of you, the reader/author. And of me, your reader/author. Consider any other joke or occasion that makes you laugh. You will find therein the basic truth of our existence: it is a joke. We are God's joke. For we are indeed gods who crap and that breaks us up. (Imagine what it can do to God!) A dialectical consciousness, then, is as near as laughter. It is experiencing and perceiving life as Both-And instead of Either/Or. The symbol I use to diagram this experience is a curved arrow as in Figure C. Given this dialectical way of seeing reality, one can return to the lists of dualisms and inquire whether as Both-Ands they do make a lot of sense. Both-And thinking is the basis of compassion for through it we see the interconnections instead of the cold separations of reality. Without dialectical thinking there is no spiritual maturity. There never was a mystical thinker, East or West, who was authentically such who did not revel in dialectical thinking. Never trust a mysticism that lacks it— or its ally, a sense of humor.

What is Christian faith if not a series of stories about dialectical events and happenings? Christmas and Incarnation, stories about God becoming human; Grace, a story about humans becoming divine. Good Friday and Easter Sunday, stories of death and rebirth. Pente-

Both   And

FIGURE C. Dialectical consciousness is a Both-And way of thinking and living.

cost, a story about Christ gone and the Spirit coming. The Sermon on the Mount, a story about loving your enemies. Being spiritual as "being in, not of the world." And Christ's advice that "unless the seed first fall and die it will not bear fruit. . . ." The Kingdom of God as leaven and as the tiny mustard seed. On and on the parables of Jesus go to reveal a non-stop dialectical artist. "Unless you adults turn and become like children. . . ." The reader is invited to return to Jesus' stories with this question of dialectical consciousness in mind. It is a question that Christian Empire Builders have seldom put to the roots of Christianity. This same question can be wisely put to any spiritual tradition, West or East.

I believe that the truly adult spiritual journey is precisely this: a journey from dualism to dialectic. From Either/Or to Both—And. Until people can make such a journey they are incapable of compassion. Neither celebration nor relief of the pain of others will truly occupy their centers. Centering will be attempted—always unsuccessfully—by competition or compulsion, by object collecting and consumerism, by controlling or being controlled. But one's divine capacities, those of Both—And, will remain untapped and untried. And from the frustration of this inability to touch bottom, to touch our roots, to become radical, will be born violence and its adulterous spouse, sentimentalism. Envy will be the bastard child born of this unholy marriage. An envy of those who are free enough, dialectical enough and compassionate enough to invite others to their own unlimits of freedom and of unfreedom. Such envy has traditionally resulted in crucifixion of dialectical persons. Hung on crosses naked and outstretched, such spiritual fools are taunted for a miracle to save them by. To save especially those who did the nailing and divided up their clothes. A miracle to flash like lightening between them and us, truth and ignorance, life and death. But even the suggestion of such miracles is a blasphemy—it presumes that our Creator did not know what she was doing when she made us dialectical, divine, animal dancers. They presume that birth cannot and does not occur from death. They are cynical for they refuse to consider the possibility of resurrections for all.

For who can dare to say that human existence is not harmonious with all other existence and that the law of energy, as in electricity, that comes alive when positive and negative interact, or of muscles that go to work when push and pull occur, or that insight that comes when a limb is lost—that these dialectical truths are not *the* truth of all existence? Do not our very bodies bear within them the truth of dialectic? We are after all bipeds, with two arms, two eyes, two ears, two legs, two sides to our heart as well as brain, two lungs, two hands. Perhaps when Jesus spoke of not letting your one hand know what the other is doing he was urging us not to judge one side better than the other but to enter into the dialectic that forms the very fabric of our being.

Authentic mystics who speak of a "nothingness" experience do so within the context of our also being divinized. It is the pseudomysticism of imperalistic spirtualists who reduce the "nothingness" experience to a dualistic and psychological put-down of an individual. Such selling of one-sided nothingness is one more weapon in the arsenal of demonic spirituality. It feeds on the hidden truth of all dialectic and for that reason deserves the title "demonic". It contains a hidden truth: That death *is* different from life; positive from negative; north from south. But its dualistic, either/or stance betrays it for what it is— a lie. A lie meant to keep people in a state of untruth first with themselves, next with others in society, past and future, and finally with God. Dualism is the ultimate lie that undermines all possibility of compassion.

Jesus, like Buddha and Francis and Amos and Meister Eckhart and Mary Daly, has stood up and called the lie a lie. It is only the truth that will make us free. And the truth is we are dialectical. The truth is we are compassionate. The world is, we are, interconnected. It is time the human mind woke up to this truth. It may even be past time and too late. This truth is holy. Its holiness is holness. It is, as all truth is, demanding of us. It demands holness of us and with that holiness. The only way humans truly experience holness or holiness is dialectically. We laugh because we need to. We cannot hold it in. We cannot not laugh. We cannot, when being true to ourselves, not be dialectical. We are not born to be liars but laughers. We *are* God's dialectic, and joke. Provided we can escape Satan's lie called dualism.

The dialectical psychology of Robert Ornstein

A school of psychology has emerged in America in this decade whose whole thrust is to recover the dialectical dimension to human awareness. The founding parent of this movement to holism in psychology is Dr. Robert Ornstein. He claims that we in the West, under the influences of positivistic science and mechanistic theories so prevalent the past few centuries, are literally using only one side of our bi-polar brain. He sees the need for our changing from a strictly analytic mode of perceiving reality to a less ruggedly individualistic one.

The analytic mode, in which there is separation of objects, of the self from others (I-it relationship), has proved useful in individual biological survival; yet this mode apparently evolved to fit the conditions of life many thousands of years ago. . . . Instead, the survival problems now facing us are collective rather than individual: problems of how to prevent a large nuclear war, pollution of the earth, overpopulation. And notice that in these examples, a focus on individual consciousness, individual survival, works against, not for, a solution. A shift toward a consciousness of the interconnectedness of life, toward a relinquishing of the 'every man for himself' attitude inherent in our ordinary construction of consciousness (is necessary).[10]

Thus Ornstein calls for a consciousness of interconnectedness, that is, compassion, as the only route for a psychology of morality in our time.

What would such a psychology of compassion consist of? The model Ornstein uses is that of the two sides of the brain. No one disputes that we do in fact have a right and left hemisphere in our brains and that the right operates the left side of our bodies and the left hemisphere operates the right side of our bodies. There is also agreement that each hemisphere is more adept at performing some tasks than others—though exactly how the two sides of the brain differ in their tasks is not altogether agreed upon yet.[11] Gestalt schools of psychology have found much to agree with in Ornstein's basic thesis, especially at the level of therapy. Gestalt therapist Dr. Joen Fagan, for example, speaks of the "rapprochement of the 'left' side of psychology (verbal, behavioral, logical, scientific) with the 'right' (intuitive, experiencing, imaging, therapeutic)." He feels that Gestalt therapy owes much to the split-brain theory of psychology. "Most of the techniques and procedures used by Gestalt therapists appear to disrupt left lobe functions and to evoke right lobe perception and memories in order to allow past and present experiences to be more adequately symbolized and integrated."[12]

Ornstein offers a "tentative" listing of the two modes of consciousness. If his hypothesis is correct, even in general terms, then his psychology offers a healing of dualisms, a way out of our either/or demonic patterns of thinking and structuring self and society. Above all, since Ornstein feels the West has overemphasized the left lobe at the expense of the right and the East has done the reverse, he challenges us Westerners to recover what is quite literally one-half of our brains. We are, he would say, a one-sided and one-dimensional people and there lies our stuckness in dualism which by definition is one-sided thinking. Following is a list that combines his findings with my own.[13]

| *left lobe of brain* | *right lobe of brain* |
| *right side of body* | *left side of body* |

Day, light	Night, dark
Clock time (control)	Suspended time (ecstasy and service in prophecy)
Linear time	Spiral time
Active (prophetic)	Receptive (mystical)
Intellectual, head cognition	Sensuous, guts, intuitive cognition
Straight	Curved
Yang, animus	Yin, anima
sky, heaven	earth
mechanistic	organic
place	space
nouns	verbs
verbal	spatial
Analytic	Gestalt
literal	symbolic

The right side of this page corresponds to the neglected side of western consciousness. Orstein's solution to this one-sidedness includes taking people through forms of eastern meditation and spirituality.

I would like to propose that Western spiritual traditions too are rich treasuries filled with insight about the neglected side of our brains, and I will develop this thesis more concretely in the last part of this chapter. For several centuries we have been under such an overbearing influence of the left side of the brain in the West that we have often failed even to ask the right questions of our own spiritual heritage.

TOWARD A PSYCHOLOGY OF COMPASSION WHICH IS A PSYCHOLOGY OF CELEBRATION

It is certain that a psychology of competition, compulsion and dualism never has resulted in creating compassionate people and never will. For the root energies that are needed psychologically speaking to unleash energies of compassion are the antithesis of the control that is implicit in competitive, compulsive either/or dualistic behavior and consciousness. Indeed, while this unholy trinity is about control, a holier trinity—one that truly makes compassion happen—would be about celebration. Psychologist Arthur Jersild rightly observes that "there are elements of compassion one can possess only at the price of pain. There are other elements that one can possess only through having known the meaning of joy. But the full tide of compassion comes from all the streams of feeling that flow through human existence." (in Eck, p. 40) He is correct, for the proper psychology of compassion is a psychology of celebration. Those who do not or cannot celebrate will take energies meant for the relief of others' pain and reduce them to compulsions, competitions or dualisms. They will destroy the social-prophetic dimension of compassion with their control-psychology. In this way "compassion" will become one more compulsion, one more moral norm, one more test for orthodoxy instead of the flowing and overflowing energy it is—an energy that flows both in the direction of relieving others' pain *and* in the direction of rejoicing with others.

Meister Eckhart, the true spiritual theologian of compassion, put it this way: "You need to love all persons as yourself, esteeming them and considering them alike. What happens to another, *whether it be a joy or a sorrow*, happens to you." Compassion is energies affecting us, "whether they be a joy or a sorrow," and that is why compassion is as much celebration as it is relief of pain. Compassion takes place at a level of consciousness wherein we recognize that "what happens to another happens to us"—it is about a shared existence, the inter-relating of all energies, those of joy as well as those of sorrow. This is why competition, compulsion and dualism wreck such havoc in the compassionate development of the individual—because by their very definition they instruct us to experience not the unity we share with others but separateness. They prolong separateness, they embelish it and institutionalize it. They make separateness an idol. Control becomes idolatrous under their powerful influences.

But the opposite of control is celebration. We have considered the unholy trinity that control presumes: what alternative trinity does celebration offer us? It is a holy Trinity of: Letting Be, Letting Go, and Letting Dialectic Happen. We will examine each of these energies in turn for it is from a combination of them that celebration occurs and is born and re-born. The Hebrew Bible is filled with pictures of the Messianic Days, the arrival of God's Fullness of Salvation as days of celebration, when wine will run down the mountainside like a river (Amos) and all will partake of a great banquet on a mountaintop with fine strained wines and excellent foods (Isaiah). Celebration is the very sign of the Kingdom and Queendom of God having arrived. The Messianic Banquet is truly a banquet, a thorough celebration, that *all*, especially the downtrodden and poor, will share in. Wine stands for the spirit that "rejoices the heart of man" and Jesus adapts this same sense of celebration symbolized by wine when he talks of new wine skins that represent spiritual renewal. And by his action in increasing the flow of wine at the nuptial celebration at Cana; and by his last meal of wine and bread.

The Biblical sign of salvation is not control (whether self-control, control of others or being controlled)—it is celebration. Thus celebration is a proper word for transcendence in Biblical thinking, just as compassion is, for celebration is one of the two basic energies of compassion. Compassion is heaven come to earth, as Eckhart put it: "To rejoice at another person's joy is like being in heaven." Heaven begins where celebration begins and control ends. One reason why lugubrious spiritualities and control-oriented spiritualities based on asceticism have next to nothing whatever to say about compassion is that they never experience celebration. I once had a student in a class who had previously been through a very, very serious program in spirituality and for the entire semester she never once smiled or laughed. I still feel for her and hope and pray that the demon of control that her spiritual training left her with might be some day exorcised. Only a psychology of celebration yields compassionate persons because it is in celebration that we learn to forget our self-consciousness, our bodies, our egos, our fears, our problems, our self-images, our positions of status or lack of status—and remember our ultimate holness and therefore holiness. For all celebration is an act of forgetting in order to remember. Thus celebration requires acts of forgetting and it is in the very energy that is expressed in celebrating (for example, in folk dancing) that such forgetting and remembering is effected. In celebration we forget the superficial in order to remember the deep. But the deep is simple and good: it invites us to celebrate.

Celebration leads to fuller and fuller compassion, whether compassion is expressed as relieving the pain of others (one fine way is to invite others to celebrate and thereby forget their troubles, not a few of which are caused by self-pity, by clinging to controls of competition, compulsion and dualism). Or as celebrating. In other words, celebration produces more celebration, energy produces energy. After a while we celebrate the relief of pain, we celebrate the good persons we are who feel pain, and eventually we even celebrate the celebration.

Celebration is not done alone even when we are alone. It is about energies dancing. Salvation as celebration touches us so deeply that it leads from the personal to the inter-personal and even the supra-personal or cosmic. The entire cosmos is touched by compassion and by celebration. Celebration moves us from the psychological to the social, from self to society, from I to We, from self to God. In this sense it becomes an integral part of the creation of the world that God accomplishes daily and of the re-creation that the world so sorely needs. Our recreation becomes the world's re-creation; and our work at re-creation becomes the world's recreation. Work and play (relieving pain and celebrating) constitute the twin energies of all compassion. But they are not dualistic—they too come together so that soon work becomes play, play becomes work and both become celebration. But play is more basic than work for in the last analysis life is a joy and a gift. Politics or our re-creating of society and mysticism or our recreating of self and others in celebration meet in the energy called compassion.

For all these reasons, then, celebration leads to compassion. But what are the steps in learning to celebrate? What is this holy Trinity called celebration? I detect three psychological experiences that add up to celebration: Letting Be; Letting Go; Letting the dialectical happen.

LETTING BE

A psychology of celebration is not an elitist psychology—each individual does not need to sit on a couch and pay by the hour for this kind of psychological release. One has to pay instead with a simpler, more relaxed way of living. One pays by letting be, letting go and letting a dialectic happen. There is sacrifice of a kind in this manner of living, as indeed there ought always to be. As Ghandi warned, worship without sacrifice is one of the deadly sins. But the sacrifice is clearly one of letting and releasing and relaxing, rather than one of ego-projection and ego-controlling. There is sacrifice involved in true celebrating precisely because there is authentic worship involved.

And what is the authentic worship that is involved in celebration? First, there is Letting Be. Letting God be. Letting ourselves be. Letting disturbances be. Letting joy be. Letting pain be. Letting beauty be. Letting be.

Letting be is reverence; it is respect. It is what all true worship presumes, for it is letting God be God, letting self be self, letting suffering be suffering, letting joy be joy. With this letting be comes a growth into being and into identity with all these important energies of our lives. It is letting mystery be mystery wherein we do not reduce mysteries to problems, but simply let mysteries be. Deep listening, acute wakefulness and keen watching are all implied in letting be. For when one lets all things be one finds great wonders even in the smallest of things. One finds God in a photograph taken between the cracks of an urban pavement and blown up to the size of a home movie screen—one searches to know *what is*, what already is, and amazing surprises occur. As Nick Weber, champion of his Royal Lichtenstein Quarter-Ring Sidewalk Circus declares, "God is a great surprise," and our need today is to be able to recognize "a free spirit like God." Let things be, Weber is saying, and even God will be. Surprises will return. God might even return. And what is celebration, after all, without surprises?

In Letting Be we learn to let others be. To let God be. And, perhaps most basic of all, to let ourselves be. And to be with ourselves. To befriend ourselves, as healthy solitude requires. We begin to learn our own holiness and goodness and then we are more fully prepared to welcome holiness and goodness in others without jealousy or recrimination. That is how deeply one is changed by learning to Let Be.

To let things be is to declare the holiness of all things. For when we sense holiness or praise holiness precisely what we are declaring is that this thing (person or event) *needs no changing*. "It is good," we are saying. (Which is what the Creator first said.) It is holy. It has something to teach us. I can be with it and learn, drink, take in, be nourished, be refreshed, be. Thus letting be is our act of reverence and respect. We are at least as capable of that as we are of compulsively trying to order the world and collect things in a compulsive kind of consumerism that reduces all the world and the whole life of mind and spirit to a kind of chess board whereon we manipulate all. When one learns to let things be, anything can happen. Even God can happen.

LETTING GO

The way we become celebrators instead of controllers is by learning to let go. "Only one who has dared to let go," Meister Eckhart warns, "can dare to re-enter." By re-enter he means to re-enter reality itself which is so full of God everyplace, every space and all the time. But it is our very clinging and compulsiveness that prevent us from waking up to the fact of giftness and holiness, of causes for reverence and celebration everywhere. Thus, we need to let go in order to let things happen and in order to let things be. "There where our clinging to things ends," says Eckhart, "is where God begins to be." The Rabbi of Kotzk is supposed to have put the following question to a group of very learned men: "Where does God dwell?" They laughed when they heard the question, saying "What a thing to ask! Is it not written, 'The whole world is full of his glory'?" But the Rabbi had a different answer. He replied to his own question: "God dwells wherever man lets him in." [14]

Letting God in implies letting other things out, not because they are things and things are bad but because of what the clinging to things does to our consciousness—it makes us clingers instead of celebrators or letting-goers. The "things" might be our bodies—how many people who say they worship 'God' on Sundays in fact never let go of their clinging to body enough to celebrate by dance, for example—our titles and positions, our stocks and bonds, our carniverous diets, our second car, our pain, or our time. Letting go might even mean letting go of letting go. When we learn to let go, we can go back to "things" and possess them without being possessive; we can even compete without being competitive; we can order and arrange without being compulsive; we can succeed without being successes; we can fail without being failures. In short, we can live again. We can celebrate. We can learn that "things" are not things but energies which can either enslave us by the demands of competition, compulsion and dualism they put upon us, or they can be part of our liberation insofar as we learn reverence and goodness from them. Truly, only those who have dared to let go can dare to re-enter.

We even have to let go of God to re-enter into a celebrative experience of God. "I pray God to rid me of God" confessed Meister Eckhart. We dance before God as David did when we also let go of God. Do we also pray God to rid us of a ladder God, a theistic God, a childish God, a perfectionist God, an all-American, nationalistic God, a capitalist ("in God we trust" on dollar bills) God, a skyscraper, up-in-the-sky God? And, of course, our learning to let go is a preparation for an ultimate letting go that will be all of ours: the letting go of life. The occasion of our death is an occasion for letting go of many, many precious and beautiful experiences: sunsets and friends, music and learning, cooking and conversation, relatives and birds' singing. And, of course, life as we know it. Surely much of the resistance to discussing and understanding death in our culture stems from our compulsive clinging to what we imagine we *have* or possess, in this case to life. But the truth is that we do not possess life or any of these true gifts of life. They have been loaned us, not given us. Even our so-called private property will belong to someone else upon our death. Possession as possessiveness is a lie, a damnable lie that condemns us to a hell of isolation and clinging even before our deaths. Death then is a very real letting go. We practice for it—and for the surprises it contains—by learning to let go well before death. Which is identical to learning to live before death. And to taste eternal life before death.

Still another obstacle to letting go is our fear of nothingness. We cling compulsively very often because we are afraid of the alternative which is apparently so unknown. And we suspect, ever so subtly, that if we did not put order into things, they would lack all order. That behind reality is a gaping hole waiting to swallow us up. This attitude toward the reality of nothingness is a very ancient one, perhaps even deserving the title of psychological archetype. The issue is: what do we do, face to face with nothingness? Do we become compulsive doers, savers, saviours, orderers? Do we despair of all somethingness? There are two great answers to this question in the West, a Greek answer and a Biblical one. The Greek answer is to create order at all costs; the Biblical answer is that, as true as nothingness is, being is even more true and more basic. The Biblical view is far more hopeful and optimistic; it invites exploration of nothingness—certainly not repression of it—but it advises: Take courage. God is greater than chaos, creation is more basic than nothingness. Thus Tresmontant says:

> It is characteristic of Hebrew thought, as opposed to Greek and Western thought, that it is not troubled by negative ideas of nothingness and disorder. Hebrew thought is not haunted by the idea of an original void that should be there 'by rights' and that has to be overcome, or of a disorder, a chaos, that has to be mastered, because its threatening presence might undermine reality. In the beginning stands, not void, but Him whose name is: 'I am,'....[15]

Faith, then, invites us to let go even of our fear of nothingness, teaching us to trust that an exploration into nothingness leads itself to Somethingness. Surprises everywhere! Even nothing leads to celebration. God even created the nothingness.

Still another dimension to letting go and to letting be is solitude. I understand solitude to be the experience of others while supposedly alone. Solitude is learning to befriend oneself, to enjoy and celebrate one's own company. But what is the key to solitude and makes it utterly different from withdrawal is that in solitude we are truly *not* alone—and we know it. We learn that there is no such thing as alone. Aloneness is an illusion that our compulsive culture has taught us we ought to fear and run from. Our dance with loneliness, like our dance with nothingness, reveals a Somethingness, the truth of shared energies everywhere.

Solitude in this sense may at first sound foreign and overly mystical to our ears because our culture's selling of love—defined always as love of two people—is so superficial. In fact, solitude is about as obvious and basic an experience as one can have. For example, one might say, "I'm going to the woods for some solitude." Fine and good, but in this statement itself is revealed the lie of those who try to tell us solitude is withdrawal, for the person declared that "in the woods" meaning *with* the woods, she or he would enter into solitude. In other words, one is never alone on this earth—or, I suspect, beyond—for there is always the earth, the water, the plants and animals, the sounds, the stars and sky. Solitude is closely related to celebration because, like celebration, it is a form of forgetting for a while. It is very often our memories that we want either to leave behind in solitude or to purify by means of solitude. It is evident, then, that solitude and celebration are closely intertwined. Both seek to get beyond noisyness and busyness for wholesome forgetfulness that leads to authentic remembering. If solitude is so closely related to celebration, then clearly such solitude is essential for celebration as well.

The fullest experience of solitude is not withdrawal but is an attitude—as celebration is—that we carry with us in work and play, whether alone or with others. It is an encounter with emptiness that carries with it a hint of fullness. It is as necessary for fullness as emptiness is; as necessary for celebration as laughter is; as necessary for compassion as celebration is. It is our letting go in order to let be. No one put the difference between solitude and withdrawal, between courage and fear, more directly than Meister Eckhart, who teaches: "Spirituality is not to be learned by flight from the world, by running away from things or by turning solitary and going apart from the world. Rather, one needs to learn an inner solitude, wherever or with whomsoever one may be. We must learn to penetrate things and find God there." Thus it is *in* "things" in the sense of events, news, work, play, people, pain, nature, music, the universe, that we are to find God and celebrate. Letting go leads to finding God.

LETTING DIALECTIC HAPPEN

In a previous section I offered a tentative listing of Ornstein's and my interpretations of the two sides of the brain, using that physiological fact more or less as a symbol for the dualisms that so rack our consciousness. The healing, I pointed out, is named dialectic. I would like to present here a brief outline of how Western spirituality could assist us in developing the neglected half of our psyches. This is especially important to consider since Ornstein and his school remain almost totally involved in an exploration of how Eastern spiritual traditions can help heal us.

In considering this outline, it is important to emphasize that healing will only take place if we are thinking dialectically and not dualistically. In other words, while I emphasize the right lobe of the brain I have no intention of replacing the former dualistic tyranny of the left side with a new one from the right. I am thinking both-and. Furthermore, as a white male who is a theologian and writer, I have developed skills of the brain's left side or I would not be writing this book and you reading it. I want to emphasize, therefore, that for persons who are not white or are not male it is not enough to develop only that side of the brain that I emphasize here. I am presuming, by remaining silent about it, that the left brain lobe needs to be developed — especially by those whom culture has not previously rewarded for such development, such as some women and racial minorities in our country. There is also an invitation here for those who, by the need to survive, have developed, often going against the cultural tide a true right lobe of the brain. Do not leave this aside in entering the left-lobe work world! "Police Woman" is no real imaginative solution to too many "policemen" television stories.

As we mentioned above, dialectic is related to laughter. In Letting the Dialectic Happen, we are, of course, letting laughter happen once again. The test of the true prophet is one who can, when all is said and done, laugh. It is no small thing that the Bible devotes an entire book (*Jonah*) to making prophets laugh at themselves. In laughter we confess that true living, true compassion, is not about control but about realizing the inherent humor of the universe. We recognize how we are both angels and animals, divine and human, right brain and left brain. We are letting reality happen, since reality is so profoundly and foolishly dialectical.

I invite the reader to explore the neglected side of our brains and psyches with me as I proceed down the list of characteristics that I have enumerated previously (see p. 87).

Night, Dark

In the Liturgy that Christians have been accustomed to celebrating at midnight Christmas services, the following reading is recited from the Book of Wisdom: "When peaceful silence lay over all,/and night had run the half of her swift course,/down from the heavens, from the royal throne, leapt your all-powerful Word;/into the heart of a doomed land the stern warrior leapt." (18.14f.) What is being said about the night and the dark in this Scripture passage which is so basic to Christian belief in the Incarnation? First, that God comes, the Word comes, especially at night. Jesus was himself born at night for we are told that the shepherds were "watching the flocks during the night" when they heard of the birth. The Resurrection also happened at night for we are told that the women who found the tomb empty arrived at the very break of dawn. Why is it that the divine comes at night? Because night is silent? Yes. But also because night is ... night. It is dark. We cannot control too many of our ideas in the dark, we are forced to listen more keenly in the dark. And to strain to see more deeply in the dark.

I once met a woman who told the following story. As she was growing up in New Orleans she and her mother were very close. One night she came home from a date about midnight and her mother was on the front porch. "Let's go inside and have a talk," her mother said. "Fine," the young woman responded, and when they entered the room she bent over to turn on the lamp. "No," her mother said. "Leave the light off. I can see you better in the dark." Can we say that? Can we welcome the dark, see better in the dark? Or are we afraid of it? Can we welcome mystery and also doubt, uncertainty, insecurity, the unknown, the hidden—and find God there? The *via negativa* developed by the mystics—Eckhart calls God the "non-God"—means that the experience of God happens especially in the dark, that it is there that God's name is revealed. The dark night of the soul is understood to be the emptiness that precedes the fullness, but it is a rich and divinely-filled emptiness that only appears to be empty by the judgment of day.

We need to ask how technology has altered our relationship to night and to dark. Now that we can enter any room at any time of day or night and, with a flick of the finger, turn night to day, it is clear that we have lost much of the Letting Be and reverence our race could once take for granted vis a vis the nighttime. To what extent is racism related to fear of dark? And to what extent is male sexism involved in putting down the night? Notice that in the Scriptural passage cited, night is called a "she." The moon comes out at night and the moon is very often a symbol of womanhood. Is a patriarchal culture, like an overly white one, condemned to putting down the night?

We must also ask to what extent a flight from darkness and night is a flight from depth and even from our origins. The depths of the unconscious are, so to speak, dark and unexplored. A culture that discourages in-depth searching will also put down night. Are we not all, in our inner depths, dark like the bottom of the ocean or the depths of space? The origins of each of us were in the dark, for the womb is dark. A flight from darkness is most likely a flight from re-birth, the fear of being born again. Moreover, almost all of us were conceived in the dark and that too makes the dark holy.

Still another insight from this Scriptural passage is the political dimension of nighttime. We are told that it was "into the heart of a doomed *land*" that "the stern warrior leapt." How often a sentimentalized faith has spoken of leaps into private souls—but the Scriptures promise a leap into a "doomed land." Redemption is political because life is political and in the dark we are more aware of this. For in the dark, our masks and personalities are down and we are less guarded; distinctions are not primary, but oneness is. In the dark we learn the truth of the unity of all things. Thus the dark is more political than the daytime.

Suspended Time, spiral time, receptivity

When we can say "Where did the time go?" or "I was having such fun I lost track of the time," we are revealing how ecstasy is, by definition, a suspension of time. It is a no-time, a forgotten time. And therefore a refreshing time. Unlike clock time which is so objective—we are either late or early or "on time"—and which is the absolute norm by which many persons are paid in a culture in which wasting time is a sin, suspended time is altogether relative. It is relative to events experienced. I once heard a radio interview in which an individual told the story of his grandmother who lived in the rural area of Arkansas and had no clocks in the house. When it came time to boil an egg she sang one verse of "Bringing in the Sheaves"—and two verses for a hard boiled egg. The results were perfect every time. It is clear, therefore, that we are free to create alternative senses and experiences of time other than the clock or objective sort of time.

Still another kind of time that is neglected in a clock or a linear approach to time is that of prophecy. When we are committed to altering the times we count time differently. Thus when we say, "It's about time that all the world's children had the basics to eat," we are pronouncing our commitment to changing the times. And this sense of bringing about a new future will alter our entire sense of time and of life itself and, very often, death too. Anyone who truly believes in the Scriptural sense of time is steeped in a sense of eschatology or the last times' having arrived—a time of justice and peace. A time that has to be carved out to truly happen and be present.[16]

Sensuousness, earth, guts, intuition

Truth comes from the guts, from our viscera and not exclusively from the head. Descartes' definition of truth as "clear and distinct ideas" does violence to our intuitions and deep feelings which are

equally important avenues of insight and awareness. It leaves aside all
the truth that is revealed in passion and therefore all the truth of pain
and of joy. The recovery of earthiness and sensuousness is so vital to
spiritual and psychological renewal that I have written a book about it
already and will develop it further in chapter five below. Suffice it to
say here that Christians should meditate on St. Francis of Asissi's one
regret in life as he lay dying: namely, that he had treated his body too
harshly. That he had taken too seriously the platonic dualism of his
culture that wanted to use the soul as a means for controlling body, instead of using both energies in a mutual dialectic of interaction. It is
no small thing that Francis insisted, when dying, to be placed naked
on the earth, who he knew as his sister and mother.

Curved, Yin, organic

Andrew Weil[17] points out how great the difference is from riding
down a straight highway such as a tollway or turnpike and driving
down back roads which are invariably curved, up, down and around.
It is a totally different energy system that is involved in the two ways
of travel. One is a basic arrow dynamic — the thrust is to arrive at some
distant place; the second dynamic is one of enjoying the interaction
along one's curved way. We have dealt with the curved and the Yin
symbols in chapter two and will treat them further in chapters four
and seven. Here lies the heart of any meditation on the global village
and therefore the essense of all global-village-spiritual consciousness:
That we are organically inter-related — all creatures — on a rounded,
curved sphere in a curved universe.

Space, verbs, spatial

The discovery that all creation is a verb and not a noun is a profound breakthrough for contemporary science (see chapter five) and
one that the greatest religious teachers have tried to get persons to see
for themselves over the centuries. Our noun-oriented and institution-
oriented culture instructs us in the opposite mentality so often, namely
that if we "knew our place" everything would be in order. But in fact,
the 'order' of the cosmos is an order of movement and motion and
energies in motion, not of static things at rest and safely in place.[18]
Surely persons who truly believe they are "sons and daughters" of the
great Verb who is God the Creator must be overwhelmed by the truth
that they are lovers and justice-makers and themselves creators. There-

fore that they are verbs and not nouns, spaces and not places. Isn't every mystical experience, that is every suspension of ego or every experience of ecstasy, a confirmation of what depthless space each one of us is? Is it not here that our fascination for the seemingly fathomless ocean or outer space truly lies? That these spaces, with which we so readily commune, remind us of our own inner space that is even more vast and more depthless?

When Christians speak of Christ as the Word, they should be aware that what is being said is not that Christ is a word as in the verbal sense of a word on a page (which, since the printing press, is what most people assume word means). The Hebrew word for word, *dabhar*, is anything but static or in place. *Dabhar* means action and Deed as much as word—it is the word that effects something, the word that creates. It is a dynamic and creative word that is being spoken of. Thus calling Christ the Word in fact falls more into the category of spatial thinking when one realizes, with the mystics and with contemporary physics, that space is a verb, a deed in motion, a universe on the move. Christians would do well to meditate on this verb and spatial awareness of the poet Adrienne Rich:

> I am a glactic cloud so deep   so invo-
> luted that a light wave could take 15
> years to travel through me   And has
> taken [19]

Gestalt, organic, symbolic

The analytic and the verbal is very useful for demarcation, for quantification, for taking apart to get to the pieces of things. But left to itself, it leaves us only with parts and only with pieces. By itself it may become piece-meal thinking. Gestalt, which is a way of picturing the wholes of reality and symbolizing them by pictures, is another way to see reality. It is truly healing in its energies and truly compassionate since it does see the wholes and their interconnections. Thus it is organic instead of mechanistic. More will be said about this in chapter eight where in fact, in exegeting the Humpty Dumpty story, we will be involved in what is basically a Gestalt experience. This organic, as distinct from mechanical, way of knowing will also be dealt with in chapter five. The importance of being able to play with symbols, become symbols, give birth to symbols, deserves the name of meditation for that is what it is—*extrovert meditation*. We will deal with how creativity as meditation develops spatial consciousness in the following chapter.

I have employed several games for developing symbolic consciousness.[20] Once when I was leading a group through these games, it happened that a Gestalt psychologist was present and he afterwards took me aside and said: "Where did you study Gestalt?" I had to answer nowhere—though I had studied Western spiritual consciousness and, by traveling that route, I was led to several Gestalt-like exercises.

This brief meditation on the neglected dimensions of our psyches and how Western spirituality has much to offer only introduces a vast and important topic. Books have been written on each of these topics[21] and religious educators of all kinds should seriously consider devoting entire programs in parish or school educational systems to exploring each of these areas—(see p. 27) for example, a month in a parish dedicated to night, to space, to sensuousness, etc. Liturgies, homilies, discussion groups, readings and lectures as well as activities could revolve around each such area for that month. True psychological healing and spiritual renewal at the psychological level would begin to happen. Persons would begin to pass from our culture's lessons of psychology as control to Biblical lessons of psychology as celebration. What I have just presented is only one abbreviated meditation. It would be an interesting exercise also to examine not only the Scriptures but also the writings of the lives of Western saints to see evidence of dialectical consciousness, of the development of space in preference to place consciousness, of suspended time in preference to clock time, of sensuousness, darkness, intuition, receptivity, earthiness, etc. Since new questions will be put to our traditions from this exercise, new and exciting responses will be forthcoming.[22]

FORGIVENESS AND THE PSYCHOLOGY OF COMPASSION

Jesus links pardon and compassion, forgiveness and celebration when he says: "Be compassionate as your Father is compassionate . . . Grant pardon, and you will be pardoned" (Lk, 6.36f.). What psychological insight is Jesus unfolding in making this connection?

It is evident that the freedom and releasement that true celebration require and that Letting Be, Letting Go, and Letting Dialectic

Happen require also demand a fundamental forgiveness or pardon. For all these activities and attitudes require trust. And trust is a kind of forgiveness, a kind of "doing it anyway," a kind of willingness to be emptied based on hoped-for assistance or support. To celebrate we need forgiveness, whether of imaginary guilt—which is the most frequent kind by far—or of genuine guilt. A compulsive, competitive and dualistic culture will heap guilt upon us for taking the time to celebrate and for living differently by letting be, letting go and letting happen dialectically. We need forgiveness for this guilt even though it be false guilt. We need to believe in the forgiveness of others and, therefore, in trust; but just as much do we need belief in our capacity to forgive ourselves, and in the Creator's willingness to forgive us. Of these three kinds of forgiveness and trust, I believe that the most basic and most difficult is the second: Self-forgiveness is a great spiritual gift. We ought to pass it on wherever possible, whether as parents or as sisters and brothers, friends or enemies. One of the greatest helps in learning self-forgiveness is learning the truth of God's forgiveness. For it is everywhere. And learning that the Creator did not make anything in creation that is guilty as such. The Biblical tradition about creation, that all of it is good, also means that none of it is guilty for being itself. We need to believe this deeply. For without believing it we will never be able to celebrate. Or to be compassionate people.

In Biblical teaching, forgiveness is a work of God's compassion and it is especially the prophets who preach the freedom that forgiveness brings with it. The "broken-hearted and the crushed in spirit" are both forgiven and freed—but their forgiveness is not necessarily as simplistic as to say: "Now *your* sins are forgiven." Their forgiveness and freedom is related to forgiving in the sense of undoing the sins of those who oppress them. Not to forgive is to put in motion a spiral of oppression and sin. Jesus repeated this same theme when he counseled persons who have a brother who holds something against them to leave their gifts at the altar and first be reconciled. Others need forgiveness as much and often more than we; and in that forgiveness lies our own releasement. The prophets, looking forward to an eschatological time of fullfillment and Messianic richness signify forgiveness as a first and definitive step toward the total renewal of creation (Jer. 31.34, Ez. 36.25).

It has been said that in the New Testament forgiveness is "presented as the entire purpose of Jesus' coming."[23] The divine prerogative to forgive and therefore to launch compassion seems to have been assumed by Jesus. John teaches that forgiveness comes from trust in

God, in Jesus and in other people around us, as well as in our own attitude of admitting our fears and sins. This forgiveness is one of the gifts the risen Christ breathes on the first Christians as a gift of the Holy Spirit.

The freedom that forgiveness brings is both a personal and a social freedom. When the Pharisees are reported as saying to Jesus: "We have never yet been slaves to anyone. How can you say, 'You shall be free?'" (Jn. 8.33), what is implied is that Jesus senses an unfreedom and a slavery in the behavior of the Pharisees that calls out for pardon and releasement. The God of the Jews is the One who liberates, who sets the captives free—free to celebrate and share the celebration we might say. We cannot forget that forgiveness, like freedom and releasement, is a political as well as a psychological category. We forgive systems that coerce and control us by replacing them with structures that release us for compassion. We shall treat this issue of structural changes in subsequent chapters. God acquits us from guilt and the slavery to guilt and sin which prevents our celebrating and becoming compassionate. For Paul, Jesus has also set us free, this time from "the spirit of slavery and of fear" (Rom. 8.15) so that "where the Spirit of the Lord is, there is freedom" (2 Cor. 3.17). Our contemporary culture, with its control-oriented psychology, has left us slaves to competition, compulsion and dualism. To move from this slavery to freedom requires our self-forgiveness in order to leave behind and let go of this unholy trinity. The forgiveness that will make us free includes forgiveness for our own anger, our mistakes, our acquiescence, even our guilt. And, as we shall see in the following chapter, even our forgiveness for creating. No wonder Jesus, who calls persons to be compassionate, put so much emphasis on forgiveness in the one prayer he left behind: "Forgive us as we forgive others," we are to pray. And from this letting go of guilt, true worship or letting go can happen and then letting dialectic happen can happen. And all this happening we call celebration, the explosion of a new and holier trinity.

The passage from dualism to dialectic demands forgiveness of the guilt we may feel for passing from clinging to objects to letting events happen. It also requires a sort of forgiveness of our enemies, i.e., that which we fear the most. In many cases this fear and hatred correspond to that neglected side of our psyches that we have outlined in the previous section. A kind of 'forgiveness' of night, a 'forgiveness' of the sensuous, a 'forgiveness' of the curved are required in order to let the dialectic happen. This is because our culture has taught us to feel guilt about entertaining another side to our psyches.

SUMMARY

To pass from the control that competition, compulsion and dualism dictate is to pass to celebration by way of letting be, letting go and letting dialectic happen. This way lies all dance, whether the dance of the atoms or the dance of the humans, and all dances in between. This way lies also the divine dance, the divine dialectic that is meant to continue creation—which is a celebration—through that newly named divinity which is human beings. For from our renewal comes our making new again and from our recreation comes re-creation. From our Letting Be, Letting Go and Dialectical Living come a new form and a new order. A form of justice and an order of love. A way of living in harmony with creation so that it can be said that a new heaven and a new earth are eager to be born. Truly, celebration is a psychology for the future instead of the past.

4

CREATIVITY AND COMPASSION:

FROM A FETISH WITH THE CROSS TO AN EXPLORATION OF THE EMPTY TOMB

We have to realize that a creative being
lives within ourselves,
whether we like it or not,
and that we must get out of its way,
for it will give us no peace until we do.

Mary Richards[1]

There will be no compassion without creativity. Whether we are talking about making work or living situations more compassionate, about making economic systems or the relationship of first and third world peoples more compassionate, whether we are facing the issues of food and famine, energy or nuclear proliferation, unemployment or overemployment, boredom or alcoholism, creativity lies at the heart of relieving the pain. We need a new way of living and working if the species *homo sapiens* is to survive. And maybe we need a new kind of *homo sapiens*. Not only science and technology need to assist the human race with creative contributions to common problems but the situation demands, if survival is still possible at all, innovations in the fields of religion, sociology, politics, psychology, ethics, art, literature, music, living styles. Without this creativity, as psychologist Carl Rogers has warned, "the lights will go out." [2]

In many places the lights have already gone out. For example, in areas like Harlem or Mexico City where employment and the pride work brings is limited to only 60% of the adult population, lights have already gone out. And drugs, crime, alcoholism and other symptoms of despair are all that remain to light up peoples' lives. In nations that can afford to spend hundreds of billions of dollars on weapons and pittance on putting people to *good* work, lights have already gone out. Violence in all its forms is an immediate issue for creative people. The earth hovers on the brink of blowing up for lack of creative alternatives to human energies. One is forced to ask whether the geometric increase in violence that comes when persons leave the countryside and pour into urban areas—whether they be Chicago or Sao Paulo—is not related to the inability to be creative in urban and industrial society and especially when unemployment is so high. Even where there is industrial employment, frustration and violence remain at a high level. Why is this? Must the human animal be violent and frustrated and mean? Is passion-with a mere wispy ideal?

Jose Arguelles suggests that the answer to this matter of violence is related to the lack of creativity in peoples' lives. Says he: "When a man is deprived of the power of expression, he will express himself in a drive for power." [3] Creativity, a power of expression, may be the richest source of answers to overcrowded prisons of all kinds and in many places. It may also be an answer to the unemployment that so racks contemporary society because, although this hardly seems to occur to our great industrialists, investment in persons whose work it is to turn others on—whether as play-actors or violinists, as story-tellers or clowns, as composers or as dancers—is a way to put many, many people to work. And "good work" it is (in Schumacher's technical use of that term "good work") for the returns are *good*. They are not the returns of gluttonous foodstuffs that ruin people's health and send them to doctors or dieticians for curing; they are not the returns of cold, hard, gas-guzzling steel that war-profiteering contractors invest in; they are not the returns of shopping malls that maul countrysides and people alike. They are the return of smiles, of relaxation, of conviviality, of ecstasy shared, of celebration. They are returns of a society at peace with itself because it is at peace within itself. They are within returns and not mere external returns. And the returns affect not only the worker (e.g., the violinist) but the participator in that person's work (which might be one person or 500). The returns of creativity are the surest returns we know of. The returns are simplicity and satisfaction and shared awareness.

In this chapter I want to explore four issues concerning creativity and compassion. First, how we can de-elitize our understanding of artist so that creativity becomes spirituality or way of life for all just as compassion needs to be. Second, how the spiritual tradition of an empty tomb frees people to overcome the fear and guilt that prevent them from being creative. Third, how creativity and Compassion are similar energies. Fourth, how the recovery of Extrovert Meditation in the West will also be a recovery of prophetic, creative, doing of compassion.

CREATIVITY AS A WAY OF LIFE FOR ALL PEOPLE

The notion that creativity might be a spirituality or way of life for all persons has been a well-kept secret indeed during the era when Jacob's ladder dominated Western mysticism.

Toward a non-elitist art

The notion that creativity might be everyone's possession and prerogative and not that of an elitist few has not been preached from the housetops of late. But is it an idea whose time has come? Are the compulsions of overwork and of competition as well as of dualism (see chapter three) related to a common *flight from creativity?* If so, then underemployment and unemployment are also related to a flight from creativity. Persons may well be content with a four-day work week, thus allowing 15% more persons to work, were they at home with their creativity the other three days of the week.

I suggest that the violence and destructiveness of Jacob-ladder-mysticism and cultural structuring are nowhere more evident than in creativity and the arts. The West over the past few centuries has put the Artist—always a capital A—on such a pedestal, and sold the artist's wares to those who want one more investment in their portfolio, that all of us not aspiring to ladder-heights have been deceived about where true art lies. Thus speaks Otto Rank:

> The art manias of modern society, with their overvaluing of the artist, indicate a decline of real artistic vigour, which is only speciously covered over by the last flicker of a snobbish enthusiasm. It is certain that artists nowadays do not create for the people, but for the few exclusive groups, particularly of intellectuals who feel themselves artists.[4]

There has arisen, insists Rank, a "professional ideology" of the artist that in fact hinders full living.

In a Sarah-circle dynamic, while there would always be room for the genius or brilliantly endowed artist, art would still belong to everyone. All would be invited to recognize their creativity, to develop it with discipline and to celebrate it with others. Eric Gill put the contrast between the two approaches to art this way: "Not every artist is a special kind of person but every person is a special kind of artist." And Erich Fromm, also in quest of folk art or art for Sarah-Circle kinds of folks, observes how telling it is that our language does not even have a word for "folk art." This lack of a word is symptomatic of something worse: the lack of art and creativity as an ideal for all.

> The word 'art' ... in the modern sense [means] a separate area of life. We have, on the one hand, the artist, a specialized profession—and on the other hand the admirer and consumer of art. But this separation is a modern phenomenon. What about a gothic cathedral, a Catholic ritual, an Indian rain dance, a Japanese flower arrangement, a folk dance, community singing? Are they art? popular art? We have no word for it, because art in a wide and general sense, as a part of everybody's life, has lost its place in our world.[5]

According to the Buddhist philosopher and poet, Kenji Miyazawa, we cannot have art both in the hands of ladder people and circle people simultaneously.

> When art is separated from its audience it becomes degraded. Nowadays, the word 'minister' or 'artist' means someone who gets for himself the possession of 'Truth' or 'Goodness' or 'Beauty.' We ordinary people don't have the power to get this kind of 'Truth' or 'Goodness' or 'Beauty.' And don't we need it. We can go our own new-found way, the right way for us. We must forge our own beauty. We must set fire to the greyness of our labor with the art of our own lives. In this kind of creation, every day becomes a pure enjoyment . . .

"What do we mean by *artist?* The idea of 'professional artist' should be tossed away. Everyone should feel as an artist does. Everyone should be free to let his inner mind speak to him. And everyone is an artist when he does this ... Here, then, are many truly free artists. Unique billions of geniuses live together in our world. Earth is heaven." [6]

This tradition that all are creators is a profoundly Biblical tradition as well. When Genesis declares that God made humanity in "the image and likeness of God," it declares that all are artists. After all, the entire story in Genesis that precedes the *imago dei* is all about one aspect of God: God as Creator. The Spirit hovering over the waters that initiates the birth of all that exists from light to stars to plants to animals and finally to humankind. To be an "image and likeness" of the Creator is to be a creator. And the biblical insight is that *all*—every single individual—are such a creator. Perhaps this creative power that is inherent in all persons and comes so close to divine power is what also renders us potentially demonic. Dag Hammarskjold used to ask: "Do you create or do you destroy?" The implication behind this question is that we are either busy creating or we are busy destroying. That there is no middle ground between the two energies since creativity and destruction, divine and the demonic, are so closely entwined. One might say that our medieval ancestors who invented torture instruments for the Inquisition as well as our present Pentagon employees who invented napalm or herbicides to kill all vegetation were being "creative." They were of course but in a demonic sense. When creativity serves the idols at the top of the ladder, then it is demonic.

Another example of a Biblical endorsement of everyone as creator is found in Genesis when the human person is said to be given the power to name the creatures of the earth. Naming is symbol-making and is therefore an act of creativity. According to psychiatrist Silvano Arieti, it is symbol-making that distinguishes us from other animals, and the Genesis story of naming the animals is a story of the power of symbol-making and therefore of creativity.[7] But the naming is not restricted to an elite on a ladder but is a power bestowed on every human person as symbolized by the first person's name, Adam, or Everyperson. Because we are namers we are creators. All of us. We need to assert this basic right and privilege and responsibility by creating.

Some people are creators as parents, some as mechanics or repairers of industrial parts, others are carpenters, lovers, cooks, gardeners, teachers, thinkers, dancers, musicians, story-tellers, laughers, counselors, or some combination of all these or of others. Creativity is not limited to an elitist field called "the Arts"; it is much more important than that. Art is not for art's sake but for ecstasy's sake, which means for the sakes of a fuller and fuller, more and more celebrative Sarah's circle dance. Art is for people's sake. Creativity is everybody's and affects all of us, whether demonically or divinely, whether by its intense presence or by its vacuous absence. It touches us much too intimately to be hoarded by a few. True creativity cannot be bought or sold— though those doing it have a right to their living. It is shared and shared back. It lies at the level of human participation, not economic or cultural dualism. Creativity is a verb and not a noun. It is an energy ever in motion. A passion that will produce commotion as much as emotion. It is political as well as deeply personal.

In the Biblical tradition all liberation or salvation is a creative act of Yahweh. Creation is not about a search for the origins of the world but about a search for human liberation, or for the origins of human history which is liberation and salvation history. For the Biblical believer, "God's creative activity is thus not limited to the genesis of the world, . . . but creation is a collective concept which expresses all the positive saving actions of God at all times." [8] This same notion is carried through in the New Testament where references to God as Father are not to be understood as reinforcing an unresolved Oedipal complex or substituting a heavenly for an earthly Father, but as references to the Creator traditions of the Hebrew Bible (1 Cor. 8.6; Mt. 11.25). In fact, by the rebirth of the Spirit, human creativity becomes divinized and the divine imagination that wants to liberate humanity is shared with the human.

If creativity is a spirituality, then it is with us at some level and in some way all our day long. It becomes a way we feel and see the world and allow the world to feel and see us. It is essentially non-elitist.

Toward a meaning of creativity

Numerous persons have tried to define art and to define creativity but none have done it altogether successfully. This is no doubt a healthy and welcome situation because should we imagine we can define creativity we might then leap to the conclusion that we could can it, package it, advertize it and sell it. In short, we would make creativity into an object instead of respecting its being a verb and a way of living. Since definitions are left-lobe analyses of events, the very frustration inherent in trying to define creativity suggests that we are involved in an activity that is more than one-dimensional, more than the work of a single hemisphere of the brain.

Nevertheless, light can be shed on our topic by considering some "definitions" that have been proposed. If creativity is a spiritual concept, much will be learned by the *via negativa* or considering what it is *not*. Silvano Arieti insists that creativity is *not* the same as spontaneity since spontaneity by itself does not make something. Nor is creativity the same as originality since, while dreams for example are always original, they are not the same as creativity. Spontaneity, originality and even surprise may be parts of creativity but they are not creativity. Jose Arguelles considers art to be born from neither the right side of the brain (psyche) nor the left side (techne) but the marriage of the two. He insists that art as spirituality is always distinct from entertainment. Art for him is "the means by which all matter may be regenerated as spirit." Art is a transformation of spirit that touches the very purpose of life itself which "*is* its transformation." The true art, he insists, "is the art of transformation" and to this transformation both the artist and the scientist must die and be reborn (283ff). It is this death and dying and suffering that true art involves and that so distinguishes it from entertainment or titillation. William Blake also insisted on the universality of creativity. Not to be an artist is to betray one's own nature. "A Poet, a Painter, a Musician, an Architect: The Man or Woman who is not one of these is not a Christian." [9] Creativity, unlike entertainment, makes demands.

Like Arguelles, Otto Rank believes that we need to transform the elitist ideologies of how the West has come to define art and artist. The artist must be able to let go of being an artist suggests Rank. In other words, creativity and art are not the same thing any more.

> The new type of humanity . . . must grow out of those artists themselves who have achieved a renunciant attitude towards artistic production. A man with creative power who can give up artistic expression in favour of the formation of personality . . . will remould the self-creative type and will be able to put his creative impulse *directly* in the service of his own personality. . . . The creative type who can renounce this protection by art and can devote his whole creative force to life and the formation of life will be the first representative of the new human type. . . . (430f.)

This almost chilling demand of letting go that Rank puts on the artist appears too much to take. But it stands as an ultimate warning against the idolatry of art, that "fine art" tradition of art for art's sake that has been so prevalent in Western civilization of late. Rank insists, much like Eric Gill, that creativity belongs to the person who creates and should be put to transformative use there. That art is for people and not people for art.

We see that creativity is a way of living that considers birthing holy and that puts birthing ahead of controlling, ecstasy ahead of objectifying and celebrative sharing ahead of conformity. Creativity as the celebrative dimension to compassion even though pain accompanies it, will be considered later in this chapter. All birthing takes discipline; it takes cognition as well as insight and form as well as ideas. To be creative then is to make demands on oneself and one's possibilities. But creativity is very gratifying and, as Jesus observed, one does not count the pain when the ecstasy of birthing is as total as it is.

Creativity *is* a way of living, a spirituality, just as compassion is. It is a way that all persons travel in responding to life and we call it "the art of survival." Everyone who survives, we might say, has proven what an artist he or she is. But of course there are qualitative differences in the way some persons choose to survive. The fullest of the arts of survival would be the creative art of compassionate living.

EXPLORING THE EMPTY TOMB AND THE RICHES OF CREATIVITY

Perhaps we would all know more fully what creativity is if we were encouraged more to participate in it. But the West has for the most part repressed creativity and very often oppressed those who came to announce it. One religious symbol in particular seems to have been a victim of this repression of creativity and another seems to have been wielded as a weapon in the service of repressing creativity.

From a Fetish with the Cross to an Exploration of the Empty Tomb

I am speaking of the exaggerated role that the cross has played in Western Christianity at the expense of a potentially equally powerful symbol, that of the Empty Tomb. The West honors fourteen stations of the cross and considers literally thousands of crucifixes and paintings of the crucifixion to be integral to its collective artistic memory. Yet how many "stations of the empty tomb" does the West know? Can the reader name even three well-known paintings of the empty tomb? In contrast, Eastern Christianity, both Russian and Byzantine, considers the risen Christ to be one of its most revered ikons.

The cross, no matter how you draw it, is profoundly linear (Figure A). How easily and how often it has been turned on its side to be a sword (Figure B). Crusades, inquisitions, witch burnings—which invariably meant the burning of old women—Jew burnings and pogroms, burnings of heretics and gay people, of fellow Christians and of infidels—all in the name of the cross. It is almost as if Constantine, upon his and his empire's conversion to Christianity in the fourth century, uttered a well-fulfilled prophecy when he declared: "In the name of this cross we shall conquer." The cross has played the role of weapon time and time again in Christian history and empire building. Thus Thomas Merton observed that when Christianity became the religion of the Empire:

> the supreme sacrifice was to die fighting under the Christian emporer. The supreme self-immolation was to fall in battle under the standard of the Cross . . . But by the time Christianity was ready to meet Asia and the New World, the Cross and the sword were so identified with one another that the sword itself was a cross. It was the only kind of cross some conquistadores understood.[10]

The cross as sword served the ladder's purpose. Thus many Catholics living today, who may have felt innocent when I replayed the Protestant Hymn "We are Climbing Jacob's Ladder" in a previous chapter, will

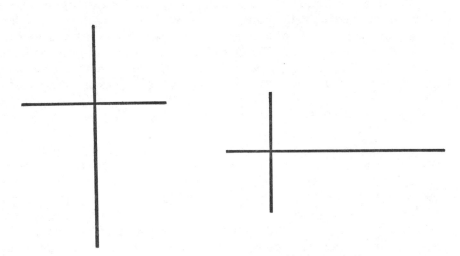

FIGURE A. The cross is profoundly linear.

FIGURE B. Often and easily the cross has been turned on its side to become a sword, thus fulfilling Emperor Constantine's prediction: "In the name of the cross we shall conquer."

recall the following marching song from Catholic Action Days not so long ago.

> An army of youth/flying the standards of truth,
> We're fighting for Christ the Lord.
> Heads lifted high,/Catholic Action our cry,/
> And the cross our only sword.

It is clear that the violent symbols of Christianity are not the monopolistic possession of either Protestants or Catholics. All have transformations to undergo.

What is most important is to enter into the symbol that, when cross and ladder reigned supreme, was so profoundly repressed in Christian consciousness. I mean the Empty Tomb. The empty tomb is the primary womb from which Christ is reborn and from which he declared, "I shall make all things new." The empty tomb is, after all, the last—and first—word of Christian belief. The cross was an invention of the Roman Empire who hung Jesus naked upon it. The Empty Tomb, on the other hand, is the product of the divine imagination. How strange that Christians should have invested so much more energy into cross than into empty tomb. It is time Christians started to explore the riches of their neglected treasure, and to initiate such an exploration I offer some of the following observations. First, a tomb is basically rounded or circular in shape, and Jesus' tomb was carved into a cave (Figure C). "Resurrection" does not mean rising up, since if Jesus had risen up in the cave he would have bumped his head. It means exiting, going out, leaving death and its shrouds behind. It is an empty tomb into which persons entered and from which one left. Being empty and having been emptied, it is not a closed circle (as in Figure D) but an open circle (Figure E). More than that, it is not a closed womb or tomb as in a narcissistic return to womb-like security and fetishness with self. Instead, because it is open and because someone has actually exited from it, it is a tomb in motion, a circle in motion. Thus a spiral (Figure F). As a spiral, it is clearly distinguished from a mere repetitive cyclical view of the universe—which Eastern philosophers sometimes espouse. The Jewish and Christian revelation is that human history, while spiral, has a direction. The direction is meant to be the increase of love-justice in the world. The spiral represents a true revolution (from the word "to revolve"), for it is a turning around, a turning from, a turning toward and a turning on. It is rebirth, Resurrection.

It is interesting that DNA, the basic ingredient of all life, is understood to be two ribbons in spiral motion (as in Figure G). A double spiral becomes then the basic symbol of all organic living. How appropriate that all spiritual living should possess the identical symbol since the Creator of physical life is identical to the Creator of spiritual life.

To emphasize the need for the Empty Tomb as a primary Christian symbol is not to suggest that the cross has no role to play in the future. In fact, a tomb presumes a cross. But there can be no question that, because the cross has played so one-sided and dualistic a role for centuries, it must be *let go of* in order to re-emerge in its fuller meaning within the dialectic of tomb-cross. One important symbol that the cross was meant to bear is the following: the cross is the cutting through (Figure H) of the ladder. When Jesus spoke of being lifted up and drawing all persons to himself, might the following not be implied: that he was to be the last victim of the ladder-powers? That his crucifixion was meant to be the last erection of the imperial principalities? That his sacrificial death was to render the ladders of the world essentially useless and to expose for all their blood-thirsty reality? That life, not death, would reign? But that the new word for life would be empty tomb, primary womb, resurrection? In this way death is truly swallowed up in victory as the dying figure, Christ, was swallowed up in the tomb and Jonah in the whale, both to be regurgitated from the

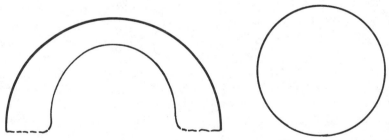

FIGURE C. The tomb is rounded and carved from a cave.

FIGURE D. The tomb is not a closed, narcissistic circle.

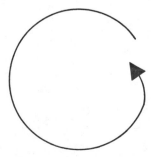

FIGURE E. The tomb is an open circle where people come and go, in and out.

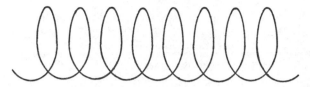

FIGURE F. When the energy of the open tomb is extended, it is spiral in its motion.

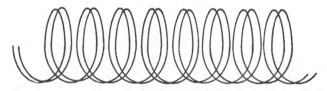

FIGURE G. The Double Spiral is the image of DNA, the basis of all physical life — and of all spiritual life.

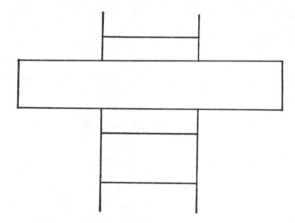

FIGURE H. The cross is meant to be the crucifixion of the ladder itself, the last erection of the imperial powers.

bowels of the earth and the great mammal, respectively. The prophet would laugh (which is the entire story of Jonah—a joke on the prophet) for death would mean life and humanity would mean divinity and the dancing of Sarah's circle would blend with the spiraling from the empty tomb to create a new consciousness in human history. A consciousness of creativity as a spirituality. One of letting go and of being let go of. One of resurrection, not repression.

Adrienne Rich comments on how the patriarchal choice of caves and tombs and labyrinths for burial "represent the female body" which in so many men "is connected with death" and with mother. Such a situation forces "a separation between the sexual woman and the 'motherly' woman; and even so, romantic sexual love is pre-vailingly associated with death."[11] The symbol of the empty tomb puts an end to this anxiety—provided people would let go and enter it. For in the empty tomb a return is re-enacted but the return is not a closed circle. Even the men who ran to the tomb, Peter and John, looked in and were amazed. But they did not stay, nor were they swallowed up by it. They moved on, very much energized. The fear of death is liber-ated at the tomb. For death is swallowed up in the victory. Above all, there is no need any longer to deny the anxiety toward mother and thus to force a vision of her as "Angel of the Home," as Rich calls it.

Still another implication of the womb-tomb oriented religious symbolism would be the release of a new kind of power. It is a star-tling fact that in Hebrew the words "compassion" and "womb" are from the same root (rehem means womb; rahamim is one word for com-passion). While much of Jewish theology is patriarchal, still there lies a world of difference in the Jewish respect for womb, from which they derive the word for compassion, and the Greek word for womb, which gives us the word for hysteria. (Hysterikos is the Greek word for womb.) A Greek-based spirituality will always flee womb energies and will reveal a basic misogyny. The suppression of compassion in the West is, I am certain, related to the supression of womb-power. Rich observes: "The idea of maternal power has been domesticated. In transfiguring and enslaving woman, the womb—the ultimate source of this power—has historically been turned against us and itself made into a source of powerlessness." (68) A womb-oriented spirituality will indeed be maternal and in creating, all persons will find that they are mothers and that they can mother others whether they be female or male, parents or childless. Such a situation would complement Rich's own concern that men learn to mother one another—and then men could relate to women more as equals and less as mother surrogates. Perhaps too much ladder and penis envy is related to too little womb envy.

Another symbol implied in womb-tomb imagery is that of the spi-ral. The spiral is an old resurrection symbol. In pre-celtic times the passage graves at New Grange in Ireland were known as the Spiral Castle. There the sun and oak kings were buried in tombs carved with spiral design and with spiral amulets. They were said to return as new kings so there is implied in spiral symbols a kind of reincarnation. The megalithic stones at Carnac in Brittany, which are thought to con-stitute the principal temple of the pre-Celtic peoples, possess a unique double ring of stones: one is lunar and the other is solar. Spiral dances include the fairy ring found throughout Celtia as well as in southern European countries. The Crane Dance of Greece celebrates

Theseus' victory over the Minotaur in escaping the spiral maze of the labyrinth. Rural England to this day celebrates Easter with a spiral dance commemorating the King's resurrection from the tomb.

The ivy and grapevine, both spiral, are symbols of rebirth and resurrection among the Celts, and in the Mediterranean the vine that represents Dionysus is meant to imply a dying with the grape in order to rise through the wine. Animals like the snake represent spiral and immortal energies especially because they shed their skin yearly. The web of the spider is a natural spiral and primitive tales often allude to its center as an entrance into the realms of immortality. Spiral seashells too are symbols of rebirth and have been found in the Neolithic graves of upstate New York along with spiral amulets and sculptures with spirals carved on their sides. The spiral, as we have seen, is also the basic shape that the nucleic acids take in the DNA molecule, the basis of life. The umbilical cord is spiralling and so too is all so-called "falling down." What looks like a straight line when an apple falls to the earth is in fact a spiral since the earth's surface is moving on its axis at the rate of 1000 mph at the equator. In space, the apple is traveling a route of a curved diagonal or a spiral.[12] To talk of spiral energies is to talk both of re-birth and of birth.

The suggestion, then, that the empty tomb is a spiral symbol is no great surprise to anyone who has considered the symbols of rebirth through different cultures and periods of time. The big surprise is this: why has Western Christianity been so slow in recognizing this dimension to its own tradition? Why has there been so much repression of the empty tomb as a symbol, especially in the Christian West of late? Surely the flight from creativity, compassion and woman has much to do with this forgetfulness. And so has fear.

ENTERING THE TOMB AS ENTERING INTO FEARS OF CREATING

In his first epistle, John comments on fear among believers. Says he:

> Love will come to its perfection in us
> when we can face the day of Judgment without fear;
> because even in this world
> we have become as he is.
> In love there can be no fear,
> but fear is driven out by perfect love:
> because to fear is to expect punishment,
> and anyone who is afraid is still imperfect in love.
> (1 Jn. 4.17f)

Notice how John links fear with fear of our divinity, the fear that maybe we too are Creators who "in this world . . . become as he is." But very simply and very bluntly John warns us that fear can be "driven out." We need to love something more than we love fear. Which is exactly what Martin Luther King, Jr, said: the fear of death is overcome by loving something else more. Then, and only then, is one free.

Creativity is about overcoming fears by entering into them and spiraling out of them. It takes courage to create. What are some of the fears that the creative person enters into and does not repress or run from? It is important to emphasize that, given our understanding of all people as creators, the fears and their resolution that we list here apply to all of us both personally and communally. They speak of our individual *and* our social condition.

The fear of death

The first fear is the fear of death. Otto Rank believed that creativity is explicable "only by conception of immortality" (47) and for that reason he defined the artist as one who wants to leave behind a gift. This definition implies, first, leave-taking. Thus the creative person has sensed the finiteness of existence. Second, it also implies a thank-you, for a gift is what is left behind. Thus creativity implies an intuition of gratitude for having lived. Creativity implies gratitude, a sense of life's having been a gift, a need to say Thank You. This aspect of creativity reveals how sadistic energies will always repress the artistic since, as psychologist Karen Horney points out, the compulsive demands inherent in sadism "never evoke gratitude." [13] The sadist is incapable of true creativity as is the sadistically oriented culture. The masochist too is for the most part excluded from creativity because to create is painful—"it always implies asserting oneself with one's particular views or feelings" [14]—and this the masochist, whose favorite words are "I can't", can seldom do. What is implied by Horney, however, is that creativity is a healing activity for the sadist or masochist in or among us. The creative person, by leaving behind a gift "not only immortalizes the artist ideologically instead of personally, but also secures to the community a future life in the collective elements of the work" (Rank, 47). Thus the solution given by the creative person to the personal and collective fear of death is to create. The creative person seeks transformation "of death into life, as it were, though actually he transforms life into death." (39) Why is creativity an intimation of death? Because the object once created "no longer has any significance for its creator, once he has produced it." And so the artist once again is driven to life experiences, which are all mortal and reminders of one's finitude. And from that reminder, the artist is driven back to creativity, to making something immortal of one's mortal experiences.

Fear of life

Rank, then, links fear of death with fear of life. Ernest Becker, in his *Denial of Death*, picked up on this same theme and insisted that it is a person or culture who represses life that also represses death. "Fear of life leads to excessive fear of death," Becker warns. "In some way one must pay with life and consent daily to die, to give oneself up to the risks and dangers of the world, allow oneself to be engulfed and used up. Otherwise one ends up *as though dead* in trying to avoid life and death." [15] Yet our culture, because it has feared life, has often preferred the quest for immortality to the quest for living. This is the case among Christian preachers who confuse "eternal life" with life after death when the New Testament tradition makes clear that this term is about the fullness of times that we already experience in this life. Emery Reves complains of our culture's fears of life when he asks: "When will our religions, our poets and our national leaders give up the lie that death is more heroic than life?" [16] When will we leave the cross for the tomb? A preoccupation with death, as Anne Douglas demonstrates, is always gained at the price of a flight from living and is basic to the sentimentalizing of reality.[17] Kubler-Ross observes that for someone who has not first loved, death "will always come too soon," whereas for those who have entered into life's energies which very much include love, death becomes one more adventure and discovery. It is, says Rank, the "fear of life which aims at avoidance or postponement of death." A fear of life will lead to neurotic repression. The creative person, then, depends wholeheartedly on living in order to break through this fear of life. "Thus we see that what the artist needs for true creative art in addition to his techniques and a definite ideology is life in one form or another." (48) The creator, we might say, worships life. Life is sacred for the creator and must needs be so.

This giving over to life and surrender to it brings about in the creative person a struggle that Rank calls "the profoundest source of the artistic impulse to create," namely that between "a complete surrender to life and a complete giving of himself in production. He has to save himself from this totality by fleeing, now from the Scylla of life, now from the Charybdis of creation, and his escape is naturally accomplished only at the cost of continual conflict" (60). The creator is thus nailed on a cross, one nail is that of creating, the other is that of living. The pain and the energy that pass from one hand to the next in turn produces the conflict in every person's life.

Fear of suffering

Our society tends to define happiness as absence of suffering and therefore we strive to invest our creative powers in building temples to security, whether they be the immortal marriage, the immortal job, the immortal corporation or the immortal skyscraper to house that corporation, or the immortal Nation with its invincible army and weaponry. One has to ask how much of this compulsion to wipe out suffering—or to buy it out in the form of insurance of all kinds—is not a symptom of a flight from suffering. I prefer Pierre Boulez' definition of what life is about. Says he, "the goal of life is not happiness [read security]; it is living." And living, as we saw in the previous section on creativity, implies suffering. In fact, the creative person—and that hopefully is all of us—takes on additional burdens of suffering by entering fully into living. All creativity is about sacrifice. The creative person sacrifices living in order to produce a work which is a gift to leave behind. The cross is not so much an object to meditate on for the creative person as it is an ever-recurring crucifixion. Jung warns: "There are hardly any exceptions to the rule that a person must pay dearly for the divine gift of the creative fire." [18] And Henry Miller comments: "they who would create order . . . must go again and again to the stake and the gibbet. I see that behind the nobility of his gestures there lurks the spector of the ridiculousness of it all—that he is not only sublime, but absurd." [19] Or, as Ernest Becker puts it, "all men(sic) are here to use themselves up" and the creative person leads the way for us (207). Like Jesus who was Son of God and therefore Son of the Creator, all creative persons, sons and daughters of the Creator, take upon themselves the dualisms and sins of humanity in an effort to weave hope and wholeness of them. Arguelles comments that "in their lives and work are revealed not only what Eliade calls the Terror of History but history's redemption, for the essence of the transformative vision is that the sufferings of history themselves constitute the process of transformation." (289)

The creative person, far from fleeing suffering, enters into it because he or she cannot do otherwise. Kenji Mayazawa advises "Do not escape from struggle; Go straight into it . . . Burn all struggle as your fuel." But in entering into this fearful arena such a person makes a wholesome and holy discovery: that letting go is not inimical to giving birth. And from this conflict a harmony is achieved and expressed. Our very fear of suffering makes us distort suffering either by making it a mountain to be avoided at all costs or by idealizing it and worshipping it. Both of these distortions of suffering—the first the act of a materialistic world view, the second the act of a perverted religious world view—treat suffering dualistically and as an object. In fact, suffering, like joy, needs to be entered into at times. If one penetrates suffering deeply enough, one emerges ready to give birth on its other, creative, side. And then, as Jesus observed, one forgets the suffering because the ecstacy of birthing is so great. A sound spirituality of suffering, it seems to me, places suffering within the context of giving birth. It does not idealize it as so many masochistic spiritualities have done; nor does it flee from it and try to buy one's way out of it as materialistic secular societies instruct us to do.

Fear of pleasure

The artist toys with his or her materials. The artist plays and, as in all play, wastes times. The artist is not paid for his or her time but for his or her work (if at all) and therefore has a correspondingly different attitude toward time than do those who necessarily count time since they are paid by the hour. But since "time means money" we can imagine that in a clock-oriented culture like ours there is a deep fear of playing and toying and pleasure. The artist chooses to enter that tomb-womb of pleasure rather than to flee from it or deny its existence.

Freud insisted that it was the artist's commitment to the pleasure principle instead of the reality principle that made the artist such a threat to society. Art gives pleasure to the artist and to those who "enjoy" the work of art. Art is play as in a *play* on words or in the question: "do you *play* the piano?" Art involves one in a recovery of childhood that is a state of euphoria capable of "regaining the last laughter of infancy." [20] Symbols become adult toys for the artist. Art, says Norman O. Brown, "is a way of life faithful to the natural instincts and therefore faithful to childhood." It is very likely that when Jesus warned his followers to "turn and become like children" he was advising political insurrection every bit as threatening to the powers of his time and place as when he drove out money-lenders from their places in the Temple. The fear of pleasure is a deeply held political issue as I have tried to indicate in my *Whee! We, wee* book, and the creative person is out in front insisting that ecstasy and pleasure are what life is about—but everyone's pleasure and not one's own private pleasure. In fact the latter kind suffers from being far too unpleasant and non-ecstatic a pleasure. The mystics through the ages have named God the ultimate experience of pleasure as I in the book referred to name our experience of ecstasy to be our experience of God. Every creative person knows this. Only such persons can live, as Meister Eckhart counsels, "without a why." They can do this because they are not always looking compulsively for the next pleasure, having, finally been filled up themselves.

Fear of androgyny

The creative person begins to blur the lines that culture draws so clearly between mother and father, female and male. Jung comments that the creative person's "own work outgrows him as a child its mother. . . . The creative process has a feminine quality, and the creative work arises from unconscious depths—we might say, from the realm of the mothers." [21] The creative urge, warns Rank, is a "bisexual urge—of begetting and of bearing, or of self-begetting and self-rebirth, which he [the artist] has fused into one" and this bisexual creative urge "is not only his perfect right but a necessity of life for him" (378). Rank rightly criticizes Jung for his one-sided and chauvinistic emphasis on passive rebirth without recognizing the active self-creative force (n.1, p. 378). Women who define their role as a basically passive one are interfering with the energies of creativity as much as men who define their role as supremely active. Neither masochist nor sadist creates, as we have seen. A fear of androgyny will accompany a fear of creating, and vice versa. The creative person dares to tempt this unspoken fear. And from this challenging of androgyny a birth happens. In creating there is "a process both of begetting and of bearing, not at the level of sexual differentiation of male and female, but at a deeper and more fundamental level: the liberation of the individual from the burden of generation by repulsion of part of the ego, which is felt as a relief and not as a loss" (Rank, 377). Creativity is a parenting experience and the creative person is challenged to become, in a certain manner, his or her own father and own mother such as Jesus insisted: One who did not leave one's own parents for his sake was not worthy of him.

The fear of guilt

The final fear that the creative person and creative society dares to entertain is that of the fear of guilt. It is clear enough that if society does not welcome openness toward death, toward life, toward suffering, toward pleasure and toward androgeny that the birther who must indeed enter into each and every one of these energies will receive considerable opposition for so entering. Guilt might well result from disobeying the long list of Don'ts that society dictates consciously or unconsciously, verbally or non-verbally. Thus there is a social guilt to all creativity that the artist also embraces as part of her or his suffering.

Otto Rank broke with Freud over the issue of Freud's reducing all creative inspiration to problems of unresolved oedipal complexes. Rank, who was himself an artist and who worked almost exclusively with counseling artists, uncovered a conflict of guilt in human efforts to create that runs still deeper than do the five fears we have treated up to now. He suggested that a basic cause of guilt over creativity arises from the creative person's "fundamental dishonesty towards nature" that is inherent in every suggestion that freedom to play is preferable to dependence on nature. Because the artist promises freedom, he feels guilty, for nature in fact requires dependency of us. All creation includes destruction and thus guilt is forever present. Creativity implies some sort of dissatisfaction with the way things are. There is revealed in this dilemma the dilemma between our being divine on the one hand and dependent on the other. To assert our divinity—as every creative person does—is to put aside our dependency. And that creates guilt. Such guilt can be seen, Rank warns, "in every process of art, and . . . is not wholly absent from play" (329). "Every productive type" has strong feelings of guilt that in turn expresses itself in an "over-evaluation of the unconscious" (424). Those who deny themselves the power of creating are running from the image of God in them and from facing the guilt that comes in daring to be true to one's divine origins. There lies here, it seems to me, the core of the cynicism that racks a society shortly before it dies of boredom and greed and self-indulgence. The decadence of cynicism is born of the flight from the authentic guilt we ought to feel at daring to be creators. The sign of such flight, according to Rank, is the reduction of art to imitation. The loss of divine fancy and divine dreams. Nothing new under the sun. All of living as one giant bureaucracy run by a God "up there" telling us "down here" what to do and be. How far we have come from John's epistle that said "even in this world we have become as God is." Loss of faith. And with it loss of forgiveness. A flight from guilt and from creativity.

The creative person can also expect to feel guilt at the sacrifice of living for creating (201) and at the break the artist makes with the past, a past that fed and nourished him or her and which is loved all the same (372). Creative guilt-feelings then are part of the price one pays for creating and ought not to scare us off from being creators. They are what most limit creativity in our time, according to Rank (425).

Forgiveness and creativity

Otto Rank is saying in effect that even if one were alone on a desert island and started creating, one would feel guilty for so doing. It is almost as if Rank is saying that "original sin" is the guilt one feels at being original and creative. In this context the redemption Christ brings takes on a fresh meaning. The resurrection is the resurrection or the re-birth of creativity. Believers are told that their faith overcomes the guilt of creativity and sets them free to be creative. Rank himself compares the therapeutic character of confession to that of the "expression" of the artist who is healed and heals in the creative work of combining dialectical tensions. There is a great need of forgiveness among artists who dare to bring something new into the world and who cannot predict its consequences for the world. For many it is religious faith that provides this forgiveness. It is here that once again "the mysterious link between compassion and forgiveness" that we referred to in Chapter One makes so much sense. People—as individuals and as societies—need forgiveness to create, just as, in Chapter Three, we indicated that they need forgiveness to let go. Forgiveness and compassion then are related because creativity and compassion are so intimately related. Jesus knew this relationship and knew it well when he said, "Be compassionate as your Father is compassionate. Be forgiving. . . ."

The forgiveness implied in creating is first, a forgiveness of self. A forgiveness of self's being true to one's ultimate origins which are divine and those of the Creator. Jesus, who is like us in every way save sin, must have felt the profoundest guilt of all—and yet this guilt did not prevent his acting creatively. If, for example, he truly destroyed death by dying on the cross and rising out of the tomb—imagine *how guilty* he felt for it! Prometheus only stole fire and see how he suffered for that act of divine courage and creativity. Clearly Jesus, who faced creativity and guilt with an utter courage, removed our guilt not only for sin but *especially* for creating. Here lies the meaning of the empty tomb and the Good News it announces. Now, in the fullness of time, in the messianic age, we can give birth without guilt. Or can we? Do we have enough faith in Jesus and in the fact that Jesus was messiah to give birth? Enough to welcome others who do? Enough to let go? Where, indeed, in all the world, is there faith like this?

There is also a forgiveness for others who create with you or even as a result of your creation. We need to forgive one another our divinity, Jesus is saying. And he is right and ought to know. Since it is because his society could not forgive him his creativity as a poet, parable-teller and vision-maker regarding God's Kingdom and Queendom on earth, that they hung him on a cross. And while there, he said again: "Father, forgive them for they know not what they do." Compassion at his own execution. Why? Because the ignorance of these persons' carrying out lethal orders was so overwhelming to him. They were utterly ignorant of how near to them the divine in fact was. Of how near to death was life. Of how near to despair is hope; and near to destruction is creativity. Of how near to earth is heaven, how near to Golgotha is an empty tomb, how near to Good Friday is Easter Sunday. Jesus forgave his persecutors in order that their misplaced creativity might be turned toward true creativity and compassion. Did it do any good? Only if we have learned the lesson: that creativity will be born only out of forgiveness.

Another example of religious faith's encouraging creativity by erasing fear of guilt is found in the story of our spiritual foremother, Sarah. It is especially telling that at the end of the episode in which she laughed at hearing she was to become pregnant at an advanced age, the following exchange takes place:

> But Yahweh asked Abraham, 'Why did Sarah laugh and say, 'Am I really going to have a child now that I am old?' Is anything too wonderful for Yahweh? At the same time next year I shall visit you again and Sarah will have a son.' 'I did not laugh,' Sarah said, lying because she was afraid. But he replied, 'Oh, yes, you did laugh.' (Gen. 18.13–15)

Sarah, we are told, tried to cover up the creativity and self-expression uttered in her laughter. Why? She lied "because she was afraid," notes the Scripture. Fear stifles our spontaneous artistry and laughter. She lies out of fear at the "too wonderful" surprises of Yahweh. And it is Yahweh who calls Sarah to task for this cover-up and insists on the truth of the situation: that Sarah is a laugher and blessed for that. And that wonder-filled events are God-given. Perhaps it is this encouragement that believers get from faith—whether New Testament faith or that of the Hebrew Bible, that is so basic for creativity and that, when it is lacking, results in timidity and flight from the courage it takes to create. This might be behind the lament of film-maker Ingmar Bergman when he says: "It is my opinion that art lost its basic creative drive the moment it was separated from worship. It severed an umbilical cord and now lives its own sterile life, generating and degenerating itself."

The creative person, then, is one who has challenged the fear of death, life, suffering, pleasure, androgyny, and guilt. No wonder the creative person has something to say after such a journey as this! From the empty tomb comes first of all courage.

We have in this list of fears an analysis of the reasons why we create as little as we do. And, perhaps, of why we are compassionate as little as we are. The way of compassion is a way of creativity and both are a way called spirituality. Every person is invited to explore these fears and not run from them, and to support one another in forgiveness and strength as each dances to the tomb and back again. We have entered into the tomb. We have seen God there and the devil. Life and Death. Where do we go from here with this newly won knowledge and awareness? We go to, and with, and in compassion.

THE CREATIVE PROCESS AS THE MAKING OF CONNECTIONS: CREATIVITY AS COMPASSION

Were I pushed to express in equation form what I understand the creative process to be, the equation would look like this: Matter plus Form yields Energy ($M + F = E$).

Elements of Creativity

The "product" of creativity is not an art object or an *objet d'art* if you prefer—such object-thinking could only take place in a period of dualistic and materialistic consciousness. The "product" of creativity is energy. If a painter paints a picture that turns people on, has them examining self, others, nature or God—then energy is the proper name for that picture and not object. The same holds for a violinist playing on her violin or a dancer dancing or a writer with his book. Energy, whose human name is ecstasy, is the proper "product" of authentic creativity.

Where does the creator or artist enter into this equation? The materials (M) appear already given, whether clay for the potter, pigments for the painter, bodies for the dancer, ideas for the writer. But not entirely. For the creator must *select* which materials to employ and which to leave unused—a very difficult task that closely parallels that of the *via negativa* of mystics which implies the leaving behind of certain materials—for example, names for God. The artist also gives form, order, style, interpretation and arrangement to the matter. This is evident with the potter spinning the clay on the wheel, with the poet playing with words and arranging them, with the musician arranging notes, chords, harmony, rhythm into a melody. Furthermore, the matter helps to create the form at the same time that the form assists in creating the matter. The truth of this fact is often lost sight of in an overly activist culture or person. Creation is truly dialectical and bi-polar as Mary Richards testifies: "Imagination in the craftsman works in various ways. There is much to ponder on here. He does not always build toward a prior vision. Often images come *in the process of working. The material, his hands—together they beget*" (114f, italics mine). That matter gives birth to form, and not only form gives shape to matter, is an important principle for understanding creativity ... and compassion. A give and take, a vulnerability, lies at the heart of such experiences. The artist is also integrated into the E or energy level of creation, for the artist is in turn energized by his or her production. Indeed, one of the biggest problems for artists is "coming down" after a fine performance or after completing a good book or a good piece. Artists must often escape society to the very extent that society appreciates them because they in turn become so high and so energized by the response that one's art evokes in others.

Is this all that is involved in creativity? A person forming energy of given matter? By no means. The very heart of being creative is seeing relations between matter and form that no one has ever imagined before or that people deeply want and need to see. It is this act of *seeing connections* that seems to form the heart of creative consciousness and that, considering Thomas Merton's definition of compassion as recognizing the interconnections of things (chapter one), suggests one more reason why the Bible identifies compassion with the womb. Perhaps compassion and creativity are in fact the same energy. For both seem to operate at the deep level of interconnections! Compassion is seeing, recognizing, tasting the interconnections; creativity is about *making the connections*.

Stages in the Creative Process

Gestalt psychologist M. Wertheimer considers the creative process to be a search for a solution or a relation between elements of a solution. The creative person's search is not for just any relation that would connect the elements but "for the nature of their intrinsic interdependence." (in Ar, 17) Thus, according to Wertheimer, creativity *is* the search for interdependence which is, in our terminology, the search for compassion. This same theme of creativity as the search for interdependence is sounded in numerous studies on creativity. Psychiatrist Silvano Arieti, in his book *Creativity: The Magic Synthesis*, points out that one purpose of the conceptual stage in creating is to "organize, since the different attributes or parts appear logically interconnected" (89). How is it that the parts are able to be conceptualized or interconnected consciously speaking? Because primary thinking or the pre-conscious first "saw" them or intuited them as such. When Arieti says that "the creative person seems to have a special access to the primary process" (180), he is saying, it seems to me, that a consciousness of inter-connections is more readily at his or her disposal. If we are to be compassionate, then, we need to tap our creative potential, i.e., our powers of seeing interconnections. Arieti even admits, contrary to Freud, that the art of humor can "lead people to experience brotherhood and compassion" (123)—a logical conclusion given our premise. Arieti talks about the creative person's need to be "in a state of readiness for catching similarities", that is, for seeing interconnections. W.J. Gordon calls this aspect of creativity *synectics* or "the joining together of different and apparently irrelevant elements." (Ar. 376) This is as necessary for compassion as creativity for the "different element" of someone else's suffering and mine are indeed seen as one in compassion.

There exist physiological dimensions to making connections. Arieti points out that the cerebral cortex of our brains is "the most complicated entity in the universe known to us." Containing fifteen billion neurons, the human cortex makes patterns and connections that are "unimaginable" in their numbers and possibilities. Each cortical cell receives about 2,000 contacts or connections to other cells. Thus the very physiological basis of creativity is also one of profound and even uncountable interconnections. A nerve net is "a population of similar neurons which are functionally interconnected so that, when fully excitable, activity among some of them always spreads to invade the remainder." Arieti indicates that at this level of making connections and of symbolic processes "the concept of strict causality has to be abandoned, to be replaced by the law of probability" (388ff), since the routes neurons travel are as fresh and unpredictable as are the insights of creativity. Is the physiological seat for creativity the same as the physiological seat for compassion?

Composer Leonard Bernstein, reflecting on his own experience, also sees the making of connections as key to the creative process.

> I sit for long nights all by myself and don't have a thought in my head. I'm dry. I'm blocked, or so it seems. I sit at the piano and just improvise—strum some chords or try a sequence of notes. And then, suddenly, I find one that hits, that *suggests something else*. The whole point of composing, you see, is not to find one chord or one note you love. *It is only when they progress to another chord or note that you have meaning.*

He comments on how this making of connections occurs.

> The mind, where all this creativity takes place, is an immensely complicated circuitry of electronic threads, all of which are connected at a certain point and are informational. But every once in a while, there is something like a short circuit; *two of them will cross, touch, and set off something* called an idea.
>
> This is the most exciting moment that can happen in an artist's life. And every time it happens . . . I say 'Gratias agimus tibi.' I am grateful for that gift, for those moments, just as I can be terribly depressed by the moments in between when nothing happens. But . . . eventually those two strands will come together, a spark will fly, and I'll be off, sailing, my ego gone. I won't know my name. I won't know what time it is. Then, I'm a composer.[22]

Bernstein would agree that the essence of creativity is the making of connections.

If making connections is the essence of creativity, then we might expect this dimension of creativity to be revealed in every stage of the creative process. Such is indeed the case if we examine the creative process in its three-fold manifestation as described by Arieti. He names three stages of creativity as the following:

A. The primary process. It is characterized by a "need for disorder" (348) and is non-judgmental, non-disciplined, or as Freud put it, there is no No or denial in the primary process, no censorship. In the primary process we play with images, symbols, the inner expressions of our inner lives. These take into account memory and traces of past perceptions, subjective experiences and impressions. Images are the "first germ of creativity" and they bring something new to life perhaps precisely because they are defective and only partial in their view of reality. According to Arieti, images themselves are dynamic and prone to making connections, for they "rapidly associate with other images" and "are always in movement . . . in a state of constant becoming. They represent the unceasing activity of the human mind" and are "a force of transcendence" that seeks to express what is not currently present (48–50). This primary process has at times been called the unconscious (Freud), "psychic reality," the "preconscious", "primitive cognition" or an activity of the right hemisphere of the brain. It produces what Arieti calls endocepts (as distinct from concepts) which are what dreams are about and what three- and four-year-old children are most familiar with. Endocepts give birth to intuition and to empathy. Music takes place almost exclusively at this level of activity.

B. The Secondary Process. The secondary process corresponds to conscious cognition or to Aristotelian logic. It operates from the left hemisphere of the brain. Its cognition is in terms of concepts or of ideas. The concept makes ideas shareable for by it we can describe, organize, predict and yet leave ourselves open to more insight by what is left unsaid and unconceptualized. A concept can become an ideal and in this way may become "one of the strongest motivational forces in creativity" (94). Just as the primary process expresses our need for chaos and disorder, so the secondary expresses our need for order. In the secondary process we choose, decide and put order and form into our imaginings.

C. The Tertiary Process. Arieti posits a tertiary process which will consist of the marriage of Primary and Secondary processes in the act of creativity. One might say that the tertiary process is the sum of the other two processes yet greater than the sum of its parts. Birthing or creativity properly speaking, i.e. in all its fullness, takes place in the tertiary process. There the meeting of the right and left hemispheres, of intuition and of cognition, of endocept and concept occurs. Here the stage of integration of the primitive archaic and primitive primary processes with the logic of one's culture to produce a new synthesis, a "magic synthesis," takes place.

Arieti takes an illustration and applies his Three Processes of Creativity to it. Says he: The primary process has an image: All that glitters is gold and responds joyfully to this truth. The secondary process becomes more realistic and declares: Not all that glitters is gold. Be realistic and don't be a fool. The tertiary process will either create a new class of glittering object or it will bestow the glittering on other substances and thereby turn them into gold by beautifying them. It is, says Arieti, "the fortunate ones among us who have the key to creativity [who] will collect and distinguish the glittering substances and form glittering classes or confer the glittering look to other objects." (410)

Thus we see that the making of connections operates at every level of the creative process: at the primary level especially by use of images; at the secondary level in denying some connections and therefore confirming some; and at the tertiary level in producing hitherto seen, unforeseen, connections that in turn others might connect with. The artist knows he or she is an artist when a fourth stage is realized and another says honestly "you have touched me" or "you have named my experience." In this way all energy becomes connected once again and the artist's ultimate vocation, to return energy to the universe by way of transformed matter, is accomplished. Participation, what D. H. Lawrence calls At-One-Ment, and what theologians call Grace, has happened. The lie of subject/object, of I/you, of Us/them, of Matter/spirit is broken through. Revelation occurs. God is us and us God. A breakthrough. A truth. An Incarnation that becomes our healing, at-one-ment, redemption. Compassion is learned and we are reminded of our holiness once again.

The creative person then is a Maker of Connections who has first seen these connections at some almost unreachable level of awareness. She or he has learned to trust that vision enough to explore it and express it. Like the Kabir who talks of swinging, the creative person learns to swing between heretofore untouchable realities. Says Kabir:

> Between the conscious and the unconscious, the mind has
> put a swing:
> all earth creatures, even the supernovas, sway
>   between these two trees,
> and it never winds down . . .
> Everything is swinging: heaven, earth, water, fire,
> and the secret one slowly forming a body.[23]

Creativity, the capacity to swing between order and disorder, between production and suffering (Rank, 43), between art and life, between child and adult, between past and future, between inner and outer freedom (Rank, 366), between something and nothing, between pain and pleasure, life and death, the cross and the empty tomb. Creativity is close to compassion because both processes are about the making of connections. That is why there is no compassion without creativity.

CREATIVITY, EXTROVERT MEDITATION AND PROPHECY

All meditation is about making connections. Introvert meditation—a journey inward—is meant to remind us of a connection already made that we have forgotten—namely that God is within us. Which is to say that God is not above us or beyond us or hovering over us or on top of us or distant from us but that God is within us. This insight is an important one in a culture of objects, things, alienation from self and one's inner self.

But there can be—and often has been in the West—too much emphasis on meditation as the journey inwards to find God within. Such introvert meditation can too easily be manipulated and controlled by self and by powers in society so that it becomes a flight from passion and a flight from compassion. It can very easily and has very often stifled our capacities to create and especially to create compassion or the experience of celebration with others and of relieving the pain of others. The exaggerated influence of St. Augustine[24] and of Descartes in the West has indeed so influenced our language and thinking that most people, on hearing the word "meditation," think exclusively of introvert meditation. Compassion is lost when that happens for there is no evidence whatsoever that introvert meditation leads in any flowing way into compassion. In fact, the numerous persons flocking to spiritual direction today in the context of introvert meditation are, according to one study,[25] coming closer to Jesus but not to Jesus' command that we "Love one another." Introvert meditation alone is not Biblical when it fails to lead to loving of the world. "To know Yahweh is to do justice" warns the prophet Jeremiah, whereas to even use the word "justice" in some introverted meditation groups today results in stares of unbelief and shock. The inner peace sought for in introvert meditation is a very puny part of Christian living. For spirituality is meant to be a peace based on justice which often must be carved out from society that so reluctantly and begrudgingly allows its birth.

There is another kind of meditation called Extrovert meditation. It is centering by way of creating. As a potter concentrating and communing with the clay, or a musician with notes, scales and sounds, or a dancer with body and body movement and space, or a poet with words, or a lover with one's beloved, or a baker with dough. Such acts of utter communion are communions based on activity and birthing. They are centering processes and they are creative. They are creativity as a meditation form. Mary Richards, who has written a classic work on this form of meditation called *Centering*, describes the reality of it. In writing or potting, she "pushes as far as I can push, to birth and death, life and death, getting then centered, unseparated ... Always I try to go toward, not formulation, but organism." (5) The senses are not bridled and put down in such meditation, they are oriented toward organic wholeness. The transformation leads "through the senses; the colors of dry and wet clay, the sensations of weight when it is solid and hollow, the long course of the fire, expectations fulfilled and the surprises, imagination already stirring toward the next form, the broken shards, the groundup slabs" (143). The bodiliness of extrovert meditation is holy, as holy as incarnation itself. "Incarnation, bodying forth. Is it not our whole concern? The bodying forth of our sense of life? ... That is what form is: the bodying forth. The bodying forth of the living vessel in the shapes of clay." [26] There can be no true incarnational spirituality without extrovert meditation.

Since extrovert meditation alone leads to action and is about action, about disciplining it for organism, it alone leads to compassion in a direct way. The riches of solitude learned by being alone in nature or with self even on a crowded subway also contribute to compassion. But without extrovert meditation such introvert meditations seldom in fact do result in either celebration or relief of pain. These experiences presume others. In extrovert meditation we learn to trust our deepest insights about images new and old and thus we learn from these images. They become our teachers. The pot not only praises the potter but teaches the potter. And this kind of learning is the work of compassion as well. In this sense, then, we can talk of compassion as meditation. When it is extrovert meditation, that is creative meditation or meditation by creativity, then compassion is meditation. For it is giving birth, the bodying forth, of justice where there was none, of healing where there was pain, of wholeness where there were only pieces.

The Creative Person as Prophet

Because of the unique inter-connection between creativity and compassion, between giving birth and giving birth to justice, there never was a true prophet who was not an artist nor a true artist who was not a prophet. Psychologist Cladio Naranjo insists that Extrovert Meditation is "the way of prophets." [27] Why is this so? Why does the creative person bring about a new future, which is in fact what prophets are about? For one thing, the creator has got to learn to listen deeply to the pain of a culture. Out of the true suffering, the *Anawim* in Biblical language, the authentic future is born. This listening implies a listening for new symbols, new images, self-made images. The Introvert Meditator takes someone else's images, very often those of the ruling elite, and ingests them. The Extrovert Meditator listens to the inner self and utters the new images from within outwards. This giving birth to new images is the work of all creative persons. It is a prophetic work. And a dangerous one.

How dangerous? Freud considered all artists political subversives. "The function of art is to form a subversive group opposing authority of the rational principle [i.e., Secondary Process from above] that builds civilization on repression." [28] In other words, because every artist is committed to the Primary Process which corresponds to the pleasure principle, every artist is a threat to the law-and-order structures and language and people who keep society in order. As Norman O. Brown warns, "art seduces us into the struggle against repression" (64). The artist is involved in making the unconscious conscious, in making the primary process at least as important as the secondary process, in making the child as influential as the adult. And the artist does this less by confronting of the accepted norms of bureaucratic change, such as the forming of committees to "study the issue," than by "seducing" us. We are seduced by the artist more than confronted by her or him. How? Artists, because they deal with images, get under our skin. Think of music, for example. The artist does not debate us or beat us over the head with logic—the artist moves us, touches us, seduces us. Such folks are dangerous, as Flannery O'Connor confessed when asked about the grotesqueness of her characters in her writing. Her response was: "All art—new and serious—is shocking and disturbing."

All artists are language-makers. And therefore language-destroyers. Not accepting the inherited language of society, they seek alternative images, symbols and expressions. This too makes them political subversives, for when you start fiddling with the way people talk and dream and report their dreams you are initiating freedoms that are not easily controlled by those who have established the norms for language and other structures of society. And the language that the artist deals with is not neutral or a neutered word. Its whole purpose is to move one. To render us vulnerable and to speak to our vulnerabilities. To lay open our pain and our joy and not to cover either up. "The purpose of a word is to reveal" said Meister Eckhart. No wonder the establishment of his day condemned him as a heretic. They wanted the language of the day to cover up. The artist explodes with a new word, a new language, a new vision with new alternatives.

The creative person, succumbing to the tension between order and dis-order, form and chaos, secondary and primary processes, is for that very reason involved in the struggle for love-justice that marks all prophets. This mark of crucifixion accompanies the prophet who comes announcing as did Jeremiah, "I have come to root up and to destroy; to plant and to make grow." Destruction is part of the creative experience. Henry Miller warns: "The task which the artist implicitly sets himself is to overthrow existing values, to make of the chaos about him an order which is his own, to sow strife and ferment so that by the emotional release those who are dead may be restored to life."[29] And Ernest Becker observes that "the creative type is one who no longer accepts the collective solution to a problem but must fashion his own." Instead of being oppressed by oppression, "the artist re-works it in his own personality and recreates it in his art" (171, 184). In this sense, the artist wants to give all. We see here the fuller implications of Otto Rank's challenge to artists in our time to let go of art in order to make art of their lives. It is a challenge to be prophetic, and what is more it is a challenge within a Sarah-Circle dynamic for *all persons to be creative prophets*. What does this mean? Becker puts it this way. "The creative person becomes, then, in art, literature and religion, the mediator of natural terror and the indicator of a new way to triumph over it. He reveals the darkness and the dread of the human condition and fabricates a new symbolic transcendence over it. This has been the function of the creative deviant from the shamans through Shakespeare" (220).

The rediscovery of the Biblical injunction that we are all creators made in the one Creator's image and likeness (Gen. 1.26) and that we are all namers and therefore symbol-seekers and image-makers (Gen. 2.19f.) is politically subversive. It means we all need to dive into the exploration of primary processes. What is politically subversive about the primary process? Images are. The experience of our own images is the first experience of prophecy: it is our first break with our parents—a break that Jesus insists on for anyone who is to follow him. Is Jesus not insisting that all his followers therefore be creative people who trust their power of image-making? Arieti writes: "Images are the first function that permits the human being not to adapt passively to reality, not to be forced to accept the limitations of reality" (50). Images constitute our first act of self-assertion, our first No! to passivity, our first No! to limits. Mysticism becomes prophecy. With visions, people need no longer perish. Thus the power of naming that Genesis speaks of is also the power of rebelling and envisioning alternatives. Arieti observes that the mystic who turns prophet uses "the primary process to sustain the secondary," since prophecy is not carried on solely at the primary level. This fact helps to explain why so many prophetic persons I know find it necessary to grow a garden. This entire section on creativity as prophecy helps to explain why, in Latin American countries when military dictatorships take over, the first group to be jailed, silenced or put up against a wall is the artists. Russia does not seem ignorant of this same pressing need. But then our own country does it much more cleanly by way of commercializing the artist whether by reducing art to entertainment or by hiring artists to write commercials. Unemployment, especially among the poorest, most oppressed, and therefore potentially most creative of our citizens also controls creativity. Those who would *not* in fact define our social sins as "ring around the collar" are seldom heard from.

Mary Richards speaks of the intimate connection between Extrovert Meditation and compassion and calls the connection itself Moral Imagination. "We are not always able to feel the love we would like to feel. But we may behave imaginatively: envisioning and eventually creating what is not yet present. This is what I call Moral Imagination" (92). But Moral Imagination is the special gift of every prophet. And there can be no compassion without it. "From the child's ability to imagine grows well the adult's capacity for compassion: the ability to picture the sufferings of others, to identify. In one's citizenship or the art of politics, it is part of one's skill to imagine other ways of living than one's own" (115). Solutions to pressing moral-political problems depend on Moral Imagination. It comes not just by sitting in an arm chair but in the very process of doing and of making. Every extrovert meditator knows this: that the best and fullest insights come in the act of creating. Extrovert meditation, then, gives birth to this new kind of power—not a power over (sadism) or a power under (masochism) which the ladder instructs us so thoroughly in, but a power with. This new kind of power, a power-with, is properly called *compassion*. It is a power to imagine with others and to be changed by this imagining. Crafts initiate one into a new kind of power. The German word for power is *Kraft*. There is no cover-up in this kind of power. "We can't fake craft. It lies in the act. The strains we have put in the clay break open in the fire. We do not have the craft, or craftsmanship, if we do not speak to the light that lives within the earthly materials; this means ALL earthly materials, including men themselves" (12).

Richards testifies to her own growth in compassion that was brought about by her extrovert meditation. One day on a beach in North Carolina, before any civil rights legislation, she noticed the segregated water fountains but also the white folks trying to get dark in the sun, a sun that shown equally on black and white bathers. "My entire feeling about the sun was affected. That's what I mean: you take it all in, the politics and the recreation and the social attitudes, the environment and spring. . . . How can we keep our recreation and our politics separate? How can we not see what our eyes behold? As our perceptions become more and more coordinated, we grow in justice" (78). The artist, true to the primary process which includes connecting all memories and traces of experiences, is involved in "taking it all in"—and in making the connections. And all justice-making and compassion are a making of connections between the oppressed and oppressor (who is also oppressed), and intuition that the sun falls on all alike and that in a real sense we are all one family. To sensitize one's perceptions—which is what all creative persons are driven to do continuously—can mean to sensitize one's capacities for learning where the real suffering lies. It is education for compassion.

Extrovert meditation or creativity does something. It does not only dream or imagine but produces. Justice too is about doing something—about carving, molding, dancing or singing alternatives. One *does* justice just as one does a pot or does a dance. The doing is outward-directed—it is toward others and toward society and this is how Rabbi Heschel describes the prophet's task. The prophet's compassion is "the opposite of emotional solitariness. . . . Not mere feeling, but action, will mitigate the world's misery, society's injustice or the people's alienation from God." It is for this reason that the prophets were not introvert meditators, they "were not in the habit of dwelling upon their private experiences." [30] The prophet does not turn inwards to find peace and calm there, for the prophet knows that peace without justice is a lie and a cover-up. Rather, insists Heschel, the prophet turns outward to find God and the God who is found is a verb and not a noun. "What the prophet faces is not his own faith. He faces God. To sense the living God is to sense infinite goodness, infinite wisdom, infinite beauty. Such a sensation is a sensation of joy" (143). It is ecstasy, the beginning of all prophetic and compassionate spirituality, as I have indicated in a previous work (*Whee*). The prophet is not involved in repressing feelings or energies but in making what Richards calls a "kind of consecration of passion." Asceticism is as foreign to the prophet's compassion as it is to the artist's work. As Heschel puts it: "Asceticism was not the ideal of the biblical man. The source of evil is not in passion, in the throbbing heart, but rather in hardness of heart, in callousness and insensitivity." In fact, the prophet like the artist arouses our passions for "we are stirred by their passion and enlivened imagination. . . . It is to the imagination and the passions that the prophets speak, rather than aiming at the cold approbation of the mind" (258). In this regard it is interesting to consider that the word "asceticism" originally meant the work of the artist and only gradually came to mean a violent flight from feeling in the name of inner calmness and serenity. The prophet, like the artist, is to wake people up and the images the prophet chooses "must not shine, they must burn." They are "designed to shock rather than to edify," (7) warns Heschel. The divine Word that the prophet calls the people back to is not a noun but a verb. Love-justice is its name. Creativity is its name. Compassion and the giving birth to compassion is its name.

SUMMARY

In this chapter we have considered how creativity itself is a non-elitist way of living, a way of giving birth wherever we are and whoever we are. As such, creativity and compassion, also a way of living and a spirituality, belong to the same family. We have explored the empty tomb and the wonders that await those daring enough to make that exploration. And we have listed some of the principal fears that prevent our entering the tomb for a fuller, more divine glance. Principal among them might well be guilt itself. It is precisely spiritual traditions, such as Judaism and the person of Jesus, that urge us to be free of such guilt—to be pardoned—and therefore to create. In this way we continue the search into the empty tomb which houses our best, divine, origins (*imago dei*) and our space for giving birth, or womb. We have presented a theory of creativity from Arieti and in doing so we have uncovered how profoundly all stages of creativity, including the physiological stage itself, are impregnated with a drive for interconnections. This drive to interconnections overlaps conspicuously with the very essence of compassion. For creativity *does* (the making of connections) what compassion *is* (the realization of the inter-connectedness of all things). That is how intimately united compassion and creativity are: you cannot have the former without the latter. And we have considered how our creative compassion is the carrying on of God's creation. And finally, we have underscored the lost tradition of meditation in the West which is meditation as creating, and whose name is Extrovert Meditation. A return to Extrovert Meditation will end our headlong flight from compassion. And our flight into flatness and boredom. For to give birth is to give wonder and healing.

5

SCIENCE, NATURE AND COMPASSION:

FROM A MECHANISTIC AND PIECEMEAL UNIVERSE TO AN ORGANIC AND INTERDEPENDENT ONE

We've now learned enough of the principles
to really carry on in a new,
completer, or grown up way,
with the Universe.
And stop forever
the idea of making human beings struggle
to see which is fittest to survive.

Buckminster Fuller[1]

Science, or whatever culture and generation takes for science, is a powerful force either to encourage compassion or to discourage it. This is particularly the case in the area of physics where society receives its basic cosmology and with it a basic framework for imagining reality. So basic is physics that not only do the natural sciences depend upon it for their basic framework but psychology, metaphysics, theology, art, economics, education and technology also take a certain physical view of the world that is derived from physics as their starting point. When physics undergoes a profound change—as it is doing in our century—all other branches of human knowledge are likewise put into a crisis. When people respond creatively, such a crisis is not at all a negative experience for, as we recall from the previous chapter, it is the creator in us who dares us to explore chaos with a secret confidence that order might be found or educed there. For chaos may well mean the beginning of a new order rather than the apocalypse of all order.

The name I assign to this new order and which comprises the thesis of this book is Compassion. But compassion, as Thomas Merton reminds us, is "based on a keen awareness of the interdependence of all" beings which are "all parts of one another and all involved in one another." Has the movement of scientific thought in our century provided us with a *keener awareness* of interdependence of all beings? I believe—as do numerous thinkers today—that physics and the bio-sciences in particular are opening up to us today truths that are as mystical as they are scientific, as compassionate as they are useful. Anyone interested in spirituality today is powerfully indebted to what scientists are teaching about the universe, about our planet, and about the inter-connectedness of all things. Therefore, in this chapter I would like to comment on five aspects of this important connection (there's that word again!) between compassion and science: first, Physics and Compassion, second, Bio-sciences and Compassion, third and fourth, Animals and Compassion, including their role as spiritual guides to us, and finally, the interconnectedness of Earth, Earthiness and Compassion.

PHYSICS AND COMPASSION

Albert Einstein might well be remembered as the Scientist of Compassion. He had compassion on us all by freeing us from Newtonian mechanisms and therefore freeing us for compassion. He freed us to see the world as whole once again instead of seeing it as independent parts in a basically static and absolutist machine. He freed us from the dogmatisms that science had fallen into after having deposed ecclesial dogmatisms from the top of society's intellectual ladder. He freed us, therefore, to be humble again. To recognize the *relativity* of our knowledge and of all constructs of the universe and universes, macro and micro, of which we are so integral a part. He freed us from absolutisms, as when he said: "As far as the laws of mathematics refer to reality, they are not certain; and as far as they are certain, they do not refer to reality." [2] Reality is bigger than we are—what a relief to know this! In freeing us from mechanistic determinisms he freed us to be compassionate once again. Four areas in particular emerge where contemporary physics, indebted to Einstein, frees us for compassion; and a fifth area takes us beyond Einstein.

Interconnections

Classical physics was based on the Cartesian distinction between the thinker (subject or *cogitans*) and the outside object (*res extensa*). This distinction allowed scientists to treat matter as objects. The building blocks of all matter, atoms, were mechanistically conceived as being solid, ultimate objects, that were pushed about and moved by external forces, the principle one being that of gravity. Matter was composed of separate objects that acted like pieces in a machine. Matter is essentially dead and inert, as billiard balls are, or appear to be. This view of reality, mechanistic as it is, provided much insight that allowed technology to flourish and allowed the "machine age" to develop since Newton. It had become too general a theory, however, so that before long all the other sciences were swept up into a basic mechanistic world-view so that we started projecting machine-like qualities on the cosmos, our bodies and our own psychology.[3] Molecular biology, for example, operates on this basic principle—just know the parts—as does much of modern medicine which specializes in intervention, usually by drugs and surgery between one's brain and one's body. Newtonian physics is also played out in much Freudian psychoanalysis and Freud himself confessed that "Analysts are incorrigible mechanists and materialists" and he was forced to reduce all aesthetic, creative and spiritual experience to a strict determinism of causes. Certain psychology schools, especially behaviorism, follow suit. It has also played a dominant role in theology, for example, in a theology of sacraments that grasps sacrament as power and mechanism—whether the Sacrament of the Word or the Sacraments of the ordained dispenser—instead of sacrament as celebration.[4]

While Newton's schema has been useful and will continue to prove useful, particularly in some areas of applied science, it has contributed substantially to that demonic situation we identified in Chapter Three as dualism. It has taught us all to think dualistically about all of reality, including us and our bodies, us and our minds, us and space, space and time, us and time, mass and energy, *ad infinitum* one might say.

Einstein offers us a better way to see the cosmos and our place (space) in it. It is a way of interconnections. It leads to organic thinking and holistic awareness wherein the universe is conceived as a harmonious process that is fundamentally interconnected. It is made up of webs or patterns that include galaxies and stars, planets and oceans, trees and birds, crystals, molecules and atoms, and we cannot separate any of these patterns from the rest without destroying them. Both organic and so-called inorganic matter are part of these patterns and only exist through this mutual interrelatedness. Moreover, according to Einstein's relativity theory, "space is not three-dimensional and time is not a separate entity. Both are intimately connected and form a four-dimensional continuum, 'space-time.' In relativity theory, therefore, we can never talk about space without talking about time and vice versa" (C, 62). Thus space and time become interdependent in relativity theory. This is a breakthrough for compassionate awareness, for space and time are such basic categories for our imagining anything in our world. (Try thinking of something that is not in space and time and you learn how basically our mechanistic preconceptions of both were shattered by Einstein.)

Atoms, instead of being the rugged individualists standing alone until pulled or pushed as Newton envisioned them, were also radically re-understood by Einstein. Atoms, these very 'building blocks' of all that exists, were no longer solid, stoic survivors but universes themselves with much more space than matter in them and where energy danced and darted. Physicist Fritjof Capra pictures it thus: if you took one atom and made it as large as the dome of St. Peter's Cathedral in Rome, the nucleus of the atom would only be as large as a grain of salt! And the electrons of the atom would be like specks of dust whirling about the dome. Einstein shattered our dogmas about matter, for example, that it was solid and stable and individualistic. What did he leave in its place? "Wave-like patterns of probabilities" which "ultimately, do not represent probabilities of things, but rather probabilities of interconnections." Interconnectedness—the clue to all compassion—lies at the very core of all that exists. Capra elaborates:

> a careful analysis of the process of observation in atomic physics has shown that the subatomic particles have no meaning as isolated entities, but can only be understood as interconnections between the preparation of an experiment and the subsequent measurement. Quantum theory thus re-

veals a basic oneness of the universe. It shows that we cannot decompose the world into independently existing smallest units. As we penetrate into matter, nature does not show us any isolated 'basic building blocks', but rather appears as a complicated web of relations between the various parts of the whole. (68)

Thus we see that matter itself contains the basic law of compassion: Interconnectedness. And so basic is this law that subatomic particles "have no meaning as isolated entities." Relationship is the law of all matter.

What I am calling this basic law of compassion applies to the macro world of the universe no less than to the micro world of the atoms. Says Capra: "in the new world view, the universe is seen as a dynamic web of interrelated events. None of the proprieties of any part of this web is fundamental; they all follow from the proprieties of the other parts, and the overall consistency of their mutual inter-relations determines the structure of the entire web" (286). We are webbed, members of a web one and all, wedded to a web. Inter-connections. "All natural phenomena are ultimately interconnected" says Capra. It is our learning this fact of the physical universe and adapting to it that will free us for compassion.

With Einstein a veritable revolution in the awareness of inter-connectedness has occurred in our scientific world view. For example, the awareness of the interconnectedness between vibration and visi-bility, of color and human moods and physiological body changes, of radiation rays and biological processes on earth, between music and the growing of crops, between chemistry and consciousness, between an individual cell and that individual's entire chemical make-up, be-tween matter and spirit. This revolution in awareness is like a revela-tion for it parallels closely the convictions of mystics over the centuries and through various cultures and religious traditions. From this mutual interconnectedness of science and spirituality a new energy is appear-ing that Lawrence Blair describes this way: "the schism between the two worlds of science and religion is beginning to heal and to merge into a single majestic river of vision." [5]

Matter is a verb, not a noun

In addition to his releasing us for compassion by allowing us to see the interconnectedness of all that exists, Einstein startles us again when he demonstrates that matter is a verb and not a noun. "Mass is nothing but a form of energy. Even an object at rest has energy stored in its mass" declares Capra (63) — matter is not nearly as dead, dull and inert as humans have presumed it to be. I once heard a potter declare that clay, the material that he worked with and loved so much, was "alive." Was he speaking only metaphorically?

"Things", "objects," "substances" do not exist in creation. What exists is processes, activities and inter-relationships which in turn give form and apparent substance. "Relativity theory showed that mass has nothing to do with any substance, but is a form of energy. Energy, however, is a dynamic quality associated with activity, or with processes . . . The particle can no longer be seen as a static object, but has to be conceived as a dynamic pattern, a process involving the energy which manifests himself as the particle's mass" (77). The basis of all reality, like the basis of all compassion, is a verb and an action. It is an action within a pattern, which at the level of compassion we have called love-justice. Once again, at the subatomic level of existence, there are no impenetrable rugged individualists. No cold-hearted unmoved movers or stoic and solipsistic loners. Instead, the high-energy scattering of recent physical experimenting show us "the dynamic and ever-changing nature of the particle world" wherein matter is "completely mutable. All particles can be transmuted into other particles; they can be created from energy and can vanish into energy. In this world, classical concepts like 'elemental particle', 'material substance' or 'isolated object', have lost their meaning; the whole universe appears as a dynamic web of inseparable energy patterns" (80).

Blair sees this passage leading from "cold cosmology of determinism" to energy or vibration — "a word deriving from 'vibrare', to share or move." Like life itself this process constitutes "the constant flux and regeneration of everything, from nebulae to pebbles on the beach" (109). Symbols from the universe around and within us are "not merely abstract ideas, but actually ciphers to the vibrationary music which knits us all together. To him whose feelings are alive to depth, the forms of snow crystals, the mandala faces of flowers, actually resonate to the awakening harmony within him" (114). The aesthetic, then, awakens us and reminds us of our connection and harmony with all beauty everywhere. All matter, whether called alive or dead, radiates energy.

From physics we are being reminded of what compassionate people like Jesus or Hosea or Buddha tried to teach: that people too are verbs and not nouns. That we feel, relieve the pain of others, and celebrate. And that this Way of living is truly harmonious with self, others, and the cosmos. And that this cosmic inter-relatedness, while it will be threatening to certain non-compassionate and nounlike people, is the only human energy that in the long run is lasting. It alone resurrects and re-energizes. The name for people, then, is a verb: lovers, compassion-doers, justice-makers. Here lies our "peace with the universe" but it is not a static peace since there is nothing in the universe that is static. It is a peace in motion, a peace of motion called justice. Which in turn causes plenty of commotion, as all energy does. In this respect Einstein was being very true to his Hebraic and Biblical heritage, as distinct from the hellenistic suppositions of Newton and Descartes. For the Greeks, being is most being when it is eternally resting. For the Jews, being is in eternal motion.[6] God is active, not passive. And now Einstein tells us that matter too is active and not passive. So too is that ultimate human energy called compassion. "This is my commandment," said Jesus, "that you love one another."

Paradoxical, Dialectical and Relative knowledge

Another contribution Einstein and contemporary physics makes to an increase in compassion is their rejection of the subject/object dualism and with it the myth of absolute objectivity that so much of the scientific world succumbed to after Newton and Descartes. This humility is more than a humility, it is in some way a confession of the way things are. And the way we know things in so far as we know them as they are. The notion that one could explain reality without even mentioning the observer became a norm for science after Descartes. But Einstein destroyed this myth entirely, revealing the immense subjectivity and relativity in all we do, imagine or think. Relativity, which is a key to compassion or the capacity to relate to those suffering more or different pain from ourselves, is the key to all thinking about motion, matter, energy of the universe. Relativity does not mean the loss of the absolute or the opposite of absolute (for absolute has no opposite)—it means the interconnectedness of all things. It is because the thinking subject is indeed part of the web of space-time, and light, and motion of all things he or she thinks about, that physics posits relativity. So does compassion.

The investigation of the Quantum Theory revealed even more about relativity and absoluteness in nature. The subatomic world itself was discovered to be full of paradox, dialectic, and the union of opposites.

Each time the physicists asked nature a question in an atomic experiment, nature answered with a paradox, and the more they tried to clarify the situation, the sharper the paradox became. It took them a long time to accept the fact that these paradoxes belong to the intrinsic structure of atomic physics, and to realize that they arise whenever one attempts to describe atomic events in the traditional terms of physics. (Capra, 66)

The principle of contradiction, so basic to Aristotelian logic in the West, seems not to hold when exploring the foundations of reality. The need for the poet and the parable-teller seems as basic as the bottom line of the universe itself. Einstein, contrary to the thinking patterns of his day, understood light to be both wave and particle. This both/and thinking is dialectical and his position demanded a new way of conceiving of both waves and particles. His hypothesis that the space-time curve contradicts the laws of Euclidean geometry is absolute no longer if space and time are not absolute. The notion of "black holes in space," which occupies many astrophysicists today, derives from Einstein's curvature-by-gravity thesis. Here too we are on the threshold of a dialectical and paradoxical way of thinking. But paradox and dialectical consciousness is the basis of all compassionate consciousness as well—because what logic can deduce for us or demonstrate to us that relieving the pain of another is relieving the pain of God? Perhaps the concept of black holes in space is a spatial joke just as humans as images of God are some kind of joke. Or that God became some kind of human. Such inversions might be more basic to the way energy operates than we have ever yet imagined. To learn to live in harmony is to learn to develop one's sense of humor as well as to learn the truths of the pain of our universe and our neighbor.

The basic force of the subatomic world is the force of electric attraction between the positively charged nucleus of the atom and the negatively charged electrons. In such a situation we see that harmony does not mean a balance-at-rest but a vibrant, bi-polar energy force that urges on all other energy. Dialectic becomes the basis of all reality! "The interaction between electrons and atomic nuclei is thus the basis of all solids, liquids and gases, and also of all living organisms and of the biological processes associated with them" (Capra, 72). We need to think dialectically because we in fact *are* dialectical—from our atoms to our dreams and all the spaces in between.

The organic Universe

To recognize the interconnection of all matter—and indeed the convertibility of energy and matter—to establish that matter is a verb and not a noun or substance, and to realize that true knowledge of matter is, like matter, paradoxical, dialectical and relative is to re-establish an awareness of the Universe as a whole. The organic universe has replaced the mechanistic one.

In an organic universe celebration in its most basic sense, or energy allowed to happen, is found to be elemental just as it is elemental in compassion. Capra notes: "Modern physics has shown us that movement and rhythm are essential properties of matter; that all matter, whether here on Earth or in outer space, is involved in a continual cosmic dance" (241). And he confesses that it was the "beautiful experience" of being at the ocean and experiencing "my whole environment as being engaged in a gigantic, cosmic dance" that drove him to pursue the interrelatedness of physics and spirituality. He describes his mystical experience as a celebration of the energies of the universe in the following manner.

> I 'saw' cascades of energy coming down from outer space, in which particles were created and destroyed in rhythmic pulses; I 'saw' the atoms of the elements and those of my body participating in this cosmic dance of energy; I felt its rhythm and I 'heard' its sound, and at that moment I *knew* that this was the Dance of Shiva, the Lord of Dancers worshipped by the Hindus. (11)

I once asked Dr. Capra what other physicists thought of his writings connecting physics to mysticism. His reply was that at first there was some scepticism until they learned what a good physicist he was, but that actually, in traveling about the country a lot, he had learned that "at least 50% of the physicists of our country are into physics because of the mysticism in it." "That would mean," I pointed out, that "there is a greater percentage of physicists who are mystics these days than priests or ministers." I once told this story in a University town and after my talk three persons came up to me individually, two women and a man, and each told me the same thing: "Don't tell anyone," they said. "But I am a professional physicist who is in it for the mysticism of it."

Yes, science and spirituality are meeting. And their meeting house might well be named: Compassion. For as long as mechanics was the ultimate explanatory science, there could be no room for interpenetration or for suffering with, celebrating with or working with. Such a science will trumpet its "value-freeness" but the more loudly it is trumpeted the more suspicious one becomes. For behind all facts lie · values and positions, as Einstein insisted. To ignore this law of the universe is to "effectively place science in the service of power, which determines the values to be served by science," as William Eckhardt warns. It is to establish science itself as a lackey of the ladder-powers.

"There are no value-free facts. Consequently, a value-free science is naive at best, fraudulent at worst, and a self-contradiction in terms." (263) It is for this reason that scientists who have not caught up with Einstein's revolution and revelation in thinking comprise that menace to humanity and to cosmology that Eckhardt describes when he says that, based on his empirical studies, "compassion was not consistent with . . . conventional science as . . . conceived and practiced in our culture today" (265). Einstein himself did not hesitate to explore moral implications of his theories,[7] even though members of the scientific community considered him eccentric and 'mystical' for so doing.

In criticizing Descartes' influence on the notion of compassion, Max Scheler points out that "the mechanistic conception of the universe makes any sort of organic point of view untenable" and all that is left is a cloudy kind of "humanitarianism or the love of mankind in general, based on an essentially 'social' conception of man's status as a being divorced from God *and* Nature." (94) Instead of a 'cloudy humanitarianism' that distance and objectivity dictate, the new physics suggests a physically rooted *self-interest* as the key to morality, for what happens to another happens to us all. Or, in Jesus' consciousness, we do indeed love others the way we love ourselves. Newton and Descartes, then, made compassion an impossible value in their world of isolated things. An experience of the unity of the universe such as Capra testifies to is an essential ingredient of a spirituality of compassion. This unity Scheler called for also: "The first task of our educational practice must be to revive the capacity for identification with the life of the universe, and awaken it anew from its condition of dormancy in the capitalistic social outlook of Western man (with its characteristic picture of the world as an aggregation of movable quantities)" (105). Precisely what Einstein launched, the awareness of the cosmos as an organism, lies at the basis of a compassionate consciousness. "Identification with the cosmos cannot really take place except within a view of things which envisages the world as a whole, a *collective organism*, permeated by a *unitary* life; it requires an organic mode of approach to things" (82). It is peculiar to Western thinking, Scheler believes, that we escaped this organic thinking during the past few mechanistically-dominated centuries.

Matter, Energy and Consciousness: Beyond Einstein

To Einstein we owe the return to organic, holistic and motion-thinking about our universe. He accomplished this feat by acting as if the speed of light were an absolute. Today frontier thinkers are going beyond that absolute and asking the inevitable question: can we know reality that lies beyond the speed of light? Is this speed what distinguishes matter from consciousness? One might call this relativizing the theory of relativity. The suspension of time and motion, it is being suggested, is what occurs when a person is in a deep meditative state. When the energy called love takes over, space and time are overcome. (In this regard it is noteworthy how many ESP experiences are between persons who love each other deeply.) Physics is on the brink of opening up cosmic vistas of consciousness that have lain dormant at least since the Enlightenment.

We now know there are 100 billion stars in our galaxy and we have made contact with one billion other galaxies so far. What is clear from these facts alone is how vast our minds are, that they can make contact with such distances of space and time. Yet, as Itzhak Bentov points out, it may be that these billion-plus galaxies that we call our universe may be merely a "tiny cell in a much larger structure" and that even that much "vaster system is again just a speck in an even vaster system, and . . ." [8] We do not know the limits—but the fact that we can know there may be no imaginable limits itself suggests our own unlimits. In some way we are as space-less and time-less and as full of motion and energy that transforms itself in uncountable ways as is the universe itself. We can travel at speeds faster than light—though our senses cannot. Who dare say anymore where matter ends and energy begins? Or where matter ends and consciousness begins? Only those who have never travelled beyond the speed of light—in other words, those who have never loved or experienced insight.

Still another suggestion that is provocative, though neither provable nor disprovable at this early stage of investigation, concerns that great unknown power that can move whole oceans and whole cities but about which we are very, very ignorant. I am talking of course about gravity. It is interesting that our language speaks of the "attraction between the moon and the earth" that in turn produces tides and of persons who "gravitate toward each other" or toward a certain life style. In other words, our language suggests a hidden connection of love or compassion that grounds us and keeps us grounded in the universe. Bentov puts the questions in a most tantalizing way. Insisting that love is an energy and not the emotion we have reduced it to, he observes: "What we call 'love' is an energy or radiation that pervades the whole cosmos. It is possibly the basis of what we know as the phenomenon of gravitation" (92). Does compassion become the basic energy of the universe? Surely this is what spiritual teachers East and West have continuously taught: that the purpose of living is to become an energy called love.

There is a profound theological issue at stake in the question of how we consider the apparently less-than-conscious elements of the universe. As one theologian puts it, "even inanimate creation 'also will be delivered from its slavery to corruption into the freedom of the glory of the sons of God'" (Rom. 8.21).[9] Paul and his commentator speak to the "freedom" and the compassion of and toward the inanimate. There is such a thing as animate chauvinism, and theologically speaking it has been declared a heresy: Gnosticism isolates the animate from the inanimate world. It was the dualistic and gnostic heretic Marcion who taught that Christ's redemption was acosmic and did not affect the universe.[10] In dualistic gnosticism, "the sublime unity of cosmos and God is broken up, the two are torn apart, and a gulf never completely to be closed again is opened: God and world, God and nature, spirit and nature, become divorced, alien to each other, even contraries. But if these two are alien to each other, then also man and world are alien to each other ..." (251) It is typical of gnosticism, continues Jonas, to teach that "man by his inner nature is acosmic; to such a one, all the world is indifferently alien. Where there is ultimate otherness of origin, there can be kinship neither with the whole nor with any part of the universe. The self is kindred only to other human selves living in the world—and to the transmundane God ..." (263). Given this insight into gnosticism, it seems abundantly clear that the spirituality that mechanistic science spawns is indeed a gnostic spirituality. This dualism is at least as much a part of us in the twentieth century as it was in the second century when Marcion lived. In contrast to this dualism is the Christian doctrine that Christ's redemption is a cosmic and universal one. (See Chapter Eight)

Still another subject being researched by contemporary physicists that a spiritual theologian cannot remain silent about is that of black holes in space. Bentov explains the theory as a sort of "gravitational collapse" in which matter becomes so dense that light itself "cannot escape the fact of the rest of the matter and is sucked down into the funnel from which there is no escape" (100f). The funnel is shaped by the curvature of space-time. But Bentov does not stop with the "disappearance" of matter but asks "Where does the energy go?" His ingenious answer, as paradoxical and dialectical as reality itself, is that it reappears in a different universe. It re-emerges as a "white hole" or the nucleus for another "big bang" and birth of another universe. While all this consideration of black and white holes remains quite theoretical, it is worthwhile to point out that the greatest teachers of compassion, such as Meister Eckhart, for example, taught that all creatures are nothing. "I do not say that they are something very slight or even something, but that they are a mere nothing," he insisted. It is important to point out that he is *not* speaking at the psychological level of people putting themselves down as nothing. This kind of repression is utterly foreign to true compassionate spiritual thinkers for, as we have seen, there is no room in compassion for either masochism or sadism. Yet it is the route that the sentimentalized spirituality of the *devotio moderna* often took. Is Eckhart speaking at the level of physics and metaphysics? Does the spiritual experience of nothingness or the void correspond to the physical reality of our origins as a cosmos from a black hole? And perhaps of the direction we are taking to return to the black hole? Thus, that we come from nothing and are madly racing toward nothing? I only offer these suggestions for the reader's consideration and meditation.

BIOLOGY AND COMPASSION

Biologists too are using terms like "holism" and "interdependence" and "organic" these days to describe their concerns and their discoveries. All this is a movement toward a compassionate consciousness and it is present wherever eco-systems are examined and explored for their interdependence. Specifically, I see four areas of particular insight about compassion and the eco-systems that contemporary biosciences instruct us in.

Living things are not separate entities

There is a movement in biology, as in physics, away from the machine anology that the mechanistic world-view espoused even in the sciences that study living organisms. Rene Dubos insists that "scientists should not be satisfied with studying the biological machine whose body and mind can be altered and controlled by drugs and mechanical gadgets. They should become more vitally concerned about the nature and purpose of man." The call is for a look at the whole instead of at the parts. "To be fully relevant to life, science must deal with the responses of the total organism to the total environment." [11] And from such a study a "new scientific humanism"—one that includes values and does not attempt to exclude them consciously or unconsciously—will be born. Far from being isolated entities, human bodies mingle and interpenetrate every time they meet in a room together. Thus Blair comments that "to sit within four feet of someone for over ten minutes is already to exchange water vapour with them, for we are as much a part of each other as are the planets in the system of the sun" (46).

Like physicists, biologists are beginning their study of the world with the destruction of the myth of rugged individualism and the separateness of things. Melvin Bernarde writes: "the deeper the analysis of the 'web of life' is pushed, the more meaningless becomes the word *independence*." [12] The very concept of "independence" is growing meaningless, warns Bernarde. We are at the end of an era, the end of a language, the end of a word. And the beginning of a new word, a new language, a new era. Cell fusion, which occupies many bioscientists today, is one example of the end of the word "independence." Cell fusion theory "violate [s] the most fundamental myth of the last century, for it denies the importance of specificity, integrity, and separateness in living things." [13] Interdependence has become a term for molecular genetics and its basic axiom is that, given the right conditions, "any cell—man, animal, fish, fowl, or insect" may be able to fuse with another. If the era and the very language of independence is ended, what will take its place?

Interdependence

The new awareness in biology is the awareness of interdependence. The biologist finds the law of interdependence wherever she or he turns these days. Thus, for example, Lewis Thomas confesses that "the new, hard problem will be to cope with the dawning intensifying realization of just how interlocked we are . . . We are not just made up, as we had always supposed, of successively enriched packets of our own parts. We are shared, rented, occupied . . . I cannot feel as separate an entity as I did a few years ago, before I was told these things, nor, I should think, can anyone else" (1–3). Our interdependence is exactly that—a dependence among one another. "We do not have solitary beings. Every creature is, in some sense, connected to and dependent on the rest" (6). We truly are a "social species" and our society goes far beyond our inter-relating with other humans à la personalism. "It is conceded that almost everywhere we are not the masters of nature that we thought ourselves; we are as dependent on the rest of life as are the leaves or midges or fish. We are part of the system." This awareness of our interdependence drives us to explore and to know this vast web of a system of which we are so integral a part, for "we cannot have a life of our own without concern for the ecosystem in which we live" (122).

Melvin Bernarde makes a similar point when he says that "our environment is a vast complex incapable of being grasped by understanding any one of its parts" (22); and John Storer, whose book, *The
Web of Life*, was one of the first ecologically oriented treatises by a biologist, gives the example of how plants themselves were saved from
themselves through the millions of years of evolution by animals. Had
animals not come along and eaten plants, thereby releasing carbon
which plants had taken from the air and trapped within themselves,
then all life—plants included—would have been extinguished from the
earth. Life is truly a life-cycle. It is spiral and circular, not linear. Not
even plants are self-sufficient. As Storer puts it, plants "build food that
makes life possible for animals, and in turn depend on the animals to
keep the cycle of life moving." [14] The fact of organic interdependence
is a principle of biology, but it is equally a principle of spirituality.
This should not shock us since the Author of physical life is the same
as the Author of spiritual life. This truth is agreed upon by Fairfield
Osborn in his Introduction to Storer's ground-breaking book: "The
most basic truth regarding our Earth-home is that all living things, in
some manner, are related to each other. This fact, while mainly important as a physical principle, carries implications even of a spiritual nature" (v). He is so correct. For interdependence is the first law of compassion which is in turn the fullest expression of the spiritual life of
human beings. Moreover, even within the organism itself we are
learning the startling revelation of the microcosm's intimate dependence on the macrocosm and vice versa—in other words, the law of
interdependence. In principle every single individual cell of our bodies
contains all the information about ourselves in its chromosomes. This
law of interdependence does not stop with our immediate bodies and
experience but extends to the cosmos itself. The stars, from which the
energies of our bodies were manufactured, are in a certain sense our
grandparents, our stellar grandparents one might say.

Cooperation, Creativity and Celebration

Still another dimension to biology and compassion is the movement
away from the *rugged*ness implied in the term "rugged individualism."
The presumption that all life is a war and that therefore competition is a
necessary and indeed compulsive dimension to living simply does not
obtain as we once thought it did under a simplistic interpretation of Darwin's survival of the fittest formula. Cooperation, rather than competition, may be the more basic rule in our universe. Comments Thomas,
"most of the associations between the living things we know about are

essentially cooperative ones, symbiotic in one degree or another" (6). Thomas urges that in place of the "social Darwinism" that we have accepted as a natural law for a century, we would do well to take lessons from chloroplasts and mitochondria, two organelles that are "in a fundamental sense, the most important living things on earth." They produce oxygen for all living things and they are the same whether in me, in sea gulls, in dune grass, in whales, in trees, dogs, skunks. "Through them, I am connected; I have close relatives, once removed, all over the place." These organelles make relatives of all of us living things! And theirs is a peaceful rather than competitive relationship. "There is something intrinsically good-natured about all symbiotic relations, necessarily, but this one, which is probably the most ancient and most firmly established of all, seems especially equable. There is nothing resembling predations, and no pretense of an adversary stance on either side" (85–87). How wise Thomas is to suggest this kind of cooperative interrelationship as a model preferred to that of competition in human affairs. For life begets life. The basic drive in the organic world is getting along, Thomas suggests, and not competition. "There is a tendency for living things to join up, establish linkages, live inside each other, return to earlier arrangements, get along, whenever possible. This is a way of the world" (147). Perhaps the "way of the world" is a rich source for learning the Way of the Creator of that world and of the mini-creators, called ourselves.

It also appears that creativity and the birthing of new births is another intrinsic dimension to living. And that the human race, through the special gift of language, is especially endowed with that imaging and naming capacity that at times seems so divine. Implied in all language—whether of words or music or dance or mime or film—are others. Language is intrinsically social and dialectic—it takes two to tango in whatever language, as they say. Language is for others and for self. Language is our utterance of a perceived interdependence. It is meant for compassion, therefore, for the sharing of passion whether the passion of pain and its relief or the passion of celebration and the re-creation it brings with it. Every speaker is an artist or creator who lives "by making transformations of energy into words" (108). Everyone an artist, everyone a creator. Language evolves, as Thomas puts it, "from words to Bach" and it challenges us to create as much as we challenge it with our ever-new, ever-imaginative creativity.

What is the direction we are borne in in passing and choosing to pass from isolated and competing individuals to cooperative and creative, symbol-making citizens of the universe? Thomas suggests—as any good theology of compassion would suggest—that the goal is celebration. The first surprise that urges us to celebrate, Thomas suggests—as Meister Eckhart suggested 600 years ago when he said "Is-ness is God"—is the very fact of our existence. That we are is enough miracle in itself, suggest both Eckhart and Thomas. "Statistically, the probability of any one of us being here is so small that you'd think the mere fact of existing would keep us all in a contented dazzlement of surprise" (165). As Becker puts it, "most of us—by the time we leave childhood—have repressed our vision of the primary miraculousness of creation," and yet we live in a world "so full of beauty, majesty, and terror that if animals perceived it all they would be paralyzed to act" (50). We ourselves, by our unbelievably organized structures, are a surprise of nature. We stand, as Thomas says, in eerie contrast to "the normal, predictable state of matter throughout the universe" which is randomness, and "we violate probability by our nature" (165). Isn't this enough "reason"—or better unreason—to celebrate?

Another dimension of existence that the biologist urges us to cele-brate is the surprising sisterhood and brotherhood that we share with all creatures, large and small. We have spent so many centuries defining the human animal in contradistinction from other species that we have for-gotten how alike we also are and how much we share in this holy time and holy space called a life-time and called a global village. There is a "family resemblance" between the enzymes of grasses and those of whales and ourselves, notes Thomas. We really owe it to ourselves and our universe to celebrate "the uniformity of the earth's life, which is more astonishing than its diversity." (3) Like celebrates likenesses.

And still another cause for celebration and letting go is ourselves. We really are as wonder-ful as we are awe-ful. If we took time to let go and allowed the space its letting be, we couldn't help but "discover in ourselves, the sources of wonderment and delight that we have dis-cerned in all other manifestations of nature" (125). Celebration is ev-eryone's then, all organisms celebrate life. It appears that the only or-ganism that can choose not to celebrate is the human being—we can be too busy "marrying a wife" (cf. Jesus' problem with this same com-pulsion in Lk. 14.15–24), or selling a stock or buying a trinket to let go, let be and let happen. That is, to celebrate with our sisters and broth-ers, some furry and some nearly invisible, some mammoth and spout-ing water, some musical and occupying tree limbs, some tiny and scurrying to turn over the soil for the rest of us. Mechanistic spiritu-ality does not allow for celebrating life because it is too oriented to ef-ficiency, too activist and too busy manipulating and being in control to let be, let go and let happen. Organic consciousness does allow for celebrating, however, for implied in all organic living is give and take, doing and receiving, doing and being.

Humility and relativity

Still another movement in contemporary biology that leads to compassion and to celebration as well is a growing reverence and respect for what is and what is so marvelously. And from this reverence there is emerging a humility in the proper sense of that virtue—*not* a putting down of oneself or one's gifts, but in fact an acknowledgement that the developed use of these very gifts leads to the awesome awakening of how ignorant we are of this very complicated and beautiful web we call life. Thomas calls upon the "nuclear realists" to interrupt their calculations of acceptable levels of megadeath long enough to wait until "we have acquired a really complete set of information concerning at least one living thing" (30). As a nominee for such a study, he proposes the protozoan *Myxotricha paradoxa* which dwells inside Australian termites. From studying them we learn how the nucleated cell is made. What Thomas is also declaring, however, is that we are so ignorant of life that we do not even know about this smallest of organisms—though we might with ten years of intensive research. Such humility is refreshing to hear about—especially for a theologian like myself who hears so many people and so many institutions who apparently know so much about God. Amazing, isn't it, that we know so little about so little an organism but possess so much certitude about God and *his* (always his) ways. Humility is a letting go of our compulsion to prove we know more than we do. One can only speculate on how refreshing it would be for the human race and its co-inhabitants of this village we call earth to have a convention of biologists, doctors, and other humans which was dedicated to "What We Do Not Know About Humanity." Of course, we would have to put a time-limit on such a gathering, lest it go on forever. But should it go on forever? That would be a devious way of preserving our endangered species, wouldn't it? Studying what we do not know would keep us from pushing red buttons and so forth in an aggressive assertion of what we imagine we do know—our dogmas and compulsions and right to be on top, for example.

Another area in which biology is uttering its humility today is that long-repressed experience called death. The human race is admitting—finally—that death is part of living and maybe, after all, we need not pretend it is not there. Confessing that he "has no data on the matter," Thomas nevertheless speculates that perhaps consciousness at the time of death makes a journey "back into the membrane of its origin, a fresh memory for a biospherical nervous system" (61). His guess seems as plausible as any other, I suppose. But the key contribution is that science is now swallowing its pretensions to immortality (inherited no doubt from the ecclesial powers it displaced three centuries ago) long enough to wonder about death again. It is "a natural marvel," Thomas observes, that "all of the life of the earth dies, all of the time, in the same volume as the new life that dazzles us each morning, each spring." But to appreciate this wonder too we must let go of our fear and ignorance of this omnipresent event. "We will have to give up the notion that death is a catastrophe, or detestable, or avoidable, or even strange. We will need to learn more about the cycling of life in the rest of the system, and about our connection to the process" (115f). It is indeed refreshing to hear biologists speak to the issue of the Communion of Saints in this mystical, cosmic, body. And with it the communion of time (past, present, future) and space that all living is about. It is indeed good to hear biologists speak with such depth and breadth for there is a hint that, maybe after all, a new energy—which may in fact be the oldest of all energies—named compassion is being listened to.

ANIMALS AND COMPASSION

I have enjoyed dialoging with some physicists and biologists and trying, to the best of my limited abilities, to encourage their stepping off the ladder of professionalism and into the circles where most all of us live, die or want to live. I want now to speak to that non-elitist scientific observation which is all of ours (everyone a scientist!) and to speak to two subjects that, if we took the time, we would all become expert in: namely animals and earth. Implied in both topics is our own self-knowledge and self-awareness, for we human beings are literally made of the stuff of both.

Ethics and savagery to animals

The word *animal* comes from the word *animale* meaning animated, which in turn comes from the word *anima* or soul. Animals are those not only with whom we share this earth and this physical universe of space/time, but also with whom we share a soul. At least that is what our ancestors taught and believed. Descartes, the philosopher of mechanistic science, took the *anima* or soul right out of the animals and declared that they were mere machines. If machines, they could be treated as brutally and bluntly as one treats a piece of metal. Contemporary philosophy, so often bloated in its development of heady language and so busy climbing the ladder away from its animality, has had practically nothing to say about the interdependence between animals and human animals. Victor Hugo has commented that philosophy "has examined only superficially, almost with a smile of disdain, man's relationship with things, and with animals, which in his eyes are merely things." [15] And Albert Schweitzer complains that: "It would seem as if Descartes, with his theory that animals have no souls and are mere machines which only seem to feel pain, had bewitched all of modern philosophy. Philosophy has totally evaded the problem of man's conduct toward other organisms. We might say that philosophy has played a piano of which a whole series of keys were considered untouchable." Schweitzer believes that "religious and philosophical. thinkers have gone to some pains to see that no animals enter and upset their systems of ethics" and he compares this kind of antiseptic academian flight from animals to the housewife who shuts the door to keep the dog off the newly scrubbed floor.[16] The ivory tower, for those on Jacob's ladder, needs to remain ivory, Lily-white. No animals need enter. Not even, especially not even, the animal dimension to the human animal. That is what the ascetic tradition in Western spirituality has tried to teach us.

One result of this flight from animals and this long silence on the important issue of our sharing this globe in tandem has been the immense sadism toward animals that has grown and become more and more evident just as, since Descartes, the human capacity for torture and destruction has also grown under the morally ambiguous discoveries of technology. There are experiments going on now and especially in our country that are not only immensely painful to animals but are often unnecessary and in which, if they are necessary, the pain may be lessened. At the risk of disturbing the reader (remember: all compassion is from the guts and bowels according to Jewish teaching), I will recount a few of these tests. The International Primate Protection League (IPPL) has researched the treatment of Rhesus monkeys and found the following situations: for the sake of military experimentation monkeys were trained by electric shock to run a treadmill for a six hour period, alternating ten minutes of running with five of rest. Following such exercises, the monkeys were put into a squeeze cage and given lethal doses of neutron rays. They were watched until they died. "The lucky ones only lived seven hours," a researcher commented, while others survived up to 132 hours. In another radiation experiment, monkeys exposed to radiation were put on a treadmill to count the number of times they would vomit. Little monkeys vomited up to fifty times before they died. Monkeys were shot point-blank in the head with air rifles at the University of Chicago in an experiment that failed, and at the University of Michigan seventy-two monkeys were killed by ramming a cannon impactor into their stomachs at seventy miles per hour. Others, with no anesthesia, were swirled about at high speeds until their necks broke or were put into restraining devices for days at a time.[17] Other experiments include the blinding of baby monkeys to see whether their mothers would care for them; the removal of glands, nerves and brain tissue from cats to study their sexual behavior; the strapping of monkeys and of bears to seats of cars and then crashing them at high speeds.

What is most disturbing about these and numerous other experiments with animals is that a large amount of them are unnecessary. A large percentage of experimenting with animals is totally non-medical. For example, in Britain, of five million experiments conducted on live animals, almost 600,000 were for non-medical purposes such as the testing of cosmetics, weedkillers and household products. In the United States, 63 million animals are experimented on annually including 85,000 primates, 500,000 dogs, 200,000 cats and 45 million rodents. "Only a third of the experiments done on live animals are for medical research" and "even more disturbing is that some experiments are of very little value." [18] No one is advocating a purist stance that would say that no experimentation whatever is useful for human survival or even planetary survival. But the moral issue of the rights of animals concerns the absolute minimizing of numbers of experiments and of the pain of experimenting. Many tests being conducted are done without any consideration given the pain of the animals whereas, in fact, the pain could often be reduced or eliminated altogether. It is in fact a gnostic and heretical doctrine that animals are spawned of evil—Biblical teaching is that animals are integral parts of a *good* creation. In the gnostic thought of Mani, animals are said to spring from abortions of the daughters of Darkness and are thus a hindrance to the light of salvation and form a prison for purity that always wants to rise upwards (Jonas, 226). The hatred the gnostic system holds for the animals of the earth seems almost played out in the sadistic attitudes many people practice towards animals in our own day.

Cruelty toward animals is an integral dimension of studying human compassion because, sad to tell, it tells us so much about the species performing the experiments. Human chauvinism is laid bare in human sadism toward other animal species. Hugo points out that animals are weaker than humans to the extent that they are less intelligent, and it is for this very reason that humans are to be "kind and compassionate" toward them. It is the way we treat the weak, be they human or animal, that is the ultimate test of a civilization. No one has put the moral issue more bluntly and more memorably than Mahatma Gandhi when he declared that "We should be able to refuse to live if the price of living be the torture of sentient beings." If people feel free to torture animals, will they not also feel free to torture one another? Is not the lack of compassion toward any being a lack of compassion toward all? Can we be part-time compassionate? Or selectively compassionate? Of course not. For compassion is a universal energy or it does not exist at all. And, among human chauvinists, it clearly does not exist.

Another dimension to the ugliness of human chauvinism toward animals is the utter lack of respect for life and the mystery of life that is implicit in such cruelty. As Schweitzer has put it, "the ethics of reverence for life makes no distinction between higher and lower, more precious and less precious lives. It has good reason for this omission. . . . How can we know what importance other living organisms have in themselves and in terms of the universe? . . . To the truly ethical man, all life is sacred, including forms of life that from the human point of view may seem to be lower than ours" (47). What Schweitzer is calling attention to is the fact that chauvinism, or what our ancestors called human pride, imagines that it knows all the answers about the inter-relation of all beings and creatures. But the truth is, as we have seen in studying what biologists know and do not yet know, that we know next to nothing about these important issues. Schweitzer is no purist; the moral norm he advocates for any taking of life is as follows: "Whenever we harm any form of life, we must be clear about whether it was really necessary to do so. We must not go beyond the truly unavoidable harm, not even in seemingly insignificant matters. . . . In each individual case they [scientific experimenters] must ask themselves whether there is a real necessity for imposing such a sacrifice upon a living creature. They must try to reduce the suffering insofar as they are able" (48). Why is this? Because, according to Schweitzer, we humans actually owe much to what animals do for us in our experimenting. "The very fact that animals, by the pain they endure in experiments, contribute so much to suffering humanity, should forge a new and unique kind of solidarity between them and us." (48)

Instead of treating animals as objects, we need to respect the interdependence we share with them. There is a gradual and growing awareness today, once again, that animals do have rights.[19] The moral issue behind this movement of animal rights concerns not only the rights towards animals but the quality of life that humans live and pass on to their own children. To harm animals is, in the long run, to harm the human animal. As John Galsworthy has put it: "Nothing so endangers the fineness of the human heart as the possession of power over others; nothing so corrodes it as the callous or cruel exercise of that power; and the more helpless the creature over whom power is cruelly or callously exercised, the more the human heart is corroded."[20] One philosopher who has not ignored the subject of the treatment of animals is Max Scheler, who observes that what lies behind cruelty is sentimentalism. A cruel person relates to elements of nature as if they were only extensions of himself that he can manipulate at will. Nature is in fact meant to be "an object of love *for her own sake*, for what is peculiar to herself and hence alien to man." Anything else is sentimentalism. And it is for this reason that "such things as brutality towards the organic forms of Nature, animal and vegetable, do not become 'wicked' merely through being regarded as a symptom of 'potential' brutality towards men, but are actually wicked in themselves" (155f. Italics his). There is, then, no compassion among those who are cruel to animals. And no compassion among a science, a philosophy or a religion that ignores our interdependence with animals.

Spiritual Traditions and animals

And this fact is indeed what religious traditions when they were truly spiritual traditions have taught world-over. As E.F. Schumacher has observed, "There have been no sages or holy men in our or anybody's history who were cruel to animals or who looked upon them as *nothing but* utilities, and innumerable are the legends and stories which link sanctity as well as happiness with a loving kindness towards" these creatures.[21] And, of course, he is right. All know the story of how, when the monks would not allow him to stay overnight because he smelled too bad, Francis found many a friend among the wolves, dogs, birds, sheep, and creatures of the wilds. How St. Anthony, whose congregation did not want to hear what he had to say, preached to the fishes and was also preached to by them. How Buddha related openly to animals and how at home Jesus was in the animal world.

This should not be unexpected, namely that Jesus treated animals with respect, for the Jewish tradition which he represented so fully was itself very concerned with the way humans treated animals. Relieving the suffering of an animal was a Biblical law according to Talmudic teaching, and so Jesus' admonition to raise a fallen ox from the pit even on the Sabbath was not out of character for a good Jew. The dietary laws were meant to limit the eating of meat and keep it to a bare minimum, and hunting for sport was absolutely forbidden the Jews. When they caught fish it was to be only by net and never by hook. Says Rabbi Dressner, "Mercy was not only shown to one's fellowman, be he Jew or Gentile, but to all living things: the beasts of the field, the fish of the sea and the birds of the air. We are taught not to harm a single living thing, not a fly or an ant, not even a spider. For they too are God's creatures. And these too suffer when they are hurt. . . . Animals as well as humans are God's creatures, and toward all of God's creatures we are taught to show mercy" (234f). Moreover, according to Jewish Midrash, both Moses and David were chosen to lead Israel because of their compassion toward animals—some criteria for choosing leaders, this.

Jesus was evidently not a human chauvinist at all. For instead of controlling animals and ordering them about, he observed them very, very closely and learned from them. In fact, so much did he learn from animals that he continually uses them as symbols for the reign of God on earth. "The birds of the air", the "sparrow falling from its nest," the fish gathered and not wasted, the sheep and the goats, the one lost sheep—all Jesus' parables that include animals reveal how humble he was toward them. He sensed the harmony and the interdependence that we share with all living things. They say Jesus was born in a stable among animals—one might say he got a pretty good start in life. And he died the slain lamb of God. Presumably the last lamb so slain.

Numerous persons—Victor Hugo and John Galsworthy among them—have suggested that Jesus' teaching that you "do not do to others what you would not wish them to do to you" or, put more positively, that you do to others as you want done to you, refers to animals and other beings who share our universe with us and not merely to other humans.

At least one great Christian mystic besides St. Francis, namely Meister Eckhart, has championed the spiritual dimension to animals and the way we interact with them. He comments on the "equality" we share with animals. "If I were alone in a desert where I was afraid, and if I had a child with me, my fear would disappear and I would be strengthened; so noble, so full of pleasure and so powerful is life in itself. If I could not keep a child with me, and if I had at least a live animal with me, I would be comforted. Therefore, let those who bring about great wonders in black books take an animal—perhaps a dog—to help them. The life within the animal will give them strength. Equality gives strength in all things." When it comes to the great gift and pleasure and power of life, Eckhart is saying, animals and ourselves are equal. There is an entire basis for animal ethics in this Eckhartian revelation. Victor Hugo predicted that in compassion to animals and plants a "whole great ethic" would be born in the West. He says: "In the relations of man with the animals, with the flowers, with all the objects of creation, there is a whole great ethic (*tout une grande moral*) scarcely seen as yet, but which will eventually break through into the light and be the corollary and the complement to human ethics" (106).

No spiritual tradition has more fully developed the spiritual relationship of humans to other animals than has the Native American tradition. Chief Oren Lyons of the Onondaga Indians comments on the Indians' attitude toward their "brothers," the buffalo. "We owe a debt of gratitude to the buffalo. They stepped in front of the white men's guns and took the brunt of the bloodthirsty time. They sacrificed themselves for us. We believe that had they not taken the brunt, the Indian people would not be there." [22]

Among the Indians there is a spiritual relationship experienced and reverenced between human and animal. Chief Irving Powless Jr. comments on the relationship between the Onondagas and the buffalo. "It's a spiritual feeling. That's how it benefits the nation. . . . With the coming of progress and the pushing of our animals back into smaller areas, not only the buffalo but our other brothers—such as the deer and the bear—are being pushed into small places, so that they are disappearing." [22] Ranchers presumed that this Indian tribe wanted the buffalo returned in order to start an industry of buffalo meat, bones and skins. Such was not the case. "The buffalo represent a spiritual thing" to these Indians, comments a rancher who has observed them. "Better than lining their pocketbooks, they're maybe lining their souls with something." On the Onondaga Reservation recently a meeting was held with the representatives of six Nations of New York State. Chief Oren Lyons addressed the group as follows: "We see it as our duty to speak as caretakers for the natural world. Government is a process of living together, the principle being that all life is equal, including the four-legged and the winged things. The principle has been lost; the two-legged walks about thinking he is supreme with his man-made laws. But there are universal laws of all living things. We come here and we say they too have rights." When Jesus commanded people to "love their neighbor as themselves," did he say that all neighbors were necessarily two-legged ones?

A century ago when Chief Seattle of the Suquamish tribe was forced to sell his land to the government, he made the following observations in his farewell speech: "If we decide to accept, I will make one condition: The white man must treat the beasts of this land as his brothers. I am a savage and I do not understand any other way. I have seen a thousand rotting buffalos on the prairie, left by the white man

who shot them from a passing train. I am a savage and do not understand how the smoking iron horse can be more important than the
buffalo we kill only to stay alive. What is man without the beasts? If
all the beasts were gone, man would die from a great loneliness of
spirit. For whatever happens to the beasts, soon happens to man. All
things are connected." Chief Seattle understands the interdependence
between human and other animals—an interdependence that is not
only physical and biological but spiritual as well—a "great loneliness
of spirit" will accompany the elimination of the creatures we share
this planet with. He continues: "We do not understand when the buffalos are all slaughtered, the wild horses are tamed, the secret corners
of the forest heavy with the scent of many men, and the view of the
ripe hills blotted by talking wires. Where is the thicket? Gone. Where
is the eagle? Gone. And what is it to say goodbye to the swift pony
and the hunt? The end of living and the beginning of survival." [23] The
end of living and the beginning of survival—the *quality* of life is what
is at stake in the mutuality between human and animal.

Schweitzer summarizes the ethics of compassion and animals in a
look at the future. He comments:

> To the universal ethics of reverence for life, pity for animals,
> so often smilingly dismissed as sentimentality, becomes a
> mandate no thinking person can escape.
>
> The time will come when public opinion will no longer
> tolerate amusements based on the mistreatment and killing of
> animals. The time will come, but when? When will we reach
> the point that hunting, the pleasure in killing animals for
> sport, will be regarded as a mental aberration? When will all
> the killing that necessity imposes upon us be undertaken with
> sorrow? (50)

In fact, those who dismiss love of animals as sentimentalism should
recall that intrinsic to all sentimentality is violence, as psychologist C.J.
Jung pointed out. It is not the non-violent person who is sentimental,
then, but the violent ones. Macho and sadistic savagery toward animals is itself an expression of sentimentality.

ANIMALS AS SPIRITUAL DIRECTORS

Because animals are so basic to compassion, and have been so
avoided by the ladder-oriented spiritualists who are so busy escaping
earth and animals, I would like to offer a brief outline of some lessons

that I have learned from animals. When I tell groups that my dog is my spiritual director I am only being partly facetious. For in many important ways, he truly is. These, it seems to me, are some of the lessons for compassionate and spiritual living that animals teach us.

Spiritual Lessons Animals Teach Us

1. That it is good to be an animal. Some of the happiest creatures I know are animals and they do not hesitate to demonstrate their joy at living.
2. Ecstasy without guilt. Animals can truly let go and let be and even celebrate without guilt feelings at "wasted time" or at letting their masks down. Indeed, they instruct us in realizing that intensity of living is more important than duration and in this sense they cure us of the platonic prejudice humans have that declares that eternity and length of duration must be the test of the goodness of things.
3. Play is an adult thing to do and needs no justifications.
4. The power and frequent adequacy of non-verbal communication. Animals are experts at the non-verbal—their language is mime, tone of voice and dance. And a truthful language it can be, also. Max Scheler comments on the meaning of a dog expressing "its joy by barking and wagging its tail, or a bird by twittering." We have here "a *universal grammar*, valid for all languages of expression, and the ultimate basis of understanding for all forms of mime and pantomime among living creatures" (11, italics his).
5. Openness and sensitivity. There can be little doubt that animals have developed or not allowed to atrophy powers of identification and sensitivity that we humans have almost totally forgotten. Many a dog, for example, on entering a room will know if someone is depressed or sad and will act to do something about it. Here Scheler also comments: "In man generally, the instinct for specialized identification has atrophied more than in most animals, and has applied itself, moreover to very *general* patterns in the life of others, whereas in primitive peoples, children, dreamers, neurotics of a certain type, hypnotic subjects and in the exercise of the maternal instinct, there remains much greater residual capacities for identification than in the average adult product of modern civilization" (31). Because the senses of animals are so often so much more acute than ours, they remind us of how limited our sense awareness often is and therefore they remind us of the need to continually expand our sense knowledge.
6. Beauty. Who cannot be caught up by the form of a seagull in flight, by the straight back of a proud dog, by the graceful strides of a

tiger, by the perfect musculature of a fine stallion? Beauty is not an appendage to human and spiritual living but of its very essence. Animals are here in part to grant glimpses of the grace of beauty. The beauty of the singing of birds is a kind of music in itself, as is the gurgling of a brook, the dashing of ocean waves against a rocky shore, the whistling of the wind among leafy trees. It has been proposed that "aesthetics may actually be a factor in evolution" of birds, for example, since "the females tend to choose the best singers and thereby help perpetuate the genes for musical talent." [24]

7. Sensuousness. Animals teach us that one can be sensual and spiritual at the same time. They know that abstractions by themselves, such as money for example, are not what living and ecstasy are about. I remember one time switching a dollar bill into my wallet and its dropping on the floor in front of my dog. He didn't bat one of his white eyelashes and had it been a thousand dollar bill he would not have reacted either. Had I dropped the wallet, however, there would have been a great game of tug of war. Why is this? Because the wallet, containing some cowhide, still retains a semblance of sensuousness. God made it insofar as nature made the cow. Thus there is some fun and ecstasy to it. It is an end and not only a means. Money, however, whatever the denomination, is only a means and is therefore not what living and ecstasy are about. This same truth that animals remind us of is also taught by children since, as Freud pointed out, "money is not an infantile wish."

8. That climbing Jacob's ladder is unnatural. Have you ever known an animal (other than the two-legged one) who liked to climb ladders? They know better. They know their place and our place is on the earth, eye to eye with the rest of the gifted creatures of the land and sea. Why should animals climb ladders when everything they need the Creator has put on earth? I once saw a bear climb a staircase in a circus when men made him do so. He was so afraid and so not-at-home when he got to the top stair that there, in front of us all, he peed from fright and discomfort. The audience laughed at this but the bear knew: there was nothing at the top of the ladder!

9. Humor. Animals bring humor into our lives, a radical, celebrative awareness of dialectic and paradox. Animals, I am convinced, love to make us human animals laugh. They are often well aware, in my opinion, of what makes us laugh and they are very often as humorous as they are humor-bearers. Animals are truly holy in their way, for all full humor is reflection of the divine good humor. A recent study on wolves, *Of Wolves and Men*, by Barry Lopez, tells the story how the author observed a wolf spend over an hour playing with a piece of dry

caribou hide, tossing it in the air as we do Frisbees. He saw wolves chase ducks amidst splashing of wings and water—all in fun. My dog once caught a squirrel—not to eat it—but to play with it. Though the squirrel was quite traumatized by my dog's invitation, he nevertheless went away completely unharmed. Indeed, it has been my experience that animals have very often retained a richer sense of humor than some persons I have met who have come from an acosmic spiritual direction experience.

10. Silent Dignity. Animals have a sense of their own worth and dignity—a pride at their own unique existence that subtly suggests that no one ever preached to them about original sin. As a result they appear at home with silence, with themselves and with solitude. I have been amazed in recent years to learn how many animals come out to watch the sun set, for example. Ducks, birds, dogs and God knows how many smaller creatures have a contemplative side to them that the human species of late has all but forgotten.

These ten aspects of sound spiritual directions to be learned from animals are only an introduction to a weighty and much neglected subject. I invite readers to reflect and expand on these basic contributions that animals make to our spiritual lives. What is clear is that God has blessed our animals and blessed us through the animals. And God requests of us that we in turn bless God through blessing the animals. For "the Lord is good to all and compassionate toward all his works" (Ps. 145).

Passion, Compassion and Human Animality

Ashley Montagu, in his book on *Touching*, tells the story of interviewing a young white woman, a college graduate. Do you want to get married? He asked her. Her answer was, Yes. Do you intend to have children? Yes, a few, she said. Do you intend to breast-feed them? Her answer was: Breast-feed them! That's what animals do!

It is good to be an animal. Ask the animals. And one can also be a spiritual animal—which is what humans are supposed to be. Ernest Becker remarks that much of human misery and human violence stems from the fact that we are an "animal who doesn't want to be one." [25] He defines the human species as "a god who shits." Becker is so right. How often the human race has pursued the dualistic folly of being either all animal and thus becoming greedy and hedonistic (the only animal it seems who is this way) or striving to be all angel and thus elevating asceticisms and spiritualisms to unnatural places and heights. We are in fact a dialectical creature—both divine and animal—and there is great joy in this and great humor. Here indeed lies the underpinning of our entire spiritual existence—that we are God's joke. A divine animal. If only we could laugh at ourselves and all our works, such as ideologies, myths, games and ever-so-serious nations, differences and goals. And our bodies. Having written a book on this vital subject of realigning the spiritual and the bodily, I learned something from reactions to that book. One suburban white mother called a journalist who interviewed me on the subject of a "sensual spirituality" and said how grateful she was for this interview. "For," she added, "I have a daughter who is college-age and now I know where *not* to send my daughter to school. I would never send her to a college where there was a priest who used the words 'sensual' and 'spiritual' in the same sentence." I bid the readers' prayers for this woman and most especially for her daughter. And please note how it is *in the name of religion* that many persons in the West have fled from their bodiliness. One truly has to inquire whether religion has done more harm than good in the West.

This is especially the case when you reflect on the latest research regarding the psychological origins of violence. A growing consensus is emerging among various researchers on how, psychologically speaking, violence originates from lack of touch and physical closeness as children. Ashley Montagu and James Prescott are examples of such researchers. Montagu cites a study in which it was found that a baby monkey can live longer without milk and food than it can without touch from its mother.[26] A flight from our animality, then, is clearly a flight *into* violence. Harmony and non-violence are learned by authentic entrance into the experiences of body and spirit and not by the dualistic control of one over the other. All this I have explored in greater detail in my book *Whee! We, wee All the Way Home: A Guide to the New Sensual Spirituality,* and I have especially developed there the profound *political* implications of flight from body (for we will project on to the body politic what we introject toward our body) and how the prophets of Israel (Jesus included) knew this powerful connection between passion and compassion, between body and body politic and spirit so well. As Rabbi Heschel has put it: "The source of evil is not in passion, in the throbbing heart, but rather in hardness of heart, in callousness and insensitivity . . ." (258). And yet, in the ever-popular and profoundly sentimental *Imitation of Christ,* every single time the word "passion" is used it is used pejoratively.

D.H. Lawrence has put the dialectic between spirit and sensuousness this way:

> Let us hesitate no longer to announce that the sensual passions and mysteries are equally sacred with the spiritual mysteries and passions. . . . The only thing unbearable is the degradation, the prostitution of the living mysteries in us. Let men and women only approach themselves with deep respect for all that creative soul, the God-mystery within us, puts forth. Then we shall all be sound and free. . . . Nothing that comes from the deep passionate soul is bad or can be bad.[27]

There can be no compassion without passion. This may be the ultimate lesson learned from animals—including the animal within us all. For moral outrage at injustice is itself a passion. And poet W.H. Auden warns that "as a rule it was the pleasure-haters who become unjust." Justice-making demands actions of us that are wise, imaginative, bodily and enfleshments of alternative living together. There never was a prophet who was out of touch with his or her animality.

Once we reject Descartes' definition of our bodies as objects that he in fact calls "cadavers," we are on our way to integrating their energies with others we constantly intersect with in the universe. This is how Descartes, the reigning influence in science and education over the past few centuries, understood the human body: "First came the thought that I had a face, hands, arms—in fact the whole structure of limbs that is observable also in a corpse, and that I called 'the body.' "[28] No wonder 'body counts' have come so easily to a culture weaned on body as corpse. In contrast, this is how Lawrence Blair understands our bodiliness. Our bodies, he says, are "diaphanous webs of pulsating form, in constant flux, which change and fall apart as soon as their underlying energies are distorted or withdrawn." The body "is beautiful and it responds to love—like all lovers—with illumination!" (133) We can no longer remain afraid, ignorant or superstitious about the mystery of bodiliness, for in that mystery lies still other spiritual mysteries. "To really *know* our bodies is to know ourselves in *depth,* and by so doing we can know much of the meaning of this cosmic flux of creativity in which we find ourselves" (134). It is important for a truthful understanding and full appreciation of our bodies to know that the very elements of which we are composed were in fact prepared billions of years ago in the stars themselves. To know our bodily selves is to be in touch with the cosmos—quite literally. Instead of putting down our bodies or fleeing from them, we ought to, as Bentov puts it, be "proud to know that the elements composing our bodies were made in these great radiant stars." (96) No wonder we, like the atoms and stars of the universe, turn to dance to celebrate our existences. A flight from the body such as much of Christian spiritualism has been involved in for centuries is a flight from body politic *and* from the cosmic body. As Becker put it, "fear of knowledge of oneself is very often isomorphic with, and parallel with, fear of the outside world." (52) The 'outside world' in this case is the universe itself, home of our origins. Eastern meditation exercises from the spiritual traditions of yoga or Tai Chi, for example, do not ignore the body or try to escape it in the name of a spiritualism. They listen to the body and they learn from the body. For, as Meister Eckhart tried to warn us, "the soul is not in the body but the body is in the soul."

EARTH, EARTHINESS AND COMPASSION

The flight from nature and earth that has characterized much of Jacob-ladder spirituality has permeated industrial society as well. Max Scheler comments that it is this loss of the sense of unity between humanity and the natural universe that has cast humanity "off from Nature, its eternal mother, in a manner which is essentially repugnant to" its nature. In such a situation "there would then be no ascription of *intrinsic* value to a love of plants, based on a sense of unity with their springing life." (106, italics his) The people our culture has come to speak of in pejorative terms as "pagans" were originally people of the soil, for the word *paganus* means one who lives in the country. Most compassionate people I know work with the soil whenever they can. Gardening for them is much more than a hobby. It is a way of life and a way of wisdom. The soil teaches us something that is necessary for becoming compassionate. What might that something be?

For one thing the gardener or the family farmer is in a give-and-take relationship with the soil. Manipulation and control are not the name of the true farmer's game. Respect, steering, waiting, patience are as much a part of gardening as doing is. The gardener then is automatically anti-Cartesian for he or she is in a relationship of mutuality and interdependence with the earth, air, water, and not a controller of it. Descartes saw our relationship to nature in the following categories: In practical philosophy, he maintained, we ought to know "the force and action of fire, water, air, the stars, the heavens, and all the other bodies that surround us" in order to "thus render ourselves the lords and possessors of nature." One needs to choose between being 'lord and possessor' and being a gardener.

Another lesson to be learned from the earth is the lesson about our own origins. We are of the earth and we are surely destined to return to the earth. There is authentic humility to be learned from our playing with the soil. St. Francis of Assisi, who knew as much about compassion as anybody, was so immensely earthy that as he was dying he insisted that he be laid naked on the ground. A commentator who was there reports that in this fashion Francis "accepted death singing"[29] for he had wanted to be returned to his "Sister Earth, our mother," as he called earth in his famous Canticle of the Sun. A rebirth happens in re-contact with the earth. The purpose of the rite among ancient peoples of placing a person on the earth at both birth and death is to "throw open to him a new and all-embracing life. The individual is resituated within the totality of being; he is brought into harmony with his own mystery and thus with the totality of his own soul . . . he participates in the totality of being and in its sacrality." [30] Earthiness is part of the cosmic sense of compassion.

The soil is far more than we imagine it to be. First of all, it is by no means inanimate. It contains a "hive of living things" that eat on one another and perform necessary operations to make the soil hospitable for other life. "Good soil is actually a living thing, and its health is a matter of life and death to the plants and animals that live on its surface. We ourselves are as dependent on its health as the smallest of its creatures." (Storer, 39) Soil needs plants as much as plants need soil—lessons of interdependence once again. And all animals need the plants, as we have seen above. So interconnected is all the soil of the earth, thanks to the action of wind and water over the centuries, that Storer can declare that "there is scarcely a square mile of the earth's surface that does not contain some ingredient from every other mile." (20) Again, back to the lessons of interdependence—this time about time and space that are facts of soil life. There is something friendly about a garden—maybe it can make gardeners friendly also. There is something motherly and nurturing about garden work as well.

This truth of interdependence of space and time is an especially sacred one in the Native American spiritual tradition wherein the earth is the veritable home where the saints and ancestors of old commune. Chief Seattle comments: "The very dust under your feet responds more lovingly to our footsteps than to yours, because it is the ashes of our ancestors, and our bare feet are conscious of the sympathetic touch, for the soil is rich with the life of our kindred. . . . This we know. The earth does not belong to man; man belongs to the earth.

This we know. All things are connected like the blood that unites one family. All things are connected. Whatever befalls the earth befalls the sons of the earth. Man did not weave the web of life; he is merely a strand in it. Whatever he does to the web, he does to himself. . . . This earth is precious to Him [the Creator], and to harm the earth is to heap contempt upon its Creator." The Chief observed the white man's ways toward the earth and was made sad and angry. "The earth is not his brother, but his enemy, and when he has conquered it, he moves on. He leaves his father's grave behind, and he does not care. He kidnaps the earth from his children. He does not care. . . . He treats his mother the earth, and his brother the sky, as things to be bought, plundered, sold like a sheep or bright beads. His appetite will devour the earth and leave behind only a desert." In contrast to these attitudes is the spirituality of the earth of the Red people. "Every part of this earth is sacred to my people. . . . Our dead never forget this beautiful earth for it is the mother of the red man. We are part of the earth and it is part of us. The perfumed flowers are our sisters; the deer, the horse, the great eagle, these are our brothers. The rocky crests, the juices in the meadows, the body heat of the pony and man—all belong to the same family." [31]

There is mystery in the earth and life there. There is, as radionics and other new explorations are suggesting, a great deal of energy and unknown potential in living plants. Of course gardeners with 'green thumbs' have known for centuries about the susceptibility of plants to moods around a home, to music, to other plants, to touch and to sounds. For we are indeed "part of the earth"—related to it as members of a family. And there can be no compassion without this strong and gentle earthiness. The antiseptic efforts to anesthetize reality by rendering our environment sterile and devoid of earthiness, dirt and tiny, unseen organisms kills compassion.

It is a gnostic heresy, a heresy by no means absent from contemporary industrial and post-industrial society, that considers the vegetable world to be one that drags us down from loftier and more spiritualized living. For the gnostics, "all plants, grain, herbs and all roots and trees are creatures of the Darkness, not of God, and in these forms and kinds of things the Godhead is fettered." (Jonas, 226)

In contrast to this dualism, Jesus was very earthy and very close to the earth. He depended on earth-stories to depict his vision of the Kingdom and Queendom of God that he was inaugurating.[32] His observations of seeds and the way things grow form an important part in his basic preaching about the reign of God. Indeed, the seed is sometimes the very Kingdom itself in his parables; at other times it stands for the Word of God—which is always a living word—sown among rocks, thistles, and good earth. He compares the godly Kingdom—not to a great cedar of lebanon or a redwood tree, but to a mustard plant which grows to be only a foot off the ground. In other words, to being close to the earth. And it will be a plant where birds will be happy to nest and no doubt to sing. It is a simple, but a welcoming, mustard plant. He admonishes his followers to learn from the plants the most basic of all spiritual lessons: "That unless a corn of wheat fall into the ground and die, nothing happens; but if it die, it brings forth much fruit." And, it is "by their fruits" that you will distinguish true from bogus spiritual people. And, in John's Gospel, he is himself compared to the vine and his disciples to being branches of the same vine. For all things are connected. The divine and the human, life and death, for instance. And the person close to the soil—as Jesus was—has learned this. In gardening we learn this ultimate law of life: dialectic. As in the Jesus story: death and rebirth. We are to be rich soil where God's seed might grow. But how will we be such if we are not soiled and vulnerable to the soil? So Meister Eckhart says: "We are the seed of God. A pear seed grows into a pear tree; a hazel seed into a hazel tree; a seed of God into God." And Eckhart, in commenting on Jesus' parable about the seed falling on good soil actually calls Jesus "the soil."

SUMMARY

We have completed our journey through physics, biology, animals and the earth. It is a holy journey with much more ground to be covered and uncovered. Many persons are sensing the need for this journey today more than ever before. For the feeling is abroad that nature, of which we are so integral a part, has many riches to teach us if we were truly eager to be compassionate, passionate dwellers in this verb called space on this sphere called global village and home. For if evolution proves anything, it demonstrates that the Creator of all things took billions of years to paint the landscapes called earth, to choreograph the dance called matter, to compose this symphony called energy, to mold this creature called homo sapiens. How appropriate it is that we let be and let go in order that this creation in its web-like entirety might flourish and return praise for such beautiful art-work.

Centuries ago, when society believed in a Ptolemaic cosmos that was geo-static and geo-centric, monks and nuns took vows of stability, thus to mirror the energies of the universe as they understood them. Today, now that we know the universe is in constant motion and is interdependent at every level, the time has come for spiritually motivated people of good will to take vows of organic interdependence and motion. The proper name for such a vow would be a vow of compassion. For as Paoli observes, "prayer that does not embrace things is not Christian. Christian prayer is 'in things.' . . . Peace is the search for justice, and the primary form of justice is the recognition that we are creatures among creatures with a responsibility for creation." (p. 11)

6

ECONOMICS AND
COMPASSION:

FROM AN EXPANSIONIST ECONOMICS
BASED ON THE 'WEALTH OF NATIONS'
TO AN ECONOMICS OF INTERDEPENDENCE
BASED ON
THE SURVIVAL OF THE GLOBAL VILLAGE

*The present convergent crises of
worldwide inflation, the energy crunch
with its attendant dislocation of the
world economic and political system,
and the looming food shortage have
combined to convince all but the most
complacent and self-deluded that we
are entering upon a new period in
world history.*

Victor Ferkiss[1]

I do not write this chapter as an economist for I am not one. I am
a citizen of the global village, however, and a theologian. Economists
who are smug with the way their economics are currently operating
will not want to hear about compassion from a theologian or anyone
else. However, they should not forget that one of their heroes, Adam

Smith, in an age that was not so overly specialized as ours, wrote a book on the *Theory of Moral Sentiments* and that he began his career as a moral philosopher. The morality he presumed for his economic system was, ironically, basically a religious one—this is one more reason for the datedness of Smith's economic theories, however, for religion as he knew it in his society is now dead. If we do not make every effort to relate compassion to economics, then compassion is only a hollow word and a pious sounding phrase. And economics becomes a highly developed form of violence.

The word "economics" comes from the words "to manage a house." Economics is about home-management—but clearly everything in economics will depend on what is meant at a given cultural or historical period by "home." Indeed, the passing of economic systems parallels the passing eras in which home was defined in a certain way. The first Christians responded to the new world-view that the joyous news of Christ gave to them by uniting in a communal life in which they shared all goods in common and in which the owners of lands and houses sold these and gave the proceeds to the apostles to distribute to the needy (Acts 2.44f; 4.32–35). This voluntary sharing with the poor later formed the basis of the monastic vow of poverty when monasticism was born as a response to a new definition given home by a new alliance between church and empire in the fourth century. Feudalism in the middle ages passed to capitalism when the lord-manor-serf system collapsed because people were leaving the land as home and moving to towns as home. Thus a more portable money system was needed for this kind of mobile revolution. The great revolutions of the sixteenth and seventeenth centuries in trade, in geographic discoveries and voyages, in the development of merchant capital, "forced a ceaseless expansion of the world market" (Marx) and brought about a new stage in economics. The new home for economics was big industry and with this stage feudalism finally gave way to capitalism. Economics underwent another giant break when the marketplace of local and in-house manufacturing was moved from family business and home-manufacturing to the factory—a movement of nineteenth century industrial expansion. The alienation or the feeling of *not being at home any longer* that the new economic system created gave birth to the Knights of Labor, the American Federation of Labor, Charles Dickens and Karl Marx as well as other critics of the economic order of their day. Labor Unions, socialisms, and communisms presented themselves as different alternatives to industrial capitalism.

Today we are involved in another economic break-up and with it a growing malaise of alienation, of not-feeling-at-home, of powerlessness and frustration the world over. This frustration is experienced in socialist *and* capitalist economics; it is experienced by employee and manager and the unemployed; by every-day citizens and by presidents of countries. People sense a chaos, a bottomless pit, over which they and their economic systems are suspended, for in fact *economics has not yet caught up with the new meaning of home in our time.* Economics is still running on Newtonian mechanistic "laws" such as Supply and Demand, with little questioning of what is supplied and for whom, and what is not being supplied and who is demanding, and how demands are channeled to manufacturers. Another "law" is that economic progress is synonymous with constant increase in Gross National Products. There is also a presumption, since Adam Smith's influential *Wealth of Nations*, that economics is primarily an issue of nationalist concern. In other words, that the proper 'home' for economics is the nation-state. People are beginning to question the frozen world of ordained economists who are unable to halt rampant inflation, to redirect resources to ensure the survival of the very poor, to guarantee employment for all fit workers, to stop the rich from getting richer and the poor from dying of starvation. People sense that our economic hierarchies are at least as much out of touch with reality as were churchmen of old who fought Galileo over his new discoveries. Fear grips people. Einstein sensed this when he said that "the production and distribution of commodities is entirely unorganized so that everybody must live in fear of being eliminated from the economic cycle." [Ein, p. 11]

What is the new name for "home" that economists have yet to adapt to? The poet has named it as follows: "The earth is your shoe/the sky is your hat." [2] The poet is more scientifically accurate than he had probably imagined, for the sky does in fact operate like a hat, shielding us from the millions of meteorites that fall against its outer limits each day and are thereby burned away. At the same time, this sky-canopy protects our oxygen supply from the ultraviolet light that would kill nucleic acids and protein. So, like any hat, the sky keeps unwelcome things off our heads and keeps welcome energies in.

"The earth is your shoe, the sky is your hat"—this is the lesson learned from the previous chapter: our home is indeed the universe and in a special way this unique planet earth. We are citizens no longer of any one tribe, kingdom, or nation, but of a planet. Our home is the world and our society is the universe—this is the lesson of interdependence that biology, physics and common awareness is driving home to us and that we dealt with in the previous chapter. People recognize the truth of this lesson more readily today, thanks to global communications and common global experiences of shared pain—

whether war threats, unemployment, inflation, starvation, etc. — or of shared joy — including music, photos by orbiting astronauts, dancers, film-makers and other celebrators of life. We are no longer isolated entities — not in our domesticated houses — not in our isolated national identities. Nation-states, though they still strut about acting like they were, are not isolated entities any longer. What is becoming clearer and clearer to citizens the world over is that the earth is *our* shoe, the sky *our* hat and both are in jeopardy. Yet economists and their politicians, capitalist and socialist, have not yet caught up with the truth that increasing numbers of citizens are aware of.

The new name for home is "global village" but economics is only beginning to catch up with what the new realities of interdependency will mean. Economist Herman E. Daly of Louisiana State University is doing his part. He writes of the need for a new paradigm or model for economics.

> Continual growth in both capacity (stock) and income (flow) is a central part of the neoclassical growth paradigm. But in a finite world continual growth is impossible. Given finite stomachs, finite lifetimes, and the kind of man who does not live by bread alone, growth becomes undesirable long before it becomes impossible. But the tacit, and sometimes explicit assumption of the Keynesian-neoclassical growth mania synthesis is that aggregate wants are infinite and should be served by trying to make aggregate production infinite. . . . Even if we wish to be neutral or 'value-free' we cannot, because the paradigm by which people try to understand their society is itself one of the key determining features of the social system.[3]

In such a situation the stand-off between capitalism and socialism — a dualism based on industrial "home" problems — is no longer the basic issue it once was. The capitalist-socialist debate pales before the survival issues that the global village faces today, and heated rhetoric from either camp only makes the situation less open to creative solutions. The socialism of the USSR and the capitalism of the USA seem equally bent on jeopardizing the fragile survival of the planet with their lemming-like race to arm themselves to the hilt so that, as of today, there are 15 tons of TNT stockpiled against every man, woman and child living on our planet.

If we are all interdependent on this planet and the planet is *our* home, then a new kind of economics and a new kind of social linkage are necessary. They will be born—provided it is not too late—from a shared pain, a shared powerlessness, that is common to nations large and small, poor and rich, pre-industrial and post-industrial. Compassion is not compassion until it touches the public arena, and so compassion too will be born only when this new order bent on relieving our common pain is itself born. In this chapter I want to employ aspects of the basic outline of this book up to now to the all-important subjects of economics in a global village. In trying to lay bare the obstacles to compassion that we have named previously and how they interact with economics, we may contribute to the process of grounding a new economics and social order: this time on compassion and world-awareness. I will first treat Newtonian science and economics, then psychology and economics, then sexuality and economics, then creativity and economics. Finally, we will be ready to consider what an Economics and Politics of Compassion might be about. This chapter will not treat any of these subjects thoroughly since space does not allow it. But the theme of compassion as a way of life would be utterly forsaken if we did not attempt such an analysis. In the course of this analysis I will be criticizing both American capitalism and Russian-styled socialism for I believe that neither gives birth to the kind of compassionate perspective that the globe yearns for. Yet, because I am an American writing mostly for American readers, and since America's ideology is so dominant an influence in the Western world, my critique is aimed primarily at our economic system in America.

FROM NEWTONIAN TO EINSTEINIAN ECONOMICS

In discussing the profound change in awareness that the Einsteinian revolution has let us to in our century, I have outlined five major myths in Newton's way of seeing reality that no longer hold: first is the passage from a mechanistic model of reality; second is the preoccupation with part or piece at the expense of the whole; third is a rugged individualism, buttressed by a Darwinian call to competitive survival of the fittest; fourth is a specious claim to "objectivity" and absolute perspective; and fifth is a questioning of the presumed split between matter and mind, matter and consciousness. Each of these movements affects economics profoundly as we shall see in this section.

Mechanistic determinisms and models

Economics has succumbed to a quest for the Laws of Economics as if the human and natural energies of production, distribution, consumption and re-cycling of energy were a machine. In such a situation issues of compassion and human concern, of injustice and justice, of luxurious living in the midst of basic deprivation, of rape of the earth, air, water and animals have no role to play whatsoever. Indeed, such moral concerns only confuse the issue of getting the machine, i.e., the economy, "going again." Since Descartes, the West and economics with it has been operating on his basic principle of Knowledge: Clear and Distinct Ideas. That which is not clear and distinct, i.e., machine-like in its simplicity, is not worthy of our attention. Descartes declared, and, it seems, almost every economist since him: "Those who seek the direct road to truth should not bother with any object of which they cannot have a certainty equal to the demonstrations of arithmetic and geometry." Thus quantity has been enshrined as the only norm for economics. In this context the observation by the influential Lord Keynes makes logical sense, although humanly speaking it is nonsense. Said Lord Keynes (1883–1946): "For at least another hundred years, we must pretend to ourselves and to everyone that fair is foul and foul is fair; for foul is useful and fair is not. Avarice and usury and precaution [meaning economic security] must be our gods for a little longer still." [4] No wonder issues of morality—justice and compassion—are not studied by economics majors. Schumacher comments on what happens when the god of mechanism and quantification becomes enshrined as an idol: "We now have this terrible fetish of measuring the gross national product of a country and dividing it by the number of people who live there to get the *average income per head*." [5] Thus the current rate of growth—the constant quest for more—is the basic measurement of economic achievement.

There are questions of direction and not only speed that we ought to be measuring in economics, suggests Schumacher, for Enough is good but More than Enough is evil. He goes on: "I find the economist's preoccupation with gross national product to be meaningless. The mere fact that some evil-minded statisticians have added together everything we did last year and announced that our gross national product rose or fell should be of absolutely no concern to anyone with any sense whatsoever. That which is good and helpful ought to be growing and that which is bad and hindering ought to be diminishing." (ibid, p. 16) What directions does he advocate for economics to take? "We should strive towards non-violence rather than a warfare against nature." (17) Schumacher's ultimate argument is that the quest for infinite growth and an ever expanding economy is an absurdity when our planet is in fact finite in size and in renewable resources. "Growth economics had become the religion of this age," he maintains, citing Walter Heller, the former chairman of the U.S. President's Council of Economic Advisors who testified that "I cannot conceive a successful economy without growth." Growth, constant growth, has become a mechanistic law of contemporary economics.

Another mechanistic law taken for granted is that of Supply and Demand. Combined with a laissez-faire attitude, this law is one of letting happen what will happen—letting the market set the price. But Americans in the past few years have learned that when *they* do not control the strings that make the market dance, questions arise about letting everything happen without any "outside interference." This is clear in the oil price hikes of OPEC. Suddenly the sacred mechanistic Law of Supply and Demand was questioned because it was hurting us. It dawned on every thinking person that the Law of Supply and Demand is not the *only* law of economics. Survival is another law. And justice. Prices, we learned, can be too high and so can profits. Other values do indeed enter into the economic equation which are after all not so simplistic as a simple machine in operation.

Industrial capitalism is not the only economic system to succumb to too much mechanism in its outlook. Gregory Baum, while admiring Marx's efforts to introduce human values into the field of economics, still faults him for his reductionism or his simplification in reducing all of human consciousness to a political and economic base exclusively, thereby neglecting the cultural and symbolic factors that operate in human history.[6]

Another example of machine-influences in economics is the alienation of the body under industrial working conditions. "The perfect worker shaped by the industrial system is the one who resembles the machine," observes Gregory Baum, endorsing Karl Marx's objection to this mechanization of the individual person. The worker becomes "a stranger to his body and to the natural environment in which he lives." (27) In this ultimate expression of Newtonian and Cartesian economics the victim is the body and energy and creativity of the worker. Time too becomes an absolute in a Newtonian and mechanistic economics so that work-time is merely punch-in, punch-out time that is determined by an absolutish clock on a wall. Time becomes a commodity we "spend" instead of an opportunity to pass in conversation, celebration or sharing of ecstasies.[7] Time is not relative to the pleasure of creative work and contribution in work but is itself subject to machine-like—after all, a clock is a machine—turning of hands on a clock. Once again, people serve the machine instead of the machine serving people.

In this context E.F. Schumacher offers a useful and liberating distinction when he emphasizes how tools are different from machines. He wants to overthrow the machine in favor of the tool. "Tools serve man while machines demand that man serve them. Tools enhance a man's skill and power while machines . . . sooner or later wind up enslaving the men who build and tend them" (Interview, p. 18). Machines end up taking the most human elements of work away from the worker, while tools leave the creative work to the worker. Interestingly enough, in the Bible the Hebrews do not have a word for *thing* but only for *tool* (*keli*). This word emphasizes what Schumacher is emphasizing: the instrumental and functional use of objects. Things for the Jewish consciousness are to be means for action and not static objects of perception.[8] Thing-thinking that results from honoring things and machines over tools is thus contrary to Biblical spirituality. It is the essence of materialism.

Still another example of machine-thinking in economics is revealed in that basic of all economic terms, goods. Goods comprise the main subject of economists—but there is a tendency to equate goods with cogs in a machine. According to Schumacher, there are in fact four categories of goods: non-renewable primary goods, such as oil; renewable primary goods, such as wheat; secondary goods we manufacture, such as shoes; and secondary goods we convert, such as services. All economics deal with these four categories but "economics, as currently constituted, fully applies only to manufacturers...but is being applied without discrimination to all goods and services, because an appreciation of the essential, qualitative differences between the four categories is entirely lacking." (SIB, 49–51) We are treating primary goods, or those we only convert and do not produce and which the earth has produced (oil and land), like manufactured goods, which, contrary to first appearances, are not produced so much as converted. In other words, we treat all goods like machine parts. Like things.

Fetish of the part

Equally Newtonian and outdated, a concept that permeates our economic thinking is a preoccupation with a part and confusion of the part with the whole. We have just seen an example of this thinking in the confusion of one part of goods (manufactured items) with all other goods. We witness such behavior in rhetorical battle cries to "save the system." A contemporary commercial on television from a multi-national corporation ends with the golden words: "The solution is the system." By "system" they mean their system or the system that is currently operating in the name of economic order world-over. I can agree that the "solution is the system" when system means the entire cosmic and eco-system that contemporary science, as discussed in the previous chapter, outlines for us. To enter into harmony with this system is indeed the solution: it is the way of wisdom and compassion. But it requires a cosmic vision, a vision of the whole, and a refusal to confuse part with whole or system.

Part-for-whole thinking is built into the very fabric of contemporary economics, so indebted to Newtonian science. Schumacher reserves his strongest language for the "process of reduction" that takes place in modern capitalism. It reduces everything to profits alone. The only whole is the part called profits. He decries an "idolatry of *enrichissez-vous*, which celebrates millionaires as its culture heroes" and which conducts an economy "on the basis of private greed." Its very simplicity—in the sense of simplistic—makes it a rather easy task to transform the earth, especially when no value questions ever have to be introduced. "Successful businessmen are often astonishingly primitive," he notes, because their life-view is so myopic. "The real strength of the theory of private enterprise lies in this ruthless simplification" that, in Schumacher's view, closely parallels the reduction of quality to quantity that scientism has been about. The simplicity of private enterprise as an economic system is "terrifying" because "it suggests that the totality of life can be reduced to one aspect—profits." One result is that private enterprise is "not concerned with what it produces but only with what it gains from that production." (SIB 254–256)

Analysis or taking things apart to understand them in greater depth is a useful, specialist kind of thinking. But it is not the only thinking we need. Persons who say more and more about less and less become easy prey for propagandists since a fetish of the part is endemic to all rhetorical thinking which tends to isolate certain factors for the sake of greater emphasis and exaggeration. Indeed, the confusion of gods with God or of part with whole is the very definition of idolatry. One example of idolatrous part-thinking that is still rampant today is the confusion of what is good for the nation with what is good for the globe. Nationalism is a species of part-thinking. National Security is one example of the results of such overemphasis on the part—as if the Global Security of common survival were not at least as important a value—and indeed a more important one—as National Security. Indeed, what good do all the elaborate National Security Systems do if, in stockpiling weapons and adjusting the nation's balance of payments by selling weapons as the basic export, a nation wakes up one day to find that the green organisms in the ocean that process life-giving carbon dioxide have all been killed off by nuclear radiation? Life is the whole; nations are a part. But we have confused the two to the great peril of all life—and even all nations. It is for this reason that the movement from a nationalistic perspective in economics to a global one is so crucial today. The "Wealth of Nations" is not an adequate starting point for economic thinking and structuring in a period of Global Village awareness and imminent self-destruction.

Rugged Individualism and Isolation of Entities

There is no way in which classical physics has so dangerously influenced economics and society than its myth that the basis of reality is solid pieces that are independent in their struggle to survive. Biologist Lewis Thomas puts it this way: "The oldest, easiest-to-swallow idea was that the earth was man's personal property, a combination of garden, zoo, bank vault, and energy source, placed at our disposal to be consumed, ornamented, or pulled apart as we wished . . . In the last few years we were wrenched away from this way of looking at it . . . It is conceded almost everywhere that we are not the masters of nature that we thought ourselves; we are as dependent on the rest of life as are the leaves or midges or fish. We are part of the system." (122) Notice how he uses the word "system." He has in mind the world system, the life-system, even the cosmic system that makes life happen and continue to happen in our globe.

Interdependency is not only the newly arrived fundamental law of the way the universe operates—it is also the law of the way nations need to operate, although nations bent on idolatrous National Security fetishes have yet to see this. Gerald and Patricia Mische point out: "We are witnessing the final death throes of the principal of national self-sufficiency." Interdependence and not independence is the key to nation-states' survival today because "a nuclear attack anywhere affects the whole species. Depletion of the ozone leaves all of us vulnerable to skin cancer . . . The devaluation of the American dollar, while it can be undertaken unilaterally, affects global economic security. And an increase of cost in Arab oil increases inflation everywhere . . . A unilateral decision by one nation to change the flow of a river within its borders would vitally affect the security of the neighboring states also dependent on that river. The list is endless. In short, all nations are vulnerable to the decisions and activities of other states." [9]

It is for this reason that the Misches in their book *Toward a Human World Order* call for a non-myopic (non-part-fetish) understanding of development which includes "Liberation for Being." This law will take into account in its understanding of development not only the economic but also the "social, political, cultural and spiritual dimensions" of living and how they all interact. (178) The number one organizing principle for such a humanizing of the earth must be, the Misches insist, "a recognition of *human interdependence*" (p. 41, italics theirs). Thus we have in their efforts a hearty example of an Einstinian interdependent and relative instead of Newtonian independent economic universe. Einstein himself would delight at this insight, for he saw the same issue as *the* fundamental issue in human affairs of our time. He said: "The development of technology and of the implements of war has brought about something akin to a shrinking of our planet. Economic interlinking has made the destinies of nations interdependent to a degree far greater than in previous years." (138) No survival is possible, he declared, "until there is a modification of the traditional concept of national sovereignty." (157)

The Misches, too, see the principle of national self-sufficiency to be an "obsolete" one that must give way to world-interest. There is a straight jacket, they claim, that Nation-States have woven for us all that keeps us tied to lack of creative economic alternatives and the straight jacket's name is the National Security State System. We are so busy policing our national interest that the globe itself may be disappearing right under our nation-feet. Power elites broker our planet for us in such a system and build us bombs instead of homes, and in the midst of it we feel alienated or powerless to shape our own destinies. This powerlessness, they claim, is "the dominant characteristic of today's national security societies." (61) The only solution to the menacing race in armament procurements is for "nations to relinquish some of their sovereignty." (97) The urgency exists for a *world* security system.

Einstein was convinced as well that a world system was the only answer. "There is only *one* path to peace and security," he declared: "The path of supranational organization. One-sided armament on a national basis only heightens the general uncertainty and confusion without being effective protection." He too observed the idol that Nationalism has become, whether communist or capitalist. "The power of every state over its citizens has grown steadily during the last few hundred years ... The state has become a modern idol whose suggestive power few men are able to escape." His solution? "A supra-national organization [that] has alone the authority to produce or possess modern weapons." He saw the United Nations as "merely a transitional system toward the final goal, which is the establishment of a supranational authority vested with sufficient legislative and executive powers to keep the peace." He was not unaware of the revolution in thinking that such a global perspective would imply. In fact, he urged such a mode of re-thinking. "We must revolutionize our thinking, revolutionize our actions, and must have the courage to revolutionize relations among the nations of the world. Cliches of yesterday will no longer do today, and will, no doubt, be hopelessly out of date tomorrow." But the stakes are of the highest: "There can be no compromise possible between preparation for war, on the one hand, and preparation of a world society based on law and order on the other." (154–157) Until there is an encompassing structural change, there will be no adequate system for interdependence, for, as Michael Harrington puts it, "an economy dominated by self-seeking units is, precisely because of that fact, incapable of seeking the common good of the 'whole society.' " [10]

Objectivity and Value-Free political Nation-States

Newtonian physics haunts us still in the form of an illusory quest for value-free and objective economics. This reductionism may be possible on a very limited scale in a laboratory or a computer print-out but it is not desirable when dealing with human affairs or other affairs of nature—nor is it, as Einstein demonstrated, the truth of the universe in which we live. Space and time, which envelop all we know and desire to know, are relative and not absolute. So is all our knowledge. To be unflappably "value-free" in the midst of a crisis of survival is to reveal one's values indeed—they are stoic ones of self-sufficiency. William Eckhardt warns that "there are no value-free facts. Consequently, a value-free science is naive at best, fraudulent at the worst, and a self-contradiction in terms. There can be no science without values." For, he insists, facts themselves come loaded with values, and to repress this fact "effectively places science in the service of power, which determines the values to be served by science." (263) The ultimate value in economics today is, according to the Misches, "the principle of unlimited national sovereignity"—a principle, they maintain, that torpedoed the best in Karl Marx's efforts to humanize economics. (190) Speaking at an international conference of scholars and businessmen held in Philadelphia in 1976, Aurelio Peccei, the founder of the Club of Rome, said that while the myth of exponential growth was now being punctured, so too must we puncture the myth of "national competence." [in Mische 260f] No Nation-State will disarm or re-orient its armaments expenditures until we can conceive of a beyond-state organization. The national security myth is common to capitalist and communist states and therefore the quest for an alternative takes us beyond the Marxist-Capitalist debate. But whatever this alternative is, it is not value-free, objective, or coldly neutral. It is a passionate quest for the survival of passion. A defense of life and of living on our common planet. The shoe we call earth is, after all, the *only* shoe we've got. And we live in it equally, putting one foot before the other no matter what ideology we maintain or are born into. Up to now the shoe has fit us all and we have worn it rather proudly. But the lie of objectivity, which is in fact a cover-up for powers so elitist and almighty that we are afraid to question them and their unimaginative questions, would have us destroy the only shoe we've got.

Mind/Matter and Economics

Conventional economics tends to define matter as the goods it produces and then treats them in a dualistic way vis-a-vis mind—as if mind were not affected by the stuff of industry or as if what is happening in economics does not affect the human spirit and what is happening in the human spirit does not affect economics. But in fact the influence is mutual. What seems to be the case is that a dynamic of contraction-expansion is at stake as the human race moves its understanding of home from house, to village, to tribe, to nation, to globe. Is it possible that the contraction of the globe is currently producing an expansion in human consciousness and that our nation-based economic systems have not yet caught up with this spiritual transformation? Here might lie much of the spiritual and economic malaise felt so world-wide today. For the dominant economic systems, USSR's brand of state socialism and the USA's brand of capital-intensive, transnational capitalism are based on constantly expanding growth. Yet people sense that expansion has reached its limits—whether expansion be promoted as expansion outwards (the proverbial "new Frontier" implicit in nineteenth century cries to "head West, young man") or expansion upwards, as is promoted in the myth of upward mobility that has captivated so many well-intentioned Americans in the past. Christopher Jencks and David Riesman conclude their study on *The Academic Revolution* by observing that "what America needs is not more mobility but more equality." (in Harrington, 342)

Expansionist myths continue to abound even though contraction is the new economic "law" of our time. An example would be the case of the super-sonic jet liner such as the Concorde. The Concorde airplane, whether to transport, titilate or amuse the few passengers who can afford to fly in it, takes 108.6 gallons of fuel per passenger on a trans-Atlantic flight while the 747 airplane takes 64.8 gallons of fuel per passenger on the same route. This consumption of fuel by the Concorde is expansionist at a time when fuel supplies are contracting. Yet the myth that it is ecstasy of sorts to be able to fly or brag about flying by Concorde perpetuates such destructive trends in aviation.

Expansion is no longer the absolute, Newtonian, law it once was. Expansion is not possible as it once seemed to be. An economic theory that remains expansionist when the world is contracting is utterly dated. It is a colossal dinosaur, gradually eating itself to death. Such a system is no longer economical for it results in costly, wasteful, violent, dualistic and competitive energies that no one in a smaller world can afford. Matter and space-time go through phases of expansion and contraction and it is evident that today we humans are living in a period of intense contraction. Our economics needs to alter to fit that new model and soon. For a system whose parts expand when the whole is contracting literally explodes. The alternative is a mindless economic system — which is, in the growing awareness of millions of global citizens, exactly what we now have. The human mind and awareness are expanding, and our physical world is contracting. And yet, we look about us and see the dominant economic systems still seeking to expand with the result that human consciousness itself shrinks. When Jesus spoke of not being able to serve God and mammon at once he was not putting down the important work of providing goods for human beings, but was demonstrating the necessary dialectic between expansion and contraction. To reduce this necessary expansion-contraction dialectic to a simplistic dualism wherein expansion is the only vital energy is an invitation to destruction. Fortunately some economists would recognize what Jesus and numerous persons of good will and decent sense see happening. Economist Herman E. Daly writes of interdependence as the new law of economics: "All economic systems are subsystems within the big biophysical system of ecological interdependence. The ecosystem provides a set of physical constraints to which all economic systems must conform."[11]

We have considered some of the implications of an economics based on Newtonian as distinct from Einsteinian physics. There remains a great deal more to be said, researched and lived. But this one lesson is certain: there will be no compassion and no rebirth or even survival of compassion as long as we remain married to a world-view of mechanism instead of relationship, of part instead of whole, of rugged individualism instead of interdependence, of nationalism and Security-State systems instead of Internationalistic Interdependencies, of value-free instead of value-oriented economics. Nor will there remain an earth or animals upon it with which to share the bodily energies we have in common. Schumacher, himself a life-long economist, warns us that "The great majority of economists are still pursuing the absurd ideal of making their 'science' as scientific and precise as physics, as if there were no qualitative difference between mindless atoms and men made in the image of God." By physics here he means Newtonian quantitative physics. We have seen, in the case of Einstein himself, some very important qualitative lessons emerging from today's physics. It all adds up to our being verb- instead of noun-oriented, to our falling in love with compassion, the verb that makes connections, recognizes interconnections and celebrates all these connections.

PSYCHOLOGY AND ECONOMICS

In our chapter on Compassion and Psychology (chapter three), we outlined the principle psychological obstacles to compassion: Competition, Compulsion and Dualism. To what extent is economics beholden to these negative and anti-compassionate energies? To what extent could economics free itself and the rest of us to a holier trinity of Letting, go, Letting be and Letting dialectic happen so that we celebrate life and its delightful goods instead of control and horde them?

Economics and Competition

Competition, a psychological idol that we have considered in chapter three, is frequently invoked as an ultimate and absolute law of economics. As such it has been roundly condemned by those who have tried to imagine a more human and just economic system, for example Martin Luther. Luther considered capital to be demonic and one of his heaviest arguments against the papacy of his day was that it was capitalistic and therefore demonic. "Money," said Luther, "is the work of the Devil, through which he creates all things, the way God created through the true word." Luther, Norman O. Brown suggests, sensed the anal-sadistic character of competitive economics in which human aggression and anal organization coincide and in which will to power, mastery and defiance take root.[12] One has to speculate as to how many Protestants since Luther have been as economically conscious as was their founding prophet.

Of late, popes too have resisted the demons of economic competition. "Competition as the supreme law of economics" is wrong and will lead to an "international imperialism of money," warns Pope Paul VI.[13] Justice or a balanced power distribution is more basic a law of economics than is competition. "An economy of exchange can no longer be based solely on the law of free competition, a law which, in its turn, too often creates an economic dictatorship. Freedom of trade is fair only if it is subject to the demands of social justice." Development of nations will "never" be assured by "the mere free play of competition." [14]

It is not only unrestrained capitalism that comes under criticism for its competitive presuppositions, nor is it only popes who object to the basic law of competition in economics. Rosemary Reuther criticizes Marxist economics for its presumptions about class warfare. "Is the endless prolongation of models of life drawn from warfare and industrial labor the best we can do in envisioning a liberated society?" she asks.[15] And she links the presumed Law of Competition with the taken-for-granted attitudes and structures of sexism. "Sexism must be seen as the expression of a primal psychology of domination and repression forged in the one-sided emergence of the male in the struggle for survival." What is the alternative to an economics of competition? A letting be, a letting go, a celebrating. An interdependence based on a sharing of the pleasures of the good earth instead of their mutual hoarding.

Competition will always lead to war, for war is but a logical and archetypal symbol of competition. All competition is a kind of war. Ecstacy, on the other hand, does not lead to competition and its logical expression which is war, but to compassion and its logical expression which is celebration.[16] The supposed Law of Competition and Survival-of-the-Fittest mechanism is, as we saw in the previous chapter, a nineteenth-century myth that contemporary biology repudiates. It is time that contemporary economics, capitalist or socialist, does the same.

The competition that is bred in individuals who are taught the out-dated myth of Survival of the Fittest (meaning the Richest) takes its most demonic expression when it is transferred to nation-states. According to the Misches, it is this "unchecked global competition between nations operating on the principle of total independence" that is the major cause to leaders of nations putting national security goals always ahead of more humanistic needs of the people of the world. (63) Competition for monetary reserves and for depleting non-renewable resources of the earth now plays as important a factor as does competition for weapons among the nations of the world. (107) What creates elitist rule, whether in a socialist or a capitalist system, is "the imperative of national security competition in an interdependent but ungoverned world" (169)—one still operating on faulty, nineteenth century biology. Competition also comprises the "major fuel" in the compulsion of ruggedly individualistic nation-states to constantly expand. (235) Competition, then, feeds the fuel of expansionism.

Like any demonic (as opposed to mere troublesome or "bad" or "wrong") position, the "Law" of Competition contains a truth in it. Some competition can be a healthy thing, as we saw in Chapter Three—it can overcome laziness and opposition to creativity, for example. In the economic arena in particular it can create alternative and at times improved services or goods. It can, theoretically at least, be the alternative to monopolizing by the giants in business, though of late it has seldom accomplished this task. Consider for example how in 1948 the 200 largest corporations in the United States controlled 48% of all manufacturing assets and today the 200 largest corporations control 67% of all assets. The top 500 corporations, which comprise only 1.6% of American businesses all told, currently control 75% of all manufacturing assets. It is clear that this useful aspect to competition is not at all being asserted in America's current economic situation. Consider, for example, how in 1941 it took 1,000 large corporations to control 67% of all manufacturing assets in this country, while today just 200 giant corporations control this identical percentage of assets, which today amounts to $350 billion. Less than 2% of the American population own these same corporations that make so many decisions about the lives of us all and about the life of our planet. The reality of "competition" is in fact lost on the scene of giant corporate economic power which is so profoundly monopolistic. Albert Einstein, commenting on his philosophy of education, calls competition the "easy method of creating individual ambition" and warns against taking so lazy an approach to creativity. The spirit of competition is wrong, he claims, and will only lead to destruction. "As little as a battle between single ants of an ant hill is essential for survival, just so little is this the case with the individual members of a human community." [17] Thus it is that even though the trumpeters of the 'free enterprise system' play their trumpets ever louder and pay their lobbyists until they grow ever fatter, the average working citizen sees less and less of his rent money, fuel money, food money or government-supporting money going anyplace. The so-called 'free enterprise' system is not at all free—it has become immensely expensive to maintain. And it is monopolistic, not competitive. Only the fittest (meaning the fattest) have survived. Even conservative columnist George F. Will, writing to his Republican friends, admits this fact. Says he: "If the GOP present itself simply as the defender of a pure 'free enterprise system,' the conservative party will be trying to conserve something that no longer exists." [18]

We have to raise the question whether our economic system and our education for it, much of which is accomplished in mythic shibboleths and unreflected cliches, does not contribute to the destruction of compassion because it is so steeped in the preaching of competition as a universal norm and "law" of economic survival. Does our economics preclude compassion by its very stress on competition? If that be the case, and cooperation and interdependence and compassion are *in fact* our proper energies for survival; then how much longer will we tolerate such stupidity and such violence against ourselves, our earth and our common good? We have reduced the very powerful motivational factor called survival to the puny level of competition—whether state or corporation or ideology or sex—whereas in fact the basis for group survival is not competition but compassion. Compassion then will become a powerful motivational factor when it is finally allowed to be announced as the practical, down-to-earth energy of self-interest and other-interest that it is.

Compulsion

We need to ask to what extent the economic training we receive encourages us to be compulsive. Is a perfect consumer not a perfect retainer and collector and, since so much of our advertising and economic stimulation is directed at getting us to be consumers, are we not being "educated" daily to become compulsive? As consumers we become walking garbage cans, people who can only mutter, if some strange person were to inquire about our philosophy of life, "I buy therefore I am;" "We consume, therefore—maybe—we exist." This compulsion seems inbred in a consumer society. As Ernest Becker observes, "modern man is drinking and drugging himself out of awareness, or he spends his time shopping, which is the same thing." [19]

No one has written more insightfully of this aspect of our economy than has Norman O. Brown in a chapter entitled "Filthy Lucre" in his *Life Against Death*. In his psychoanalysis of money, which is Freudian in its base, he points out that the calculating personality who makes the "ideal type of *Homo economicus* is an anal character." Max

Weber also notices the connection between the "capitalist spirit" and the anal character. Money falls into the category of the sacred, Brown maintains, because it is about guilt and its expiation. "The whole money complex is rooted in the psychology of guilt." [20] In such an economy work becomes a compulsive act of expiation from guilt, "man must punish himself with work." (272) Here again we see why it is that Jesus linked compassion with pardon, and especially with self-pardon: for compulsiveness is the sign of a person who cannot be pardoned or feel pardon or give pardon. The economic life of a nation or a person becomes oriented, not around the enjoyment and sharing of life's enjoyments, but around the compulsion to "organize a life of nonenjoyment," (270) and pain instead of pleasure becomes the norm of such a culture. Masochism and sadism reign as its primary energies rather than celebration and letting be, letting go. A compulsion with money implies a compulsion with time ("time means money") and therefore the inability to let go of time, i.e., to experience ecstasy and celebration. (Have you ever noticed how little laughter goes on in banks? They are almost as bad as most churches because of their sobriety and constipation.)

Money can be so compulsion-making because money is a pure object. One cannot have an I-Thou relationship with a dollar bill. Money is dead. Putrid. "Excremental" to use Brown's phrase. People who are in love with money or instruct others to be so are people in love with death, teaching others to love death. The relationship to money is not one of eroticism or of play but rather, insists Brown, the money complex is "a manifestation of the death instinct." (290) Compulsive needs such as the quest for money generates suck all other needs into themselves much as a vortex sucks all that passes its way into itself. The compulsion regarding money swallows all other perspectives to living such as celebrating, relieving one another's pain, letting go and letting be. Moreover, a quest for money is intrinsically frustrating for it can never be satisfied: there is always more to be had or won or lost or multiplied. Truly compulsion brings its own death. A smothering kind of death with objects. A drowning in money and the problems money buys. A suffocation by things. A life without pleasure or the pleasure of sharing of pleasures. Life become compulsion. Life become death. Pleasure itself is reduced to the *buying* of pleasure—which is the destruction of pleasure since pleasure, an authentic basis to living, is of its essence an act of inter-dependence. Pleasure, unlike money, does not presume subject/object relations but overcomes them. It presumes unity, give and take, in and out, hot and cold. It presumes, in short, a dialectic. But give and take is precisely what compulsion cannot tolerate. Compulsion must always be in command, always commanding, always buying or always selling. In compulsion there is no room for dialectic but only for control. Control becomes the "name of the game" in a compulsively constructed world-view.

Not only does our economics instruct us to be compulsive retainers as consumers but compulsive expanders as well. Historian Carroll Quigley writes that we live "in a cancer society in which growth has become the enemy of life,"[21] but in which we still keep "investing in growth" anyway. How ironic (or is it appropriate?) it is that a society of run-away economics has as its most feared disease the disease of run-away cells, the expansionist disease called cancer. We have been instructed to expand—if the GNP does not go up, if the stock market does not rise in volume, our newscasters are downcast and pass on their sad spirits to the rest of us. Yet all growth, as cancer teaches us, is not necessarily a good thing. As Gregory Bateson puts it, "less oxygen can be 'better' than more. It all depends on the context." [22] Capitalism takes its very name from its fundamental law of constant growth. Compulsive growth under capitalism has produced on the one hand "unprecedented material productivity" that some members of society can indulge themselves in and on the other "unprecedented social recklessness." [23]

The psychological word for persons who are compulsive in their need for expansion is *greedy*. Greed seems to be an energy built into our economic system now that it has evolved to be as efficient in its desire to expand as it has. Greed is the condition of never being satisfied. Greed produces dissatisfaction. Greed obscures the boundaries between need and desire—too much greed destroys a society's ability to delineate need. One result is that economics, instead of being the important and service-oriented contribution to society that it needs to be, becomes preoccupied with trivia. Titillating trivia is imagined, manufactured and sold. Pick up any of the "Gift Magazines" that are given away on airplanes and you will learn how real an economics of trivia has become for the upper echelons of America's economic ladder. You may be thrilled to learn, for example, that you can now purchase a sterling silver money clip that contains a miniaturization of your business card at $24.95. Or for $7.95 you can purchase a "lovely little crystal ring caddy" that prevents your rings from going down the drain when you take them off. "Keep one in your bedroom, one in the bath, one in the kitchen." [24] One wonders how civilization has survived so long without these products!

What is at stake is more than a nuisance of gadgets in our lives. What is at stake is life itself and the quality of living. For when industry turns to manufacturing and promoting such trivia, it means it is turning *from* other goods that might indeed deserve priority—such as mass transportation, to name just one example. Luxury goods are not morally cute or neutral; they are bought by the few at the expense of other goods for the many. An economy that puts more and more of its resources into luxury and trivial items is thereby declaring that it is an elitest economy for the elite. It is about as far away from compassion as an economy can get. It is a profoundly sinful economy, as the prophet Amos insisted, for it ignores the "ruin of Joseph" in its midst, that is to say the poor, while it plays at its luxury living of ivory beds and stall-fattened veal.

> Woe to those ensconced so snugly in Zion
> You think to defer the day of misfortune,
> but you hasten the reign of violence.
> Lying on ivory beds
> and sprawling on their divans,
> they dine on lambs from the flock,
> and stall-fattened veal;
> they drink wine by the bowlful,
> and use the finest oil for anointing themselves,
> but about the ruin of Joseph they do not care at all.
> That is why they will be the first to be exiled;
> the sprawlers' revelry is over. (Amos 6.1, 4–7)

The former head of NBC and Curtis Publishing, Matthew J. Culligan, himself confesses that the death of the competitive enterprise system of the United States will take place because the "principle compulsion of most people running American businesses today" is to make short-run profits. "The disease is greed," this former corporate boss declares.[25]

Nolan Bushnell, a man worth $10 million, offers a profound revelation of the economic system of which we are a part. Says he: "One of the things that's really neat about business is that it's the ultimate game. You keep score with dollars and there are a lot of interesting people playing it." [26] This explanation goes far to explain the psychological appeal, especially among the compulsively competitive, of capitalism. But it also reveals a poisonous and rancid side to such a system: it reveals a hint of sadism, for Karen Horney points out that it is one of the characteristics of the sadist that his emotional life is so empty that he needs continuing thrills and excitement.[27] It also reveals the utter betrayal of the seriousness and morality of economics; for economics, in such a trivial world-view, is reduced to a play-thing. The human questions of distribution of the goods of the earth and the survival of one another get shelved for the sake of "the ultimate game." No wonder so many business people I have listened to have been intellectual, moral and psychological adolescents. Economics for such persons plays the same psychological role as being a football star did in high school days of yore. It is time that such persons, if they must play games with themselves, do so by themselves and not by using up the scarce resources and goods that the rest of the human race needs to survive. If capitalism is indeed the "ultimate game"—as one of its winners, Mr. Bushnell, claims—then it is time for a more serious economics to take over our country. Money may be a game for the rich; but it means survival for the poor. Let our adolescent gamesters meditate on that for a while. For the game they play is a deadly serious game.

The compulsion for game-playing and for reducing economics to trivia cannot go unchecked. An economy based on compulsive expansion and on quantitative game-playing with money is doomed because money is intrinsically infinite (just as numbers are) in its potential for expansion. For many, it is now evident that the more money you earn the more you will spend. One person has called this an "irrefutable law of the marketplace"[28]—money by itself will never be enough. Who has ever heard of a satisfied capitalist? Henry Ford was interviewed this past year and was asked: "When is enough enough?" And he had to answer, "When there is always a little bit more." This compulsion for more, this compulsion to expand, is what makes the economic system we now are part of utterly obsolete and demonically dangerous to the survival of our planet. It renders all citizens utterly incapable of appreciating the epistle of John when he writes:

> If a person who was rich enough in this world's goods saw that one of his brothers or sisters was in need, but closed his heart to that person, how could the love of God be living in him? (1 Jn. 3.17)

Who can say, in a compulsive culture of expansion and greed, when "enough of this world's goods" was enough?

The truth is that it is one of the ironies—indeed illusions—of our time that capitalists call themselves conservatives. In fact, capitalism is a compulsively expansive and therefore destructive force. It is expansive and destructive not only to the earth and the environment but to the human psyche and spirit, feeding as it does on insatiable desire and manufactured desires. The one who conserves is in fact the one who resists the kind of expansive, greedy, capitalism that wraps itself so piously in cloaks of conservatism.

It is this world-view of compulsive expansionism and greed taken as an economic system that sociologist Marie Augusta Neal attacks when she calls to the non-poor, namely that one-third of humanity that is profiting from the present global economic arrangements, to practice letting go. "What should they be doing who are advantaged by the existing system? Perhaps developing a theology of 'letting go.' ... What is called for on the part of the non-poor is relinquishment." [29] But how will a people know what letting go is, and how to do it, if compulsion to possess has dominated their entire economic upbringing? Here is where conversion, in the full religious sense of the term *metanoia*, enters. *Leviticus* (chapter 25) speaks of the need to return the land to the whole people every fifty years or jubilee year, for "the land cannot be alienated from the people in perpetuity" and the Gospels too "mandate the poor to take what is theirs." "No right of ownership supersedes human need" and "no matter who possesses food it belongs to hungry peoples." (105) There are only two ways to relinquishment: violence and nonviolence. The haves will not readily surrender their privileges and it is on this conviction that Marx and his followers have posited that only violence will bring about relinquishment. The non-violent path, however, is that associated with Jesus' remark to the rich young man to sell what he owned and come follow him. Repentence in the Gospel (Lk. 3.1–11) is "directly associated with restoring goods to the poor" (107) and again we learn why Jesus connected compassion to pardoning. To be pardoned is also to repent, and to be repentant is to seek new, more humanly oriented and less compulsive economics.

Dualism

To what extent does the economics we possess instruct us willy-nilly in dualism? To a very great extent indeed. There is the dualism between employer and employee, employed and unemployed, those who own their homes and those who don't, stock-holders and non stock-holders, national economics and international economics, buyer and seller, consumer and manufacturer; rich and poor, haves and have-nots, third world and first world, exporter and importer, socialism and capitalism. The list seems endless and as if it could continue indefinitely. And it could. For intrinsic to all mechanized views of reality are the subject/object pieces that form the basis of that world-view. Such an economics, one based on mechanism, is also based on essential and absolutist dualisms. That is the kind of economics we were weaned on, all of us. But must it always be so?

A deeper truth than this "Law of Economic Dualism" is a Law of Economic Interdependence. The rich and the poor are not only separate but are inextricably related to one another. For the rich to remain rich, certain persons must remain poor. It is this relationship that is the most fundamental of all of the facts of economic life. Because economics is not just about fact and figures and objects but is ultimately about people, it is also in an ultimate sense about a dialectic. Economics that is not dialectical is a lie and an abstraction. For then it is not about living at all but only about the manipulation of objects. But we all know how important economics is to our living . . . and our dying. All economics is telling us how to live our lives and not merely how the market leads its life. How do we change from the presumptions about dualisms in economics to the deeper truths about interdependence?

One might begin with a reflection on the following facts of economic life. I live in the Chicago area. In general the poor in Chicago—most of whom are black or brown—live on the south side; and the executive classes—a vast majority of whom are white—on the north shore. There is great pain on the south side manifested in unemployment and the spiral of sin that unemployment brings with it including loss of self-worth and pride, envy, crime, prison, broken homes, drugs, parentless children. But there is also a great pain on the north shore that material prosperity has brought with it. Its most evident manifestations are alcoholism among the adults and boredom and purposelessness among the youth, which are very often expressed either in drugs or alcohol. An example of the former pain is the following story that a north shore cab driver relayed to me. He said that each weekday morning he spends his first one and one-half hours of work filling his taxi with booze and delivering a bottle to the same large homes each morning for the wives who live in them. These persons, having just put their husbands on the commutor trains to go downtown and run our culture's economy for us, drink all morning, shower and play bridge, etc. in the afternoon. Alcoholic wives of successful and wealthy directors of our economy. Pained victims of the dualistic economics we have. Harrington is very close to the truth when he observes that we have become "incapable of dealing with our own prosperity" and when he warns that "we are more threatened by our affluence than by our poverty." (348, 331)

A second example of the north shore pain at our economics is the youth. I recall meeting a seventeen-year-old young man who told me that he was envious of those black youths who knew at an early age that they were fatherless children. Why? Because, he said, "I only recently learned that I am a fatherless child. Oh, yes, my father still lives. But he is so busy at his work, dashing about the world, that never in my life have I had a single conversation with him. I too am a fatherless child but I have only recently discovered it. I have had to live all these years with the lie that I had a father." One more victim of the dualistic economics we possess. Larry Ross, an ex-president of a giant conglomerate who is now employed as a consultant to executives tells of one officer who had a private dining room with his own chef on beck and call. Unfortunately, all he could ever eat was well-done hamburgers or well-done steak because he had an ulcer. He ate Gelusil by the minute.[30] This same ex-president predicts that "twenty corporations will control about forty percent of the consumer goods market" before long, and he testifies that the "jungle game" of climbing up to the top on the basis of competition is not healthy even for those who make it all the way up. "I've been to the mountain top. It isn't worth it." (537, 540)

What conclusions can we draw from these stories? That the present economic system is a pain to us all. Whether unemployed or very successfully employed, its demands on all are too great. Pain, not pleasure, is being passed on. Dualism and not dialectic. For the evident fact emerges that the north shore and the south shore are inextricably related just as two persons on a teeter-totter. When one is way up the other will be way down—and that is no way to have a playful game of life or economics. We are dialectically and not dualistically related to one another. It is time that our economics took cognizance of this fact of all life. There is a profound connection—an inter-connection—between the alcoholism and boredom in Chicago's north shore—where the haves live—and the desperation of Chicago's south shore—where many have-nots congregate. Both places suffer from violence and joylessness. The crux of their common plight, the pivot for their single teeter-totter, is Chicago's Loop which is where the economic power conglomerates make our economic decisions for us all. The only long-range solution to the violent teeter-totter on which we are members and to the violence that is being perpetrated on poor and rich alike is to reconstruct our economics. It will need to be reconstructed on principles of dialectic, letting go and letting be instead of taken-for-granted assumptions of absolutest laws of dualism, compulsion and competition. It will be an economics based on people instead of on objects. On people and their ecstasies—their joys and their pain. An economics of interdependence of all peoples and of all the goods of the earth. It will be an organic rather than a mechanistic economics. Instead of concerning itself with the *Wealth of Nations* as does the Bible of economics by Adam Smith, it will concern itself with the poverty of the Globe—it will be dialectical in its approach to national and international economic interdependencies. Rather than perpetuate the dualistic, competitive and compulsive ideological ranting and military buildup between capitalist and socialist nations, it will strive to link the different systems wherever possible. It will practice dialectical economies and not just talk about it. For example, I recall a conversation I had with a Polish economist ten years ago in Warsaw in which he told me that the "number one" problem in their economy was that the West would not accept their currency. If the West would accept their currency, he argued, their economy would become even more linked to the West and more interdependent, thus lessening an exaggerated dependency on Russia and at the same time assuring more basic consumer needs for their own population. Are economists thinking globally about such matters as currency recognition?

SEXUALITY AND ECONOMICS

In Chapter Two I identified the primary sexual issue in compassion as that of passing from worshup and the sacralizing of upness, verticalness and Jacob's ladder to the dancing of Sarah's circle. We also considered in that chapter the legitimization that mystical symbols of up-ness as transcendence give the ever-increasing gap between the haves and have-nots. Here I would like to explore what, if any, role economics plays in inspiring either the energy of Jacob's ladder or that of Sarah's circle.

To move from climbing Jacob's ladder to dancing Sarah's circle in the economic and political sphere means our moving from one kind of power to another experience of power. "For one person to have power, others—or another—must be powerless," warns Adrienne Rich.[31] And that kind of power—power over/power under—is the system that Jacob's ladder represents and that we experience all about us. Rich wants to replace power over others with a transforming power which alone is the "truly significant and essential power" and which women knew well in prepatriarchal society. This power was learned especially in pottery-making—a fact that Mary Richards also demonstrates to be true even today among potters. How does economics become a transforming power instead of a perpetuation of power over? It becomes a transforming power to those who refuse to accept its claims to absolutism and divine or national infallibility. The first step of transformation in Rich's view is "to refuse to be a victim" (246)—that is, to leave the ladder and its implications that some of us need to be down and victimized. With this refusal, economics as a transformation is already beginning, for with the conversion of the masochist begins the conversion of the sadist. Of course, it will be a *new* economics.

Another strategy is to encourage those who man the upper echalons of the ladder to join the rest of the human race and to start combining love with work instead of dichotomizing the two spheres of energy. In overcoming this dualism between work and love, action and feeling, it is hoped that some holness and compassion might re-enter the spheres of economic and political influences—but the spheres will need to be reshaped, transformed, in order to tolerate values that have been so conspicuously absent for so long. Thus Rich advises—and Reuther does also—that "the most revolutionary priority that any male group could set itself" would be to assimilate men in large numbers into a comprehensive child-care system. (216) For in such a situation men would cease to be children and would enter into the "full experience of nuture." They would begin to develop their "undeveloped capacity for sympathetic identification" and would learn something of mothering one another. In other words, men might begin to learn compassion instead of always projecting it onto women. "As long as women and women only are the nurturers of children, our sons will grow up looking only to women for compassion" Rich warns. (211) And the institutions they occupy—namely our dominant economic and political ones—will be void of compassion, assigning that exclusively to the women's sphere of domesticated concerns. The release of women from exclusive occupation with domestic chores may also humanize the work and ladder world—or else make the pressing need to replace ladder worlds with circle ones even more urgent. In this scenario the presumption is that women, because they have learned something of compassion from interaction with children and from being closer to the earth and Sarah's dance, will also be more demanding of the work world and accept less passively than do men its amoral shibboleths and its dualistic and competitive presuppositions. Once they have seen the phallic hierarchy from the inside, they will shout the truth to the rest of us: "It's not worth it; it's not for real; we need a new economics, a new politics, a new way of living."

Even though our earth is round, our patriarchal economics remain ladder-like and with it the very name God and the name Justice and the name Compassion have been betrayed. For when you have a system that is ladder-like as in Figure A below, energies of all kinds including religious ones are ushered in to insure the survival of the ladder. We have seen how Jose Miranda demonstrated that this betrayal happened in Western religion with the very words "mercy" and "justice." Originally *saphat* meant Justice and the just God was the one on the side of the unjustly oppressed, the poor, the widow and the orphan. As the ladder grew in influence and power, however, the very name for God as justice was altered to God as Judge. Instead of standing with the poor, God became judge *over* the poor, aligned with the powerful at the top of the ladder. The poor could no longer call on God as a steadfast partner in justice-making but had to appeal to mercy, which became a buffer between the God of Judgment and the simple, non-privileged people. Thus appeals to mercy and to the God of mercy in fact accepted and encouraged the status quo. Mercy became a tender feeling but had nothing to do with changing structures or liberating people. Compassion then became synonymous with mercy and the word "justice" was exiled into introverted areas of religious concern about one's "righteousness" before God.

How far God-talk wandered from the Biblical tradition of God as Warrior on behalf of the oppressed, of God waging war for the slaves and the forgotten, of justice as what people need to crave instead of what a Final Judgment metes out to the powerless. "The true meaning of *saphat* is not 'to judge', but rather 'to do justice to the weak and oppressed.' " [32] Compassion becomes the carving of justice which is often an assertive kind of work, as in Psalm 143: "In his compassion he destroys my enemies." Those who remain close to the earth may be further from the judges who preside so handsomely from on high, but they live more closely to the justice which comes from below and which alone is a divine name. (See Figure B)

Amazing things happen at the top of the ladder where men and their manly corporations become buddies to one another. The rich, for example, receive more welfare that the poor do in such a ladder economy. According to Philip Stern, discriminatory and inequitable tax concessions give 2.2 billion dollars to 3,000 families whose incomes exceed a million dollars. According to Mr. Stern tax handouts to the wealthy amount to $77 billion annually—or twenty five times the amount we pay to support all the American poor who wander about at the bottom of the ladder.[33] This summer the House of Representatives has voted a tax deduction of $16.3 billion. Whom is it for? According to one critical analysis, it is "in all essentials, a handout to the very rich." Already capital gains deductions in the tax code amount to $11 billion annually and this bill adds another $1.9 billion. Two-thirds of the deductions in the new bill will go to taxpayers who make $200,000 or more per year or to 3/10 of one percent of U.S. taxpayers. The average income of the families who will receive this windfall is $400,000 per year. Each of these families will receive tax breaks of $30,000 from this bill. In contrast, the bill that was voted down would have provided tax relief to 98 per cent of the population of the country. Who lobbyied to get this tax relief for the wealthy? Mr. Charles Walker, one-time lobbying manager for the American banking industry who is head of the American Council on Capital Formation.[34] Justice Douglas was not talking idly when he said that in America we have socialism for the rich and "free enterprise" for the poor.[35]

The perpetuation of ladder economics perpetuates the lack of compassion that so characterizes our aggressive culture. It puts power in the hands of a few at the expense of the many who are, quite literally, at their "mercy." Popes have spoken out against such a system, encouraging instead a decentralized or Sarah-Circle approach to development. "At every level the largest possible number of people should have an active share in directing economic development." [36] Yet the irony of this statement is that the institutional Catholic Church, male dominated and patriarchal as it is, hierarchical and uppity as it often has been, remains part of the ladder structure we are criticizing. Which only goes to demonstrate how insidiously rooted the Jacob's-ladder syndrome is in the dominant institutions of the West. So insidious that their very spokesmen can condemn lack of participation in other spheres of living while not questioning their own.

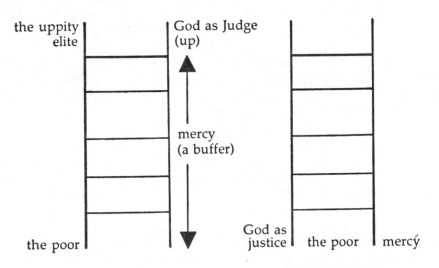

FIGURE A. If God is Judge, mercy is buffer.

FIGURE B. If God is Justice, mercy too is justice.

Another dimension to sexism in economics is how the ladder-differentiation is split along sexual and racial lines. A.T. & T. is the largest private employer in the country. Among its one million employees, 80% of the females earn less that $7,000 annually, while 96% of its white males earn more. The Equal Opportunity Commission has called A.T. & T. "without a doubt the largest oppressor of woman workers in the U.S." [37] Racial discrimination also raises its head in these ladder models because 64% of Spanish-surnamed employees and 79% of black employees of A.T. & T. also earn less than $7,000 annually. Since this same company could afford to pay $3 billion in 1970 to its stock and bond holders who reside in the upper 1.6% of the economic ladder, it is clear that the workers at the ladder's bottom—especially women, blacks and hispanics—are subsidizing the continued good fortunes of that tiny elite at the ladder's top. [38]

It is not only salary differentiation that reveals sexism in our corporate economy but also the role that women are to play for that ladder. They are reduced from being makers of products—which their foremothers were who worked on farms or made cloth in their homes only a century ago—to being consumers of products. Thus, they are pictured as essentially passive to a system that is essentially active. As Anne Douglas points out in her study on women in the industrial nineteenth century, "women no longer marry to help their husbands get a living, but to help them spend their income." [39] Most of the advertising of products was directed at women for whom shopping now became a "feminine occupation." Reuther comments on this same sexual-economic formula: "Women became the chief buyers and the sexual image through which the appetites of consumption are to be stimulated to buy the products of consumer society. Women become a kind of self-alienated 'beautiful object' who sell consumer goods to themselves through the medium of their own sexual image. The home becomes the voracious mouth to be stimulated by every sensual image of consumer capitalism." [40] Here indeed is another definition of 'home' in our day—that of the "voracious mouth." Here lies much of the idolatry of Family (always with a capital F) that the consumer society and its giant institutions invest so heavily in, for the family becomes the basic cell; the first rung, of the ladder economy. Spiro Agnew declares that "the family is the cell of society." He should have added, "of consumer society." Greed, with its voracious mouth, is taught in that particular rung of the ladder these days or unless the family becomes critical and compassionate.

What happens to men who compete on the sexist ladder-climb upwards? A curious dimension to the all-male corporate existence is the role that gossip, backbiting and jealousy plays as one climbs up and up. As Larry Ross testifies: "Gossip and rumor are always prevalent in a corporation. There's absolutely no secrets." All that is holy is reduced to the overpowering appeal of the ladder itself. Corporate directors "really play God . . . They're interested in keeping a good face in the community—if it's profitable. You have the tremendous infighting of man against man for survival and clawing at the top." For at least one of his bosses, "there was nothing sacred in life except the business." Why did Mr. Ross leave the ladder? "I left that world because suddenly the power and the status were empty. I'd been there, and when I got there it was nothing. Suddenly you have a feeling of little boys playing at business." (534, 539) These little boys playing at business are unfortunately the little boys with the greatest influence over our priorities in education, medicine, international politics, legislation, industry, for they comprise the key-positions on boards of trustees of almost all of our institutions of research and "higher learning." More often than not, they are the ones to become advisors to presidents.

Another myth that is perpetuated as long as persons remain uncritical of the worsh*up* motif in the ladder economy is the myth that middle class living is what America wants for all its citizens and for all citizens of the world. Each American uses thirteen times more gasoline than the average citizen of Latin America. Who are we kidding? Who are we lying to when we imagine that we want Latin Americans to become like us? Should they succeed, we ourselves would no longer be able to sustain the life-styles we do, dependent as they are on the private automobile. It is a bold-face act of stupidity or a straight-out lie to preach middle class living as we know it in the United States to other countries. The earth's non-renewable resources such as gasoline will not tolerate such hypocrisies. When will the ladder give way to the circle? Reuther believes that "women's consciousness, the consciousness of all oppressed people, becomes redemptive when it reveals a cohumanity beneath the master/slave distortion as the authentic ground of our being, and fights its battle in a way that takes its stand upon and constantly reaffirms this ground." (B, 117) In other words, the new struggle away from the ladder and into circles will itself be the new way. A way of compassion which is dialectical and not dualistic. And this new way will never be able to occur within the structured society we now possess. For "the liberation of women as a caste is impossible within the present socio-economic system. Only in a new system, a restructuring of reality in all its basic interdependencies, especially in the relationship between work time, place and the domestic support system, can women emerge into the full range of human activities presently available to the dominant class and sexual caste." (111) There will be no birth without death. Most mothers know this. Many non-mothers who have spent themselves climbing ladders would just as soon forget it. But unless a seed falls into the ground and dies, nothing is born. No economics that is worthy of the name human economics, and no politics worthy of human ordering and organizing. Nothing is born.

CREATIVITY IN TODAY'S ECONOMICS

We have seen above how the decisions about what goods a society will produce and who will do the consuming are decisions that are made at the top of ladders mostly for those who dwell at the top of ladders. The so-called Law of Supply and Demand seldom asks the question: supply of what and for whom? And by whose demand? Who is it who is demanding the new model car every year or the sterling silver money clip instead of basic housing, public transportation, etc.? The 'creativity' that goes into making sterling silver money clips is a decadent creativity that is luxury-oriented and not people-oriented. It does not deserve the spiritual name of creative any more than do the manufacturers of the gas ovens in Hitler's Germany. It is a demonic creativity, which is the betrayal of the God-given likeness and image that human persons possess in order to create celebration and justice, not greed and war-like competition.

Creativity in today's economic system seems mostly limited to that art of creating demand for what must be for the most part unwanted supplies. I refer of course to advertising. Advertisers hire creative people to create demands where for the most part there were none previously. For example, in 1976 corporations spent over $400 million on television commercials aimed at young children alone. The average high school senior—the 17 year old—has seen over 350,000 commercials on American television. In the year 1948 American companies spent $4.87 billion on advertising while in 1976 it spent $33.42 billion. At $33.42 billion per year, who can deny that Selling is one of the biggest industries in the entire country? In terms of amount of dollars pumped into the economy, Selling ranks just between General Motors and Mobil Oil as an industry in itself. Advertising expenditures between the years 1975 and 1976 increased 18.5% nationally. Who are these persons and corporations or corporate persons that we allow into the intimacy of our living rooms and bedrooms, to speak with our small children and to influence our teenagers 350,000 times over? The leading U.S. Advertisers in the year 1976 were—in the order of their expenditures on advertising: Proctor and Gamble Co., General Motors Corporation, General Foods Corporation, Sears, Roebuck & Company, Warner-Lambert Co., who sell drugs and cosmetics. Among them, these visitors to our homes spent in 1976 $1.451 billion dollars on advertising. No one has ever asked me but I wonder if you and I, the recipients of such largess, might not prefer the cash instead? [41] What does advertising do to our potential for compassion? What does it do for our potential to direct our energies of desire and fantasy toward relieving the pain of one another and toward celebrating with one another? When engaged in on a mass scale for the sake of mass 'education' and mass profits, it destroys us. For what advertising is is an institutionalized and highly creative effort to create greed in a person and in society. And greed will always lead to competition and never to compassion. For greed begins with a competition in oneself, that is, a gnawing dissatisfaction with what one already possesses and therefore its very starting point is one of *creating dissatisfaction*. Advertisers do not want to win us over to loving something we already are or already have, but they begin by convincing us that we are not yet what we should be because we do not yet have what we ought to have.

There is a spiral of destructive dissatisfaction endemic to all advertising and it is an eternal spiral. If you were to please every advertiser you met on TV for an entire year and buy everything that he wanted to sell you, what would happen next year? It would all be 'surpassed' and your Cadillac for 1978 would be outdated in 1979. The spiral of materialism is eternal and never ends. There lies the ultimate alienation that all advertising is about. Like Sisyphus, whom we met in Chapter Two, the materialist is *never* satisfied. A consumerist culture will never be satisfied nor know what satisfaction is about. For the heart is not made full or satisfied by any or even all of the things that the religion of materialism and its preachers of advertising want so desperately to sell us. "Where your treasure is, there your heart will be," warned Jesus. And the treasures that lead to compassionate living are not buyable for they are less objects than they are experiences. Above all, experiences of ecstasy and the sharing of ecstasies. Ecstasy alone satisfies. Ecstasy and the faith to see oneself through the long task of sharing the ecstasies with others in this world. Greed never asks when is enough enough? It knows nothing of limits. Therefore, it knows nothing of the true pleasures that life is about. It is utterly ignorant of celebration.

Karen Horney warns of the sadistic dimension to advertising when she points out that the sadist plays a "game of attracting and rejecting, charming and disappointing, elevating and degrading, bringing joy and bringing grief." [42] For the sadist, she points out, "exploitation becomes a passion." The ladder, its sado-masochistic energies very much in tact and on Go, perpetuates such sadism time and time again in its advertising as well as in its interpretation of the news that it sponsors whether on television or in newspapers crying titillating headlines. If you absent yourself a while from American television news and then return to it I believe that you will find that the news blends more and more with the advertising—or is it the advertising blending with the news?

Advertisers, we are learning, will stop at nothing to make us greedy for their product. They do not hesitate to destroy our language, for example, and will manipulate any sacred structure whatsoever for their own ends. "Ginger ale tastes like love" we are told—or sold. In this telling that is pure selling, what happens to the word—once sacred—called 'love'? Some psychologists suggest that it is the very repression in our society that advertisers thrive on. Since our population is "generally stroke-hungry" a large number of enterprises, such as massage parlors, Esalen, the American Tobacco Company, and General Motors, are engaged in selling strokes, or implying that their product will obtain strokes for their consumers.[43] Thus it is our repression of body that produces so much oppression in the body economic. Strokes, rather than celebration, become a reigning concern in such a society. The creative advertisers are very capable of sentimentalizing the sacred, as in the well known commercial from Xerox, Inc. of "Brother Dominic," a fat monk who needs a copy machine to fill his vow of obedience. The actor in that commercial (yes, there is an actor!) says that he is portraying monks in a "sweet, nice way," and declares that he has had little critical reaction from any genuine monks (apparently he thinks 'genuine monks' watch television and its commercials!).[44]

The opening notes of Beethoven's Fifth Symphony are being employed to sell us pain reliever and the Prayer of St. Francis is being used to sell us hair conditioner.

Why is so much money, talent and compulsion built into the giant advertising industry? I have always thought that if a product were 25% as good or as necessary as advertisers tell us, that advertising would hardly be necessary. What people need they usually manage to hear about and to acquire. More and more I am becoming convinced that our nation's industries spend the amount they do on advertising because they know as well as we all know that we, in fact, do not need these products all that badly. In other words, in the system we have, we are being sold trivia that no one really needs. Maybe we should be breeding other kinds of products—the kind that persons really need. Then our advertising costs would be drastically reduced and with that our compulsive lack of satisfaction.

I believe that there is a place for some advertising. To announce the information that a useful product is available is a service to the community. But big advertising has taken a demonic stand by so manipulating what is legitimate that advertising is no longer a question of information but of making a whole society greedy. It distracts,—social sin is reduced to 'ring around the collar'—titillates—notice the sexual manipulations so often contrived in advertising—and makes false promises. Thus it degrades us all. For it destroys that unique gift that a human being can make to another, namely a promise. It reduces all of life to the level of having, of dualistic buying-selling, of entertainment. Advertising is a demonic expression of creativity most of the time today and it renders us more fit for dying than for living—consider what percentage of advertising is for cosmetics—the painting of the body so akin to what undertakers do for us one day. Drug and cosmetic companies comprised 20% of the 50 largest advertisers in America in 1976, the expenses topping $1.75 billion. Apparently folks need an awful lot of convincing to become cosmetic buyers since that industry as represented by these ten giants spent a median average of 9.6% of its sales on advertising.[45] Advertising on the massive scale we are involved in renders us more fit for competition, envy and greed than for compassion, celebration and letting go. A culture raised on advertising is sure to be more interested in investing in military exploits than in the peace that justice can bring.

TOWARD AN ECONOMICS OF COMPASSION: SEVEN PROPOSALS FOR DISCUSSION

We have established in Chapter Four that there will be no compassion without creativity and no creativity without imagination. Instead of our creative people being manipulated by our uneconomic economic system either to manufacture luxury goods that no one needs or to sell us ever-whiter detergents and teeth, softer bathroom tissue and longer-lasting deodorants, it would be healthier to use our creative powers to imagine and to implement an economic system that was truly compassionate. The time has plainly arrived to bring about economic alternatives that are more Sarah-circle in their dynamic and that will therefore make possible once again a way of life that is more eye-to-eye and less violently and compulsively ladder-like. One that reflects Einstein's universe of interdependencies instead of Newton's world of absolute isolation.

Economics is far too important and basic to the lives of all of us to be left to some kind of impersonal, quasi-divine and immutable Laws of Economics which were formulated in the nineteenth century under the exaggerated influence of mythologies derived from Darwinian Survival of the Fittest Laws. The ordained economic hierarchy who advise presidents represent an elite that has failed utterly in imagining basic solutions to the real economic realities of unemployment, violent employment, grotesque distribution, wealth, racism, sexism, inflation and competitive violence built into our economic system. I once listened to a live TV interview of one of these anointed ones who was President Nixon's main economic advisor. During the depths of the recession of '73–'74 he declared that: "Those who are suffering the most from the recession are the stock brokers." These economic priests should be served notice that hierarchies, whether sacred or secular, ought to either get off their high horses and down where the people live, work and play or they ought to step aside. They should recognize that as people learn that the word "hierarchy" means sacred and that transcendence is not up, they will no longer tolerate secular and mammon gods hiding at the top of ladders behind the skirts of religious mystical language that the believers of true religion no longer believe in.

Following is a basic guideline for discussion that I would propose for a compassionate economics containing seven points.

Local Control over Economics

I would like to see economics that encourages instead of discourages the small business owner or small farmer. Such an economics implies a non-elitist language and a thorough training in economics of interdependence instead of rugged independence. It also requires a removal of red tape, of giant bureaucratic intervention. A decision needs to be agreed upon about what amounts of merchandizing constitutes "small" businesses. One reason that small business continues to be a victim in the marketplace today is the propaganda that big business feeds about the "free enterprise system." It is imperative that small business people learn to disassociate themselves psychologically, mythically and economically from big business. The monopolies that the conglomerates create destroy the small business farmer, grocer or jeweler, and all the while the large groups propagandize about the need for non-interference of government agencies. In Kansas this past year I was told by family farmers who have worked the land there for generations that within ten years not a single family farmer would be left in that state. At present a quarter of a million family farmers leave their land yearly in America because they can no longer compete with the agri-businesses that are taking over the land of this country.[46] Non-interference for the small business person—Yes! For the large ones, No! Small businesses would do far better linking up with lobbyists of consumer agencies with whom they share so much in common than with lobbyists for large corporation interests. For what makes small business human, compassionate and a contribution to society is that in such a situation the buyer and seller look each other in the eye. It is a Sarah-Circle dynamic. There is a potential for knowledge and therefore for human understanding that is utterly lacking from the top of our skyscrapers.

Simplification of income tax structure

The tax laws we now have are elitist—only accountants and lawyers can interpret them—and therefore those who can afford these specialists, especially the giant corporations, get the most mileage from them and, of course, from the legislative and judicial systems. How many small business people, for example can even afford the time or cost of court usage? Would it really be difficult, and would it not cut drastically the bureaucratic ballooning in IRS, to simplify the tax structure into a pattern that resembles the tithing of old? For example, a straight tax on income that might read as follows:

5% for those earning $10,000–$15,000
8% for those earning $15,000–$30,000
15% for those earning $30,000–$75,000
20% thereafter

With no deductions, no write-offs, etc., except for dependents. Those who earn less than $10,000 would simply not pay income tax.

Money that is earned by work should be untaxed or taxed minimally, while money that is earned by money ought to be greatly taxed. For anyone who has money to play with can afford to pay more taxes. People would be willing to pay income tax if they were convinced that, first, the tax were equitable and did not include constant welfare for the rich and the large corporations and, second, they saw results from their taxes in the form of decent housing, transportation, education, health and protection.

Institution of land-tax

Outside of people, land is the most precious resource we know. All property presumes some kind of relationship to land, if only to store it. The relationship we all have to land is a sacred one, for no one of us created it ourselves and we will all return to it. And yet much land in America goes unused, abused, or becomes reduced to the status of one more object possessed. By taxing land more than we do and in a special way, we will be able to tax work and income derived from it considerably less. (Thus the reason for relatively light taxing in the previous section). A land-tax is meant to correct the monopoly of large corporations, of absentee landlords, and of State control. As such it would seem to be a useful device in a period when more and more observers were heard to remark that United States, home of multinational corporations and USSR, the granddaddy of State Control, seem to have more and more in common. A land-tax would tax all land but not improvements on the land and in this way would encourage initiative and jobs, rather than discourage them. It would run the land speculator and the absentee landlord out of town.

Henry George, an American pioneer in the land-tax movement, sees his movement as an alternative to Marxism and as a radical solution to an unjust economic system that rewards the speculator and puts millions out of work. In effect, he asks that everyone pay rent on whatever land he or she is occupying and that this rent be the only basic tax that a person pay. A land tax would encourage farmers who actually farm instead of those who speculate and, he feels, it would increase productivity, ingenuity and the creation of jobs. It would also lessen bureaucratic interference since basically it is simplifying the law code. Wealth would become "equally distributed. I do not mean that each individual would get the same amount of wealth. That would not be equal distribution, so long as different individuals have different powers and different desires. But I mean that wealth would be distributed in accordance with the degree in which the industry, skill, knowledge, or prudence of each contribute to the common stock ... The non-producer would no longer roll in luxury while the producer got but the barest necessities of animal existence."[47] Just as we enslaved the one source of wealth, human beings, in the name of an economic institution for centuries but finally learned we could live without slavery, so we are still enslaving the second source of wealth, land. "The other source of wealth—the more passive one—is still held in bondage by a foolish‘ economic system," [48] and only when land is 'freed' from land speculators who sit on it or charge great rents for it without improving it will people themselves become free.

I do not know the full extent of the ramifications of George's economics though I do suspect that some basic income tax will still be required. But his starting points are impressively compassionate—which is more than can be said of the economic system we now grapple with. He says, for example: "Civilization is co-operation . . . What has destroyed every precious civilization has been the tendency to the unequal distributions of wealth and power." He believes that his system "will greatly benefit all those who live by wages, whether of hand or of head" and, because he is an American, he does not scare off Americans with talk of "nationalizing" the land or private property. For many Americans the latter carries with it a myth of self-independence. For all these reasons I believe that further investigation of a modified tax on land programs as George describes it might well be worth the efforts of our imaginative economists who are also compassionate. Several cities such as Pittsburgh and Baltimore already have adopted versions of George's land tax.

Emphasis on Distribution Rather than Production

Growthmania and myths of infinite possibilities of economic growth delude us all and distract us from the real purpose of economics which is to make a liveable home for our human family. Instead of idealistic mythical visions served up by so-called secular scientists whose world view is more mythical than that of most theologians even, we should begin economics with facts. The fact of economic life is that the poor are increasing in numbers and the poor are getting poorer while the few rich are getting richer. Anyone who visits a supermarket and observes the retired person on a fixed income having to turn down fresh vegetables and basic meats knows this fact of economic life. (I have observed, however, that very few of our very wealthy ever do their own shopping in supermarkets; and I wonder how many of our comfortable economists do either.) Harrington puts the starting point of economic facts of life this way: "We have in this country a *majority*, composed of the poor, the near-poor, more than half the workers and the lower middle class, which does not even have a 'moderate standard of living' as defined by the Government itself." (337, italics his)

What do we do about this situation? Economists sensitive to it call for a distribution revolution to replace our production compulsions and I agree. "Material growth as we have experienced it over the last century in *no* way has resulted in increased equality among the world's people. To the contrary, growth in its present form simply widens the gap between the rich and poor." [49] Boulding comments: "The essential measure of the success of the economy is not production and consumption at all, but the nature, extent, quality and complexity of the total capital stock, including in this the state of the human bodies and minds included in the system. . . . This idea that both production and consumption are bad things rather than good things is very strange to economists who have been obsessed with the income-flow concepts to the exclusion, almost, of capital-stock concepts." (p. 127) And Daly insists that "the important issue of the steady state will be distribution, not production." (19) The global home demands of all of us, economists included, a broader look at distribution of the basics for living. This necessarily means a cutting back on the luxuries that, as Keynes points out, while they may "satisfy the desire for superiority, may indeed be insatiable" in the desires they arouse and the production they require. John Stuart Mill also warned of an economics based on "consuming things which give little or no pleasure except as representative of wealth." (cited in Daly, 26) Who can say that an economics infused with the desire to distribute would not open up all new industries and job opportunities for many, many persons? The encouragement of those who create what Schumacher calls "good work" ought to be a priority in any humanly-oriented economics. This implies the encouragement of small businesses, of the uses to which land can be put, of the hiring of artists. Has anyone considered how many persons would derive not only employment but also delight and ecstasy by the hiring of mimes to walk our streets, clowns to invade our offices and factories and commuter trains, of musicians strolling through neighborhoods, of conductors organizing and leading neighborhood symphonies? In this kind of *good* work lies the end to unemployment, underemployment and even overemployment because a lot of overemployed are compulsive do-ers who have not learned to receive from the creative ones of society. The rewarding, for example, of inventions that truly save energy and that put people to work instead of eliminate persons from work, the rewarding of kinds of work that bring home-life and work-life closer together—all such rewards should be part of the fabric of a humanly based economy.

Skilling the hard-core unemployed where they live

Around forty per cent of Harlem youth are unemployed and yet Harlem needs improved housing, shopping, safety, street-cleaning, parks, child-care centers, etc. All of these jobs—carpentry, policing, cleaning of streets, beautifying of parks and caring for children—can be done by local residents. And they are the ones who should do these jobs for from a commitment in group activity, community can happen. From a learning on the job, individuals committed to such neighborhood recovery work would also learn skills that can assist others in the neighborhood. An investment in materials and basic skilled leaders, who in fact do not have to be top dogs either in pay or expertise, would go a lot further than the money that otherwise will be lost in crime, prisons, drugs, or that ineffable loss of capital called the snuffing out of a potential citizen at an early age. Joe Selvaggio, director of Project for Pride in Living (PPL), has done exactly this in Minneapolis and St. Paul, proving the feasibility of it and demonstrating the community results of hope, pride and initiative that can follow from it.[49]

Making Economics Global

Economics must be world-oriented and world-aware and not merely nationalistic. Adam Smith's *Wealth of Nations* has been described as the first study in political economy "to constitute it for the first time as a separate science." It is, says J. Bullock, "the best all-around statement and defense of some of the fundamental principles of the science of economics."[51] This may have held true for the nineteenth century (though it may also help to explain the World Wars that have so characterized this century). But there is no future to our shrinking globe without a global economic perspective. We need to pass from a perspective on the Wealth of Nations to a perspective on the Wealth and Poverty of the Globe. With that perspective all else might change into a compassionate way of group-survival. Thus Barbara Ward and Rene Dubos can declare that "we have to place what is valuable in nationalism within the framework of a political world order that is morally and socially responsible as well as physically one."[52] Economics, like all sciences, must become truly inter-dependent.

Economics as an Ideal and Motivating Factor: Towards an American Socialism

There is an intangible that is at stake in this 7-point Economic dream that can not be put in dollars and cents but is not thereby un-important. In fact, it may be the single most important contribution of this or any other economic vision. It is the human factor of motivation, of idealism, of myth that arouses generosity and team-work and for-getting of one's own problems in working with others. *Time* magazine (and I deliberately cite *Time* because it is such a spokesperson for the 500 biggest American corporations that it admires so greatly and of which it is one) admits that Socialism is winning two battles around the world today. The battles are both very much related. One is the contribution that socialist societies make in what *Time* calls "quality of life" issues such as social services, education, medicine, employment. *Time* confesses that "state-provided social services are one promise that socialism has kept ... The essential human services provided by Marxist-Leninist states often match and sometimes top those in West-ern democracies." [52] It would seem that this accomplishment, which even *Time* confesses to, is an important one from the point of view of compassion.

The second battle that *Time* confesses Socialism wins at is that of idealism. "In his ongoing debate with the socialist, the capitalist is at a disadvantage, unable to compete rhetorically with socialist idealism ... Instead of a noble 'new man,' capitalism offers only the 'old man,' whose self-interest in profit—even though it may be condemned as greed—will ultimately benefit the commonwealth." (p. 36) This last as-sertion takes more faith to believe than does the Trinity itself! *Time* goes on: "The quintessential capitalist, whether or not he is religious, rejects the idea of man's perfectibility on earth." Here lies the moral and spiritual malaise of the West: our basic economic system, and here I cite not its critics like Karl Marx but its spokes-media, is pessimistic. Lacking in vision and hope and therefore in motivation. It is incapable of stirring us to cosmic vision or compassionate sharing or generosity. Therefore it has nothing intrinsic to it with which to capture the imag-ination of youth (who are not as easily fooled by the enticements of greed as their parents apparently are). It may accuse socialism of being "fundamentally utopian" which *Time* does but in doing so it reveals why socialism and not capitalism appeals to youth and other idealistic segments of the world: That socialism, for all its claims to being mate-rialistic, is also compassionate. Yet capitalism's only effort at spirituality is in terms of sentimentalized, profit-oriented religion or in terms of philanthropy.

Given this lack of spiritual challenge in the capitalistic economic system as even *Time* itself confesses to, it is clear that the economics we now possess (or does it possess us?) is doomed. For it cannot rouse the hearts and minds and hands of people. Individual self-profit is *not* in the long run what economics is all about. It is about people, not profits. About the poor, not the wealthy. About conserving the goods of the earth that need to be conserved, not about the fast profiteering that destroys non-renewable goods for other generations. Nor is competition as universal as capitalism would like us to believe. We need — the people need — an economics of interdependence. Yet how many of us have been invited to create or debate such an alternative economic system? Most of our 'education' in economics amounts either to, first, making money in the system we've got or, second, inciting us to worship the 'system' we have today by way of ideological propaganda and to hate the "other guy's" system. It is time for some creative alternatives.

Should the alternative be called Socialism? Sociologist Robert Bellah points out[54] that Americans resist that name born of a foreign philosophy developed in nineteenth-century Europe and associated as it is with philosophies of atheism from the same period. For many the term "socialism" has been tainted with too much expansionism, too much bureaucracy and too much dualistic fighting with capitalism to be very useful as a name for an alternative economics.[55] Yet, since an Economics of Interdependence and Compassion is what we seek and it is also what in theory socialism seeks, we should not isolate ourselves from what the socialist tradition can teach us. The time has come for our own adaptation of the socialist principle to our country's situation.

I have lived in American society and in its economic system for thirty-eight years. In those years I have observed the violence that that system perpetrates in very subtle ways — such as the building of greed by its mammoth advertising mania, its established unemployment and compulsive overemployment, its now-rampant inflation, its coddling of the over-wealthy (thirty senators in the US senate are millionaires), its ignoring of basic priorities such as health care, decent education, safety, housing, food, transportation and access to beauty for vast percentages of its citizens, its succumbing to an economy of luxury and trivia, its rendering of people into consumers and of festivities into orgies of buying and spending, its corruption of the media, its rendering citizens ignorant of their own economic system and bigoted toward alternative possibilities, its lack of idealism that can stir youth and old alike to work toward new and common visions, its pandering to decadence of the comfortable, its idolatry of rugged individualism that destroys a sense of the common good. I am now convinced that capitalism with its presuppositions is incompatible with compassion.

Therefore the time has come for a new kind of socialism—an American effort toward a truly democratic socialism. It would need to go beyond slogans and rhetoric and deal with complex issues of modern economics. It would reflect the uniqueness of our country and its peoples—its size and variety, for example, and will not merely borrow blindly from other efforts at socialism. Many of these efforts, as is well known in America, have failed at being both democratic and socialist—one thinks of Russia, of totalitarian regimes in Africa, etc. Yet there are many lessons to learn especially from European and middle European experiments with socialism. Socialists need to be patient people—after all, capitalism has evolved over eight centuries in the West and socialism has been with us for only one century. But this is precisely the point—recognizing the need for more creative expressions of socialism, expressions that truly utter Michael Harrington's goal of the "maximizing of human freedom and potential." It is time that Americans started to make the constructive contributions that they can make to a more compassionate economic system. But compassion will not be built in a day nor in our lifetime. The "quick fix" that McDonald's Corporation has taught Americans to believe in, the fast food fad, is not the way to set economics right.

The basic model for socialism is truly Sarah's-Circle, unlike capitalism's which is just as truly Jacob's-Ladder. Can America, which pioneered Sarah's Circle as a political ideal in the 18th century regain such courage and imagination to invent Sarah-Circle as an economic model for the 21st century? Here lies the most basic challenge that a spirituality of compassion hurls at us today.

SUMMARY

In this chapter we have considered the interdependence of economics to other levels of consciousness and compassion treated in this book: Namely, to psychology, sexuality, creativity, science and politics. We have called for an economic system that reflects the reality of the world we live in to replace that which only protects the privileges of the economic elite. I have presented a seven-fold path to consider in debating such an alternative economics. The key to the new economics will be Interdependence, the newly recognized "Law" of our world.

The basis of this Economics will be corporate and spiritual works of compassion. Do not tell us whether our economy is growing in Gross National Product yearly: rather, tell us whether our world-wide economics are accomplishing the following: housing for the homeless, feeding the hungry, educating the ignorant, caring for the sick, humanizing the prisons, creating good work for the unemployed, encouraging technology with a human face, celebrating with the forgotten, passing on nature's energies to other generations. This would be an economics of Interdependence. An economics as if the creation we lived in mattered.

The ultimate principle in any economics of compassion is that it is to the self-interest of all of us and it is to the private and greedy interests of none. Or, in Gandhi's words, there exists "enough for everyone's needs, but not for everyone's greed." Such an economics presumes that we have learned the difference between need and greed. Clearly we have a lengthy education ahead of us.

7

POLITICS AND COMPASSION:

FROM AN ELITIST AND LADDER-LIKE SOLUTION TO POLITICAL ISSUES TO A JUST SHARING IN A SARAH-CIRCLE BODY POLITIC

If humanity is shaped by its surroundings,
its surroundings must be made human.

Karl Marx[1]

he word *politics* comes from the word for citizen. It is about our being and acting and being acted upon as citizens. It would seem that, if politics means being citizens, then a logical question arises: citizens of what? Who are and who are not citizens? The Greeks understood themselves to be citizens of a city-state, the Romans of the

Empire, Americans of America, etc. Today's Global Village realities are challenging us to conceive what world citizenship, being citizens of a common global village, is all about. Such citizenship consciousness and activity come up against hard and serious opposition, well organized and well financed, not altogether unlike what the first generation of American citizens faced when they stood up to King George and his policing of the colonies. Tellingly, the word *police* shares the same roots as the word for politics or citizen. In some countries and among some citizens, police is the closest one gets to politics. When citizenship becomes reduced to policing, perhaps something is amiss in the body politic.

THE NEW MEANING OF POLITICS

For many today, politics has become confused with politicians so that it appears to be one more game at assuring individuals their security in their compulsive and competitive climb up the political ladder. To yield to this meaning of politics is to surrender true citizenship activity. The struggle of groups through the ages, of blacks, of women, of the non-landholding whites, for their rights as citizens has been a struggle for a citizenship based on Sarah's Circle. The struggle goes on.

Furthermore, politics is a caretaker for the economies of a people. One might say that politics polices a people's economics. As the economics goes, so goes the politics. An economic system that puts greed for some ahead of necessities for all will require a Jacob-ladder, elitist politics to insure its precarious, ladder-like, existence. These ladders in turn create bureaucracies to sustain their weighty selves. Bureaucracy is common to all elitist and ladder structures, whether they be governmental, religious, educational or medical. Indeed, Ivan Illich, basing his documentation on the records of professional administrators themselves, estimates that 25% of hospital costs today are spent on feeding the bureaucracy that administers the hospitals.[2]

It is evident to reflective persons today that politics and economics are about as interdependent as two energies can get. The reason why so many persons no longer affiliate themselves with any political party in America may be that both of the two options we are given have been bought by the same, unimaginative and elitist economic hierarchy. There was a day when the democratic party, for example, represented the country's struggling working classes. But what party represents the hard-core unemployed today? The victim of crime today? The non-elitist or the persons not striving up the ladder today? The handicapped? The aged? Union wages are often so high that only the fittest workers can enter the union. More and more persons are becoming aware that political systems are the caretaker structures of economic systems. There will be no fuller participation in the democratizing of politics until we have begun to democratize the economics of our country—there lies the reason why fewer and fewer Americans bother to vote. When they say they "have no choice" between the candidates, they mean it. Structurally speaking, no major party in America is offering the creative options that the people know they need. Neither is willing to question what in fact the people are questioning: namely, the elitist economic system we are saddled with.

The political parties play with trivia, hiring the same agencies who sell us soaps and lipstick to sell us their candidates. What political party is even asking questions like: is economics about wealth or about poverty? About National Output figures or about International cooperation? About GNP charts or about people starved, killed, unemployed and without pride? What is the difference between need and luxury? What non-titillating goods could our industries be manufacturing for us all? What are the goods in our lives that all of us only borrow and rent and that we need to preserve and conserve for future generations? When is enough enough? When is too much too much and too little too little? How do we pass from a Wealth of Nations mentality to a Poverty of the Globe mentality? Is it possible to construct a socialist economics that is basically non-bureaucratic? If so, how? How do we pass from a concern about quantative growth to a commitment to qualitative growth? How do we pass non-violently from the philanthropy implicit in welfare to a re-structuring of society wherein all will be able to contribute their talents to the common pool of resource? How do we overcome the dependency that is so endemic to a system whose power is more and more in the hands of fewer and fewer? How do we recover the vision that freedom is for everyone, and were it for everyone then security would not have to be the compulsive need of the elitist few? How do we build an economy around the spiritual and corporal works of mercy instead of around corporate profit and private greed?

Our common home has indeed changed in our time with our discovery of the global village. So too has the meaning of 'wealth.' Human beings with their hands, imaginations, hearts, voices and visions are the primary resources we need to conserve and develop. How do we do this except by providing housing for all, work for all, health for all, education for all and celebration for all? Here lies a priority list. And we cannot do this in our present world without also an economic-political system that is interdependent, not competitive; international, not national; supranational, not super-power dominated, and at the same time local and not State-controlled. Here lies an agenda for creative persons to debate our common economic political futures.

In this chapter I would like to take three instances of political, i.e. citizenship, issues that concern all caring persons today and all compassionate persons: the issues of Energy, of Medicine and of Education. Decisions we make in the next decade concerning these highly political issues will, I believe, point to whether we are capable at all of devising a more Sarah-Circle economics and politics. They constitute a trinitarian litmus test for our compassionate futures. To address these issues is to ask whether compassion itself has a future or not.

THE POLITICS OF ENERGY

There is a basic difference between energy gotten from oil and coal or energy derived from the sun. The former kinds of energy are ladder-like and elitist for it takes immense amounts of expertise, capital and specialization to derive fire from coal, gas or oil under the earth. In contrast, sun energy is potentially democratic and Sarah-circle.

It is this fact of the democratizing of energy that is at the heart of the opposition to and slowdown of solar-energy research and distribution in our country. Our federal government is currently budgeting 95% of its research moneys into non-renewable energy sources. The government and the oil executives have been misleading the public into thinking solar energy is expensive and have also been involved in a self-fulfilling prophecy by continually pumping billions of dollars into the oil profiteers while choking most efforts at solar-energy research. According to a United Nations Report, the photovolactics that form the basis of solar energy could be reduced drastically in cost if only $1 billion were invested in research. ($1 billion is less than the cost of a single large nuclear power plant.) However, four of the ten most commercially active photovolactic companies have already been bought up by giant oil firms who are giving signs of wanting to monopolize the sun as they have monopolized what is under the earth. We can be assured of this: that the day Esso imagines it owns the sun we will have solar energy on a mass scale, though not a cheap one.

The day following Sun Day, Mobil Oil Corporation launched a publicity campaign to discredit solar energy and in doing so spent more on its advertisements nationwide than Sun Day's total budget. It is clear that solar energy "has become an unquestionably political issue" [3] — and economic one, let us add. In the past few decades, the federal government has subsidized the elitist energy sources to the tune of $150 billion of tax money. Part of this money has been fed back by way of lobbyists in Washington to guarantee that the interests of the beneficiaries of this windfall are maintained and sustained. One more case of socialism for the rich and entrenched ladder-top corporations of our culture. E.F. Schumacher has put the situation succinctly when he says: "With the rise of the importance of solar energy, we have the rare opportunity of either standing by and watching an attempt to create a new monopoly before our eyes, or we can add our support in an effort to see that solar energy is developed and used for our best benefits as individuals, as a society and as a world." Clearly, the economic and political lines are being drawn about our future in energy.

The issue of solar energy cuts across ideological lines of capitalism/socialism. Yet it will create new jobs, it is cheaper in the long run, it is benign and it is capable of local control and operation, while it modifies international rivalries over oil, gas and coal. In short, it fulfills the basic criteria we have set up for a compassionate economic and political system. The myth that nuclear power is an answer to energy needs continues to hold sway only where the facts have been repressed. A nuclear reactor that produces temperatures in the trillions of degrees is equivalent, Armory Lovins points out, to "cutting butter with a chainsaw." [4] The storage of atomic energy wastes will always be unresolvable and its dangers are finally being publicized. Professor Robert Jungk of the University of Berlin points out that the dangers of nuclear reactors lead to such stringent security precautions that such energy "will eventually lead to growth of a police state." Third World countries, if they adopt nuclear energy "will become all the more authoritarian," he predicts. What would constitute authentic progress, he suggests, would be "the development of a decentralized technology, a technology which is humane and gentle." [5] This kind of energy would be what Lovins calls the "soft" or what I have called the Sarah-Circle energies of sun, wind and hydro power. "Hard technologies are huge, centralized and nonrenewable sources such as nuclear and coal-fired plants." [6]

We know of no safe storing of nuclear wastes whose life-time for emitting dangerous radioactivity into the atmosphere and into the soil or into the waters of the global planet is 200,000 years. If we care anything at all about the life that is to come after us, it is time that we laid to waste the myth that nuclear energy is a healthy substitute for oil-driven energy systems. The citizens living near the West Valley nuclear fuel reprocessing plant south of Buffalo, New York, have learned that to protect their earth from radioactive contamination might cost $1000 per gallon of the nuclear waste. In their case the bill could come to $600 million.[7] We should invest more into research that will guarantee more gentle and less violent ways of firing our industry and our homes. For our attitude toward energy reveals our political, economic and spiritual consciousness.

POLITICS AND HEALTH CARE

A similar case obtains in the instance of health care the world over. One can distinguish between soft and hard medical care. It is the hard kind, such as overly specialized hospitals, overly aggressive surgeons and overly fat drug profiteers engage in, that is behind the 330% (sic) increase in medical costs in America over the last twenty years. (At the same time the overall price index rose only 71%.)[8] Discounting inflation, health costs in America rose by 42% from 1969 to 1974 alone. Similar statistics obtain among all the industrialized nations. Therefore the issue is not merely economic greed on the part of the privileged classes at the top of the medical hierarchies, nor is it a matter of political parties of the left vs. political parties of the right. The issue concerns what we mean by health care: "The rationalization is motivated, not by politics of the left or the right, but by the sheer necessity to secure more effective use of scarce and expensive resources," warn commentators on the International medical scene.[9] The issue is hard vs. soft medicine. Violent vs. non-violent medicine. Elitist vs. non-elitist medicine.

Soft medicine would resist the competitive and machismo myth that a healer conquers the body or conquers disease. It would resist the dualism between mind and body with its implication that mind, in this case technological inventions, is the cure-all. Instead, it would respect the power of the brain—not to be confused, as dualists do confuse it, with the mind—to heal one's own body. Soft medicine would work without surgery and without drugs for the most part to release the brain to heal the body. In soft medicine the doctor is an artist who practices the art of healing, which includes listening intently to the patient and encouraging the patient to listen to his or her body. For the doctor who is still an artist respects the body and knows that "no man or group of men can repair the body. The body must always repair itself by a growth of new cells replacing the old, dying and dead cells of our bodies." [10] Such a doctor studies "the normal first in order to understand the abnormal better." He or she has a reverence for the body and the brain's capacity and desire to heal the body and sees his work mainly as removing the interference between the brain and the pain in the body so that the brain can do its work of healing. He or she practices letting be and letting go.

Soft medicine would respect the traditions of the art of healing that humankind has developed over the centuries and not presume that the latest is necessarily the best or that the most expensive, most dramatic or most highly priced and magnificent technology is the best. Acupuncture, for example, has been healing persons for over 5000 years and yet the medical establishments of this country still think chemicals instead of electrical energies—the latter form is the basis of acupuncturists' impressive successes over the centuries.

Soft medicine implies a respect for feelings. However, feelings are not what so many ladder-like persons in our society who make up the medical hierarchies are adept at. As Dr. Charles puts it: "It's no wonder we are still in the dark ages of understanding in regard to our health when we cannot communicate our feelings to each other better than we can. Doctors cannot communicate with other doctors regarding feelings either." [11] Feelings are in fact excluded from hard medicine. They do not show in laboratory tests or X-rays, blood tests or urinalysis. A soft medicine will urge the patient to be responsible for his or her own health care and to listen to his or her own body. "The only time the body does not manifest the truth to you is when you have taken into your system some inhibiting drug or chemical which interferes with the normal channels of communication from the affected part to the brain, (the nervous system)." [12]

The introduction to the human body of chemicals or the cutting up of the body by surgery is what I would call hard or violent medicine. And yet, this is the medicine we lay persons have been instructed not only to expect to heal us but to respect and even worship. "We have all been taught to think chemically about our health, not electrically. The allopathic medical Doctors think chemically and they head all the government and educational agencies and facilities concerning health in all our universities, colleges, high schools and grade schools. They head all health departments in political parties and all medical divisions of health insurance companies. . . . Why do you think our young destroy their bodies and their health with upper's and downer's? They are led by chemical thinking people who make billions of dollars selling it." [13] The media contribute an overwhelming amount to the selling of hard medicine with their titillating profiteering regarding heart transplants and their very destruction of our language in talking about the "miracles of modern science" or talking about doctors as saviours.

Hard medicine is costly and elitist. Only persons locked away for years—much as seminarians of old—who emerge with the aura of myth about them to perpetuate the closed class and caste, the new clerical caste, that our society anoints as "doctor" can practice it. This elitist core of ordained graduates for the most part seeks the upward mobility of the medical ladder, maintains its elitist language and contributes to the alienation of patients from their own bodies, perpetuating a myth that only they have the "answers" to others' diseases. For the most part hard medicine has lost the art of healing and instead has become beholden to technology. Doctors frequently become almost as hard, unfeeling and cold as the machines they delight in operating.

Twenty-eight months ago I was in a serious automobile accident. Since that time I have gone to eight separate medical specialists—some for as many as eight visits apiece—and have had one double operation. I have spent over 400 hours either in hospitals or the waiting room of doctors' offices (Illich points out that the average time spent with an internist in Germany today, no matter how many hours one spends in the office, is 1.7 minutes—this comes close to my own American experience as well). My costs have exceeded $7500 to date. Yet my pain was reduced in my neck, where I had the operation, but has increased steadily in my wrists, hands, feet, arms and knees. This month the doctors wanted to operate again—this time on my right wrist. But I received hints that after that operation would come a suggestion to operate on my left wrist, my feet, both my knees; they said I would be on crutches for three months following that operation.

As I shuttled faithfully and docilely from one specialist to another over this two and one-half year period, I received definite impressions from some of these doctors that, if they were a wrist specialist I should tell them nothing about the pain in my knees; and if they were a back specialist I should keep silent about the pain in my elbow. Truly, these hard medical people are Newtonian and mechanistic in their outdated body awareness. Finally, I made the break with them on these grounds; whether they knew it or not, I knew that my body was an organic whole and that pain in one part was related to pain in another. I also knew that the wrist, on which they wanted to operate—and all operation is violent and always leaves scar tissue that can never heal itself—was not the core problem. I told them all along that the problem was my elbow.

I contacted the doctor who has written the two articles I have referred to above; his name is a fictitious one in those articles for hard, political, reasons. I spent two and one-half days with him and in that time I received more relief from my pain than I have received from the previous two and one-half years of medical specialists. For the first time since the accident my feet and knees are not paining me all day. I also had all my questions answered—something that other doctors, verbally or non-verbally, have taught me they were too busy to answer or I was too stupid in asking. I have been given techniques to practice on myself and with the help of a friend, to continue the healing process that my body wants to do. Those visits with Dr. Charles were the first time I have ever heard God spoken of in a doctor's office—his is a reverential view of medicine. I learned more about my body in those 60 hours than I had in my previous 38 years of existence. My entire bill was less than $150.00. Dr. Charles confirmed my own diagnosis, pointing out that at the elbow is one of the principal acupuncture points for the entire body. I am still reeling from the consequences of having learned how truly ignorant—in the sense of ignoring of the truth—our medical hierarchies are.

I have received a definite impression from my numerous hours in doctors' hospitals and offices that doctors today are almost afraid to touch the body. They prefer to touch it with machines which are very often immensely painful to the patient. I found doctors trained in hard medicine to be among the most no-touch people I have ever met. In contrast, Dr. Charles spent each of my six one-hour visits with him working *on my body.* I have been made to wonder whether sadists are not persons who are ultimately afraid of the body also. For frankly, I have found much of elitist, high-cost medical care to be sadistic.

I am a convert to the movement in soft medicine. Neither I nor Dr. Charles is suggesting that there is no place for some surgery or even on occasion some drugs. But I am suggesting that our ladder-like, violent and non-feeling medical establishment, more committed to industry than to healing, has led us astray and continues to do so. That the political issue of people who are patients getting in touch with their own right and responsibility to heal themselves is a critical political battle the world over. I am encouraged, for example, by those parents I know who are choosing natural childbirth or by persons committed to preventive medicine, to good eating habits, to family massage and laying on of hands and energies. Only this commitment to soft medicine will de-monopolize the elitist medicine we now worship to the tune of $95 billion a year in our country.

Anyone who imagines that hospitals, for all their bloated incomes, are compassionate places today has not tried to survive in one. "The frequency of reported accidents in hospitals is higher than in all industries but mines and high-rise construction," warns Illich (31). I spoke to an intelligent woman who was hospitalized for many weeks who told me the only hospital employee who made her feel better was the cleaning personnel who, unlike almost everyone else, had time to pass humanly and humanely.

Having myself been a victim of our high-paid professional elite who made me feel guilty for my pain because first, I was taking their valuable time or second, I was probably faking it ("it will all go away" one told me a year ago) and who made me feel more dependent and essentially masochistic than I had felt in years, I find myself more and more in agreement with Ivan Illich, who declares that "by turning from art to science, the body of physicians has lost the traits of a guild of craftsmen applying rules established to guide the masters of a practical art for the benefit of actual sick persons. It has become an orthodox apparatus of bureaucratic administrators who apply scientific principles and methods to whole categories of medical cases" (253). How elitist has medicine become just as costs have tripled? The number of specialists has doubled in the past fifteen years and currently fifty percent of practicing physicians are specialists in America. The medical industry, like other American industries, has grown into a capital-intensive, quantitatively oriented, ladder-oriented, violent business. It is for this reason that Illich advocates that "the deprofessionalization of primary care" would constitute the "most important single step in raising national health levels" (227). Yet, this is not his private conclusion alone, but that of the World Health Organization as well. Illich calls for a Sarah-circle response to health that he calls putting autonomy ahead of industrial modes of production. (266) When it comes to the basic direction for health to take, I am in agreement with him. I seriously question the health insurance remedies now being proposed in congress and by the President if they are only going to be pumping more money into a system that has revealed itself to be so unhealthy in so many basic ways. Medicaid and Medicare have been a financial windfall for the not-exactly-starving medical elites of doctors and drug and insurance companies, and one questions if the latest schemes are not equally ladder-supportive. More basic questions of Sarah's circle must be faced before merely pumping more of the taxpayers' resources into what we now call medical care. How appropriate it would be if religious hospitals and those in health care for professed religious reasons were to leave the violent and elitist institutionalized hard medicine and enter the prophetic fields of soft, holistic medicine wherein all citizens are taught the principles of healing themselves.

POLITICS AND EDUCATION: EDUCATING FOR COMPASSION

One of the ironies of what has happened to education in our time is that secular education has become sacred education and so-called religious education has very often lost touch with the sense of the sacred in the universe. I will treat these two themes in this section.

Toward a meaning for education

One problem with expecting academia to teach us in compassion is that the very word 'education' has lost its meaning. For the most part we have reduced education to job preparation or to diploma getting, making it one more commodity that a consumer consumes. That is why Mary Richards' definition of education as "a process of waking up to life" [14] is so refreshing. Waking up is what all education ought to be about. Waking up to life and its mysteries and its solvable problems and the ways to solve the problems and celebrate the mysteries. Waking up to the interdependencies of all things, to the threat to our global village, to the power within the human race to create alternatives, to the obstacles usually entrenched in economic and political shibboleths that prevent our waking up. Indeed, I believe that all spirituality is about waking up. Paul said this: "You know the time in which we are living. It is now the hour for you to *wake from sleep*, for our salvation is closer than when we first accepted the faith. The night is far spent, the day draws near." (Rom. 13.11) And Jesus advised: "Stay awake, therefore! You cannot know the day your Lord is coming. Be sure of this: If the owner of the house knew when the thief was coming he would keep a watchful eye and not allow his house to be broken into. You must be prepared in the same way. The Son of Man is coming at the time you least expect." (Mt. 24. 42.44) This theme of waking up is also integral to Eastern spirituality, as in these warnings from the Kabir.

> Oh, friend, I love you. Think this over carefully. If
>   you are in love, then why are you asleep
> . . . .
> My inside, listen to me, the greatest spirit
>   the Teacher, is near,
>   wake up! wake up!
> Run to his feet—
>   he is standing close to your head right now. You
>   have slept for millions and millions of years.
> Why not wake up this morning?
> . . . .
> Friend, wake up! Why do you go on sleeping?
>   The night is over—do you want to lose the day
>   the same way?
> Other women who managed to get up early have already
>   found an elephant or a jewel. . . .
> So much was lost already while you slept . . . and that was
>   so unnecessary![15]

This entire book has been intended as an education and therefore a waking up to compassion. Like all authentic education in compassion it has pointed to the inter-connectedness of all things, including the interrelatedness of values and all things and all nonthings. The ultimate value we have labeled as the survival of the planet by way of the increase of love-justice in the world. If survival is the natural law, interconnectedness is nature's principal law. This truth ought to be taught as the core and center of all efforts at education.

Recovering the "secular" in Secular Education

So-called "secular education" is not secular at all since to be secular means to be non-clerical and non-hierarchical and non-elitist. What is in fact the case in industrialized societies today is that education has become education *for* hierarchy and for insuring the sacralization of the secular. An education for anointing those on ladder tops, an education up the ladder and how to stay on the ladder top. So-called "secular education" is not secular at all for it does not prepare us to live in the world (*saeculum* means world) of the cosmos and the universe. It does not prepare us to be either good cosmic citizens or to be good global citizens. Rather, it prepares us for a man-made artificial world of ladder-climbing, competition, specialization, nationalism, part-thinking and part-acting,—in short for control instead of for celebration. Secular education has become a contradiction in terms. It perpetuates violence.

Claiming to be value-free, it is in fact racked with the values of the ladder-climbing culture and the economics and politics that it represents. The true values of world survival and global survival, as we have seen, are values of interdependence. But when these authentic values are repressed and whitewashed, then we have the grotesque situation of flag waving as an educational value. This flag waving at times takes the expression of nationalism and at times the expression of organized sports from grade school through college. It also takes the form of corporate flag waving and few are surprised to learn that representatives of drug manufacturers are actually lecturing to medical students in our high-class medical schools.

E.F. Schumacher believed that all education is about values. It is more than "know-how," since know-how "is no more a culture than a piano is music." Why is the transmission of values the essence of education to Schumacher? "We think and feel with them, . . . they are the very instruments through which we look at, interpret, and experience the world." He suspects that what people most want from education is "ideas that would make the world, and their lives, intelligible to them. When a thing is intelligible, you have a sense of participation; when a thing is unintelligible you have a sense of estrangement." [16] (84)

If education is about values (as Schumacher suggests) and about waking up (as Richards suggests), then this whole book has been about education. It has been about our waking up to the exiled value called compassion. Since the word education comes etymologically from the Latin word meaning to lead away from, it has also been about leading out from Jacob's ladder and into Sarah's circle. Here lies the true meaning of revolution (to revolve, to turn around) — education is about revolution in the sense of people on a ladder learning to look *around* them, and not just above them, to see and feel, and then to lead out from the ladder and form new energy systems. Here lies true spiritual and compassionate revolution and education. A value-oriented education, one oriented toward compassion, will be one that not only tolerates feelings as integral to educational growth, but develops, as psychologist Jersild insists, a "widening of the range" of one's feelings. A compassionate person needs to be at home with one's own feelings in order to sustain and not run from the deep feelings of others. "Compassion is not the emotion of the weak but the hard-gotten property of the strong," notes Jersild. (200–206) The situation we have today requires the extension of feelings of just outrage and other feelings world wide. A truly 'secular' education interested in the survival of the world would be teaching such values and feelings along with intellectual tools for responding constructively to them.

Waking Up to World Religions

One waking-up exercise that the survival of our global village demands of us today more than ever before is the waking up to world religions. E.F. Schumacher believed that there are two places to learn wisdom: from nature and from religious traditions. We have, under the aggressive impetus of mechanistic science, ignored and indeed jeopardized both of these schools of wisdom. It is time that we attended these schools once again—not in the dreary and dusty way that education in its moribund state has become in many places, but in a revitalized, re-energized state of active healing and living compassion. For wisdom is compassion and compassion is wisdom.

Education has become an elitist thing available to an elite and to those aspiring to be elite and to those whom the elite deign to award scholarships as a kind of philanthropic crumb from a well-heeled table. The biggest and busiest of our giant educational institutions are hardly big and busy about learning compassion, much less teaching it. In the United States we have the unbelievable situation of entire university systems not even teaching courses in religious traditions. And then we wonder—or do we?—why so many of our youth turn to emotionalized religious sects or to drugs or to some other avenue of potential wisdom. We have, for the most part, in education at the university level today what Ralph Emerson accused Harvard of having a century ago: "all of the branches of knowledge and none of the roots." Often when schools do deign to allow departments of religion, they are staffed by religious rationalists who can give dates and numbers for other peoples' religious conversions—Lao Tsu, Buddha, Nicolas of Cusa, etc.—but have nothing to say about their own. In other words, religion is one more *object* among the subjects that a school teaches. But how can anyone teach faith without faith? True, there is an intellectual content that can be analyzed, compared to other traditions, etc. and even an agnostic could teach the content. But spirituality or a way of living—which is what compassion is—cannot be taught without living or trying to live it. Clearly, then, the university system is not at this stage in history a worthy place to go to learn compassion.*

*There are, of course, some exceptions to this situation. Where I am now working, we have developed an entire program in spirituality that is built around the ideas of compassion enunciated in this book and truly tries to integrate them. Also, it should not be denied that even learning

Max Scheler emphasized this theme of world religions in his study on compassion early in this century when he said: "Our greatest need at present is to bring about a long-term reciprocal adjustment between the Western ethos and that of Asia, and especially India; so that eventually Asia should learn to cultivate the western ideals of *humanitas* and the non-cosmic love of persons in God, while we of the West should cultivate in ourselves the sense of emotional identity with the living universe." [17] The mutual waking up that can occur when persons living and understanding their diverse spiritual traditions meet has seldom been tried and so we hardly know what depths of renewed human energy and creativity and courage might result from such meetings. Of this we are sure: that education as waking up and as edge-ucation, preparation for making the edge the center and for stretching to this edge, the kind of education that all living faiths desire to offer their believers, has never been more urgently needed.

Education for the most part is operating on a Newtonian model of isolated atomic subjects which are objects. It is time education learned to flow once again and to interconnect. The effort at "interdisciplinary courses" is for the most part a dismal failure even in the small colleges, saying nothing of the large ones. That is only a band-aid-like approach to solving the isolation of different departments. For a university truly to become unified once again something else is needed. When the Middle Ages, operating on a Jacob's-ladder model, looked for a unifying source and goal for all education it chose theology, the so-called "Queen of the sciences." I am not for reinstating such a Queen, nor replacing her with a King, for we do not need the ladder at all. What we need is a center, not a ladder. A centering from which all education worthy of being called human and therefore edge-ucation, will derive. I think we now have the center. The new mandala. The global village. The cosmic egg. With all its interconnections. Survival. Compassion. Compassion, understood in the sense in which I have developed it in this book, is the proper central force from which all edge-ucation should flow. We ought to re-organize edge-ucation, beginning with primary schools (which are often closest to being so centered), to secondary schools, to college and university, to adult education and certainly to all religious education. The re-organization should have world-survival as its common motif. A value we ought by now to be able to agree on. Then all branches of learning will have a

---

about compassion—which is the extent to which most schools are equipped to teach—is not nothing and can be a beginning for a way of life.

common root, whatever their varied roots. All persons learning economics or physics, biology or math, philosophy or music, will be able to interact once again with others. As a start that would not be shocking in expense or restructuring, edge-ucators might open each semester with several days dedicated to compassion in which all students will be present. At this general gathering representatives of the various disciplines could address themselves to the question of what their discipline is accomplishing for compassion. The very outline of this book lends itself to being a starting point for such spiritually ecumenical—and not merely religiously ecumenical—convocations. Persons meeting in small groups which would be interdisciplinary in their make-up could then discuss the major presentations. Each semester could end with the same kind of convocation, with students and teachers alike evaluating their year on what contributions they have made in their field to compassion. Compassion needs to be taught, criticized, grown into, added onto—that is to say, our understanding of compassion needs these dimensions of intellectual and emotional growth. For truly as William Eckhardt has put it, "the world is dying from lack of compassion."

So that this kind of instruction take place in formal education, it is imperative that religious traditions start making contact with their own best roots. I seriously wonder whether compassion is not the one value (at least) that *every* major religious faith of the world wants to teach its believers. Consider, for example, Dr. Suzuki's description of the Buddhist experience of interconnectedness known as *Avatamsaka*. It is

> a state of complete dissolution where there is no more distinction between mind and body, subject and object. . . . We look around and perceive that every object is related to every other object . . . not only spatially, but temporally. . . . As a fact of pure experience, there is no space without time, no time without space; they are interpenetrating.[18]

With this teaching of compassion so common to all faiths in mind, I would like to turn to one world religion, a Western one, for a brief glimpse into some of its insight about compassion. While I have made numerous references to compassionate wisdom that can be learned from the Western traditions of Judaism and Native American religion, I will here concentrate only on Christianity as an example of what a renewed faith, a faith renewed in light of the demands of compassion, might explore.

Five Christian Doctrines Pointing to Compassion

It is evident that Jesus taught and lived compassion and I have dealt with such matters in previous chapters. I want to sketch here some typically compassionate doctrines that Christianity possesses in its storehouse of doctrines which it ought to start re-discovering and re-searching, and sharing. Christians who start asking rich questions of their tradition concerning compassion may well find that their empty tomb is rich not only with the hope that resurrection brings but also with old and new insights on the way of living resurrectedly that is called compassion. Following are doctrines that are rich in compassion and deserve much re-discovery, re-searching and sharing.

1. The Reign (Kingdom and Queendom) of God. The announcement of the Kingdom of God constitutes the central message of Jesus in the Synoptic Gospels. God's reign is already present and it is yet to come in its fullness. It is not the same as the Church, though the church has often blurred the distinction in its lack of theology and thereby smothered the richness of the doctrine. Indeed, believers are to be "seekers for the Kingdom" according to Paul (Col. 4.11) and the Kingdom consists of justice, peace and joy (1 Cor. 4.20). The Kingdom is to be a person's first concern, that for which one would surrender everything (Mt. 6.25–34; 13.44ff), and such a conversion to the Kingdom will mean doing the works of compassion or mercy (Mt. 25. 31–46). One might say, then, that the Kingdom of God means the Coming of Compassion. That is why it is godly—it is "compassionate like your Father in heaven is compassionate."

But Jesus' teaching on compassion and the Kingdom arouses still more insight on what compassion is all about. "Asked by the Pharisees when the kingdom of God was to come, he gave them this answer. 'The coming of the kingdom of God does not admit of observation and there will be no one to say, 'Look here! Look there! For, you must know, the kingdom of God is among you.'" (Lk. 17.20f.) Jesus speaks here of time and of space. First, the question addressed him was about the *timing* of the Kingdom—"When?" his disciples asked. And so in his response the word *is* is all important. Jesus is emphasizing the presence of the kingdom, its nearness and operation in his own day and history. His message is that the kingdom "has arrived." The kingdom of God—which means compassion—has now begun. There is Jesus' time-response.[19] Regarding space, Jesus is equally emphatic. Do not confuse the Godly kingdom of compassion, he is saying, with institutions or place or, one might say, rungs or places on a ladder. The kingdom is impossible to see if you are object-oriented for it is not an object! It is a verb. Where is this verb? "Among you, in your midst," Jesus says. Thus compassionate consciousness for Jesus presumes awareness and consciousness, and that is why the wealthy, as Jesus counsels over and over, will have such a hard time recognizing the Kingdom. Because they are trained in object-seeing instead of amongness-seeing. Amongness consciousness is the consciousness of interdependence. Jesus saw the necessary link between interdependence and compassion.

It is telling that through the centuries, under the influence of introverted spirituality, Christians have frequently translated the unusual term Jesus uses here (*entos hymon*) as "within you." Within is where the soul was understood to be located for a certain period in history, and Hippolytus, Origen, Athanasius, Ambrose, Jerome and Bede so translated it. Others, however, such as Ephraim, Cyril of Alexandria, Theophulact, translated it as "in your midst" and still others, Tertullian and Cyprian, as "within your grasp." Amongness, not withinness, is the key to the Kingdom. And the messianic age, the age of salvation for all, is now here. Compassion is at hand.

Another example of Jesus' "amongness" consciousness applied to the reign of God occurs in Luke's Gospel: "What shall I compare the Kingdom of God with? It is like the yeast a woman took and mixed with three measures of flour till it was leavened through." (13.20f.) The dough becomes "leavened all through" by the yeast—amongness is yeast's unique property or characteristic—as is to be the reign of God according to Jesus.

2. The Mystical Body of Christ. Another Christian doctrine that says much about compassion is that of the mystical body of Christ. Christians believe, or say they do, that Christians themselves form a body politic that is the body of Christ on earth now that Christ has left the earth. In this act of faith, "the Church is viewed as a sort of magnetic field, charged, as His body, with Christ's power, and, as His fullness, one with Him." [20] This doctrine of the Spirit of Christ permeating those who come after him is a dynamic one that teaches that the 'soul' or vital principle of this body politic is nothing less than the Spirit of Christ. Christ, the Son of God, The Incarnation of Compassion, becomes incarnated once again in a new kind of body, this time a group body or body politic. All dualisms give way to the interrelatedness of God and people. "There is only Christ: he is everything and he is in everything" (Col. 3.11). The new creation is a unity, an inter-connectedness that underlies all compassion. This new body is filled with the fullness of Christ (Eph. 1.22f.)—fullness overflows into

fullness. Body into body. I into We. When one part of the body suffers *all* its parts suffer.

What a far more compassionate—and biblical—perspective on the word "body" this is than what most Christians have come to react to when hearing the word 'body'—namely one's own private and too passionate machine that one owns like a piece of property. In fact, what is needed to recover a true belief and therefore a truer living of the mystical body is an awakened attitude toward our bodies, for in the West it is precisely the put-down of body and flight from body that has contributed to the mystifying and therefore the 'impracticality' of the doctrine of the mystical body. Thus Fritjof Capra observes: "The experience of one's body is, in fact, emphasized in many Eastern traditions and is often seen as the key to the mystical experience of the world. When we are healthy, we do not feel any separate parts in our body but are aware of it as an integrated whole, and this awareness generates a feeling of well-being and happiness. In a similar way, the mystic is aware of the wholeness of the entire cosmos which is experienced as an extension of the body." [21] Body is not I in this doctrine—it is We. The Body Politic is the Christian expression of the Kingdom of God, for the mystical Body of Christ is meant to carry on the compassionate works that Jesus did in his lifetime on earth. There is unity in diversity, there is a living organism *among* human beings, compassion is possible. These are some lessons of the doctrine of the mystical body of Christ.[22]

3. The Cosmic Christ. The doctrine of the mystical body of Christ, like any true religious belief, demands something of the believer—in this case, the capacity to think organically and not mechanically. It led Paul quite logically to still another expression of profound interconnection: that of the cosmic Christ. Paul writes:

> God wanted all perfection to be found in him and all things to be reconciled through him and for him, everything in heaven and everything on earth, when he made peace by his death on the cross. (Col. 1.19f.)

Notice that "perfection" here means the making one, the unveiling of interconnections, the peace that compassion brings. Paul says, "all" are reconciled, and this means the entire universe and all of its parts from atom to animal to mineral to vegetable. All breathe the new creation whose name is compassion. Unity. Harmony. Indeed, Paul extends his mystical-body doctrine which we have seen as body politic to include the cosmic body when he says that the Creator "has let us know the mystery of his purpose . . . that he would bring everything together under Christ, as head, everything in the heavens and everything on earth" (Eph. 1.9f.). All the separatist worlds of creation have been organically healed, organically graced, to form one body with one head. The cosmic body of Christ becomes one again because Christ now exercises a "cosmic dominion over principalities and powers." [23] There is a great gathering "of all the powers in both the material universe and the world of the spirits" and the gifts of the Spirit pour forth to every limb of the body.[24] Christ is not an object of worship but an energy among us—the "Risen Christ"—that allows us to see cosmically once again. History is newly created in Christ, the Son of the Compassionate One.

4. The Communion of Saints. The word "saint" has unfortunately been the victim of dualistic tendencies in Christian history so that a word that once applied to all members of the Body of Christ has now come to mean for most people someone who is dead and, most likely, a freak of a person at that. (You know that she or he is a freak because saints are so rare, we are told). In fact, the doctrine of the communion of saints means the communion of all, regardless of life or death, living or dying, sinful or pure, in heaven or on earth, past or present or even future. The powerful doctrine of the communion of saints cuts through all prejudices favoring linear time, absolute space or place. The communion of saints means that all energies who ever lived as persons are interacting with us now as well—provided we are, to borrow Fuller's language, "tuned in" to this truth. It is on this basis—that the body of Christ is not an elitist place only for the living—that prayers of 'intercession', that is to say, of caring and compassion bear weight still. Compassion, this doctrine teaches us, does not cease with this life. Why should it, if it is truly a perfection of God? Compassion continues. No energy, especially no such beautiful energy, is lost.

The doctrine of the Communion of Saints, then, is a doctrine of raw and radical hope, for it suggests that the universe does not, after all, use us up, but that the fullest of all energies, compassion, goes on and on, out and out, in and in, wherever it is welcomed or called upon to grace us. This sense of the overcoming of space and of time as ordinarily conceived parallels much that physics is suggesting about the relativity of space and time. Space and time, the doctrine of the Communion of Saints teaches, is relative to compassion. The ultimate truth of interconnectedness does not cease when life ceases. All energies are connected. Especially the good and the beautiful ones. The Communion of Saints puts the lie once again to the mechanistic myth of isolated parts for it teaches that "there are no fully isolated individuals even" after death.[25]

5. Dialectical Doctrines in Christianity. Dualistic religion has time and again smothered the essentially dialectical spirit of Jesus and of faith in Jesus. Jesus' own teaching is replete with paradoxes that reveal how dialectically he saw the world. "Anyone who wants to save his life will lose it; but anyone who loses his life for my sake, and for the sake of the gospel, will save it." (Mk. 8.35) Or, a phrase frequently repeated, "the first will be last, the last first." At times he talks of bringing peace, at other times of bringing the sword. His life story was itself a story in paradox: Death on Golgotha has become a rebirth at Easter. Death begets life. The Christian belief in the Incarnation is nothing if it is not dialectical — to truly believe and therefore act as if God became a human "in order that humans may become God," as Meister Eckhart put it, is the depth of paradox. So often and so easily Christian theology has succumbed to the temptations of dualism and rendered Christ a God or an Angel or anything but the animal (*homo sapiens* variety) that constitutes so important a dimension of the dialectic that his Incarnation was all about. The heresy for this one-sidedness is named docetism and it, alas!, has inspired many a so-called Christian spirituality.

Another example of a dialectical doctrine in Christianity is that of the Trinity wherein the persons are three but one, the same but not the same, different but one. The Trinity is an energy of dialectic, filled with spirations and generations and filiations. Even though many creative minds wanted to play with this belief and did and were often labeled heretic, those many heresies surrounding the Trinity were invariably heresies of dualism. The mainstream orthodox teaching on Trinity was always a simple matter of reaffirming the dialectical and non-reducible insight about shared unity in the universe and even within the Creator of the universe.

All heresies are heresy because they are dualistic and to the extent that they are dualistic. Orthodoxy in the fullest sense of that word (meaning "true opinion") is always meant to be about dialectic, for paradox is the truth behind all truths in our universe. It would seem that all sin too is a climbing up to dualism and away from the truth of dialectic.

Christian Sacraments, instead of being objects of ritual, are meant to be celebrations of dialectical experiences among believers, the living out of interdependencies of all creation, matter and spirit, local church and great church, saints, who are all of us, and sinners, who are all of us, of the future that is now and the future that is not yet.[26]

We have, then, in this brief sketch of five Christian doctrines, a hint of the education for compassion that is lying coiled and ready to spring to action for those who will investigate the Christian tradition asking good and radical questions: such as, for example, that question that is the beginning of all wisdom — What can I learn from you about compassion?

SUMMARY

What is needed in politics today is a separation of church and state when "church" means the hierarchies of elitist power structures that in their giantism, over-industrialism and violence have usurped the rights and the responsibilities of citizens. This situation of clerical usurpation by the so-called secular powers is evident in the examples we have considered of Energy, Health care and Education. (It is not for nothing that Illich calls today's hospital the Cathedral of our time.) Perhaps what the human race needs in order to survive and therefore learn to live compassion is a common bonding and binding — what religions have called vows — that would support oneself and be a support to others in pursuit of the truths of interconnectedness. Could those seeking compassion make public pledges to pursue Sarah's Circle, Letting Go, Letting Be and Letting Happen, creativity, an integration of science and survival, an economics and with it a politics based on interdependencies, a love of the global village and a desire to see it survive? These vows would constitute public commitments to global citizenship: to a new meaning for the politics of energy, of medicine and of education. If all education is meant to be edge-ucation or leading us and preparing us to live on the edge, then in a common political consciousness and new structuring we will actually be constructing a new sense of soul. A new sense of salvation.

8

COMPASSION
AND THE HEALING OF
HUMPTY DUMPTY
THE GLOBAL VILLAGE
AND US:

FROM THE SALVATION OF THE PRIVATIZED SOUL TO THE MENDING OF THE CRACKED WORLD SOUL

A beggar crouches in his own filth,
Displaying stumps of fingers, running sores;
He says the egg of the world is cracked,
And from its wounds
Poisoned tears fall, like rain over Jakarta.

Constance Urdang
"Living in the Third World" [1]

Myths contain wisdom and a trip into our mythological childhood may well make us wiser concerning the meaning and practice of compassion. Among the noteworthy myths of the youth of most of us is the tale of Humpty Dumpty. It deserves our careful and adult attention. It may serve to make us whole again.

HUMPTY DUMPTY: AN OVERVIEW AFTER THE FALL

Humpty Dumpty sat on a wall,
Humpty Dumpty had a great fall.
    All the king's horses,
    And all the king's men,
Couldn't put Humpty together again.

This is clearly a poem about power and politics, and therefore, one can presume, about economics, for the king's horses and the king's men did not ride out on their horses to attempt to put just anyone together again. They honor power. It is also a poem about pain, brokenness and the struggle to make whole. It is necessarily, then, a poem about salvation and holiness for wholeness and holiness are one. It is also a story about an accident—a fall that is a great fall. It would seem that the fall could be blamed for almost all of our lack of holness if we so wanted— and yet such blame would be misplaced, for Humpty would not be in pieces if he had fallen from just any place, for example off a curb or from a chair. It is the wall that has so much to do with the fall being a "great fall." Clearly the wall must be a very high wall and perhaps, Humpty is a very delicate individual. The combination—high wall and delicate person—together creates a fall that is a great fall. But what is this wall that is so great and so destructive? How did Humpty get up there in the first place? And who, pray tell, is Humpty? Is Humpty worth the effort of all the king's horses and men to mend him? Is there a ray of hope in the poem insofar as it appears, even to the king's men, that there is a possibility that Humpty might be mended after all? But clearly the king's horses and the king's men are not the ones to accomplish the task. The sexual imagery in this poem is frank indeed—for it is the *king's* horses (kings are male and often symbolize male aggression, especially in days before the automobile) and the king's *men* who fail so utterly at their hoped-for healing. Nothing is said of the king's women. But we must delve deeply into the Who, Where, Why and When of Humpty Dumpty's historical plunge.

Humpty on the wall

What was Humpty doing when he fell off the wall? He was sitting. So we know what he was *not* doing—he was neither celebrating nor relieving the pain of others, for neither of these actions of compassion are accomplished while sitting. Might he have been contemplating or wishing he were contemplating? Perhaps. For one thing, he was on top of the wall—as in 'at the top of the ladder'—and, as we saw in chapter two, according to the mind-set of those raised to climb Jacob's ladder what lies at the top is contemplation. How did Humpty get to the top of the wall or ladder? Did he climb? Was he born to be at the top of the wall or ladder? It is very likely that he was in some way of an elitist class since we do know that the *king's* horses and men were sent to rescue him and royalty of any stripe hardly send their own horses and men out to care for the hoi polloi. What is at stake in this fall from the wall is an elite who define their task on the top of the wall as sitting or contemplating. A non-elitist world-view or spirituality will not find itself on wall tops in the first place and so will not have to call upon the king's horses and men to save them from falls. Compassion will not force anyone to climb up walls and ladders but will find a fitting home nearer to the earth.

One has to ask if Humpty knew what he was doing up on the wall-top, if he knew the dangers and risks he was taking with his own life, psyche, or soul. Was he embarrassed to have put the king's horses and men to so much trouble in a vain effort to revive him? If he had life to live over, would he still choose to sit on a wall? It's not unlikely, however, that Humpty, like so many others who were born into wall-climbing, never woke up to the dangers inherent in it and never even reflected on what price he and others might be paying for his 'right' to sit on a wall at all. His climb or the climb of whoever it was that put him there may well have been completely unanalyzed, uncriticized and unthought out. Maybe, after all, and this would be a supreme irony to wall-climbers, Humpty fell off the wall because, being so high up, the air was too rarified and the lack of sufficient oxygen rendered him so dizzy that he came tumbling down willy nilly. One has to pity Humpty. Which is not at all the same as extending compassion toward him. If Humpty had had some truly compassionate people around him in the first place, they would not have allowed him to climb a wall to the detriment of himself, the king's horses and men, and all those he left behind on earth who would not and could not sit at the top of the wall. (One wonders if he crushed any of these when he plunged to the earth from the wall.) But alas! It is evident that in the entire kingdom where he lived, there was no one who applied compassion to Humpty Dumpty. Not even—and this is the saddest truth of all—Humpty himself. Perhaps the word "compassion" had not been uncovered yet and was still covered over with sentimental sighs and wimpy feelings of pity. In that case it may well have happened that, just prior to scaling the wall for his last contemplative sitting, Humpty was patted on the head by good-willed but unthinking people who told him "to get a good tan" while on the wall top or to "enjoy the view" from the summit and maybe even to "bless the crowds" as they huddled below where the earth and plants and animals meet. Poor Humpty. These sentimental and uncritical people, imagining they were loving Humpty, in fact sent him to his piece-meal death.

Being so high up on the wall, Humpty no longer had his feet on the ground. A precarious place on which to perch—out of touch with the soil. How did Humpty, a sterile egg, expect to become fertilized sitting way up on his high perch? Jesus said that a seed becomes alive by falling and dying to the ground—yet Humpty, with his shoes well buffed and shined no doubt, was nowhere near the ground. He was not grounded; he was far from his roots. No wonder that when he fell the earth did not welcome him softly and warmly but offered instead its hard side with the result that Humpty broke into so many pieces. Meister Eckhart says, commenting on Jesus' admonition to let the seed lie in the earth, that "Jesus is the soil" and our souls are the seeds. But Humpty is all egg and no seed. He has fled the earth, fled the soil, fled the place where the Son of God was most at home and is still most at home. Jesus knew well the importance of soil for seeds and growth, for he elaborated on the problem of getting things to grow in his parable about the sower who went to sow a field. I doubt that Humpty, high on his wall, would have fared any better than the seed that was sown on rocks or in the thicket. No soil, no soul. That is a lesson from Jesus, from Meister Eckhart and, in a negative and painful way, from the tragedy of Humpty Dumpty. For Jesus the "kingdom" or reign of God is *on earth,* God's will is to be done "on earth as it is in heaven," and "the field is the world." (Mt. 13.38). Humpty would never have fallen had he been nearer to the earth.

Humpty off the wall

The fall of Humpty and the inability of the king's horses and men to correct that fall represents also the Fall of the Fathers—the Death of the Fathers in so far as they are afraid of Mother Earth. Such Fathers are dead not because they are without power—for horses are very powerful and so too are kingly men—but because they represent a wrong *kind* of power—a power that is outdated and therefore deadly. Theirs is a power to control instead of a power to heal. It is a power over instead of a power with. It is the power of power instead of the power of nurturing and celebration. One sensitive person I know recently had a dream in which a church filled with pulpits suddenly collapsed. The powers that be are too kingly and too manly to survive. Implicit in Humpty's fall is the fall of the twin powers of rationalism and scientism that have ruled the psyche and even the globe for the past few centuries. While technology has sometimes been a good child of this parentage, at other times it has proven to be a wicked and dangerous offspring. What is increasingly evident is that the power of these powers did not include compassion. It also lacked a cosmic vision. Like gnosticism of old, it left people dread-filled and lonely in the universe, for it taught that humanity was so distinct from creation and so separate from it (Descartes saying that our thinking set us off utterly from all of creation and from animals) that we experienced an utter loneliness here. We had lost our way (spirituality) and our home. The seventeenth century represents this awful awareness of our lostness, and Paschal expressed it for us when he said: "Cast into the infinite immensity of spaces of which I am ignorant, and which know me not, I am frightened." [2] And Nietzsche prophesized the chaos that the twentieth century would rain upon the inhabitants of earth when he exclaimed: "Woe unto him who has no home!" Existentialism would represent this same dreadfulness and loss of home in the mid-twentieth century.

But the fall of Humpty Dumpty and the blatant inability of the modern world's kingly men to reconstitute him is in fact a "happy fall." For a new beginning follows on old falls. Life from death. And what people are aware of today is that existentialism's nihilism, that is traceable to the emergence of scientism in the seventeenth century and is paralleled in the gnosticism of the first few centuries of this Christian era, is dead. What Jonas calls existentialism's "contempt for nature" parallels the gnostic contempt for nature and is itself fallen and broken. The acosmic perspective of the past few centuries of Western thinking is fallen and broken. And with it, its ugly stepchild called nihilism. "The disruption between man and total reality is at the bottom of nihilism," advises Jonas (340). Thus the recovery of humanity's relation to "total reality" by today's science (chapter five) as well as by today's feminist thinkers (chapter two), artists and psychologists (chapter three), and even today's economic and political prophets (chapters six, seven) is the new birth that Humpty's fall makes possible. Compassion is no longer passivity when it is truly placed in the matrix of a cosmic world view. It is in fact "the acosmic position [that] comes to express itself in a general morality of withdrawal, which develops its own code of negative 'virtues' " (Jonas, 276). Today organized religion, by such means as the Second Vatican Council, is urging believers to find God in the world and in the process of transforming and re-creating the world. Christianity is no longer a faith of withdrawal or a faith of acosmic, introverted beliefs. It is rediscovering its origins as a compassionate, outgoing, world-changing, way of life. (cf. chapter one) It is separating itself from the Humpty Dumpties of the world.

HUMPTY DUMPTY AS WORLD EGG AND COSMIC EGG

Who is Humpty Dumpty?

Every child's book I ever read on Humpty Dumpty made it clear by the pictures that accompanied the text that Humpty Dumpty was an egg. A person as egg, an egg as person. A personable egg—one might even say, a "good egg." *Not* an egg-head, for the egg was very much the whole of Humpty Dumpty. Humpty's being an egg might help to explain why it is that he was so vulnerable to falling and breaking, for eggs are vulnerable and quite delicate, often subject to cracking and breaking open. Because Humpty is a person-egg, we know that he or she is not merely an object but a mystery full of potential and unimaginable possibilities, as every egg is. Since Humpty is not an object, we know that Humpty is far greater than might be perceived at first glance—that the energies and vibrations that Humpty gives off may extend in many, many directions. An egg after all is the beginning of something or someone. Who is this person who is in embryonic form in the person of Humpty Dumpty? Better, who *are* some of the persons Humpty reminds us of?

Humpty Dumpty as World Egg

Humpty Dumpty is a patent reminder of the oneness of our world and of its interdependence, for Humpty is clearly *one* egg and not several. We are dealing here with not only a sort of mystical intuition that one might expect from a mystic but with the convergence of mystical *and* scientific visions as one gets in the biologist Lewis Thomas. Thomas states that the world, seen from the perspective from which the astronauts photographed it, is alive. "Viewed from the distance of the moon, the astonishing thing about the earth, catching the breath, is that it is alive . . . the rising earth, the only exuberant thing in this part of the cosmos." It is alive like an organism is alive, organized and interconnected, a truly interconnected, a truly mystical body. "It has the organized, self-contained look of a live creature, full of information, marvelously skilled in handling the sun." Lewis' favorite analogy for the earth is that it is a cell. "It is *most* like a single cell." For it does what cells do. It carries on life. "We should credit it for what it is: for sheer size and perfection of function, it is far and away the grandest product of collaboration in all of nature. It breathes for us . . ." [3] Bentov agrees, for if not only energy and matter but also consciousness and matter are exchangeable, then, our planet lives. "Matter contains or *is* consciousness . . . If this is the case, then our planet must be a very large being! And the sun an even larger one." [4] And Blair declares that "the earth is a mysterious, living being." (53)

Humpty invites us to consider the world as an egg—a whole system, as something greater than the mere sum of its parts, as a miracle bigger than—and more fragile than—a machine. Its operation implies what Buckminster Fuller calls the "synergy" or system-behavior and not merely parts behaving on one another. A world egg is one, but systematically so and designedly so. There is order to such an egg. And Humpty also lays bare the truth of the frailty of such an egg. For Humpty is nothing if not a vulnerable, a broken and potentially irredeemably broken world egg. Humpty is a microcosm of our macrocosm. The egg of our Egg.

Much more is implied in Humpty as world egg. First, there is the interconnection among numerous cultures' explanations of the origins of the universe, for the myth of the egg is found in Egyptian, Finnish, Druid, Persian, Indian, Chinese, Phoenician and Greek myths. In the Vedas, the world grows out of an egg that is divided, one half becoming the earth and the other half the heavens. The sun is the embryo of the egg. Such a doctrine is a startling reminder of the interconnectedness of all things, of the basic unity of our cosmos that is even bigger than world egg, the cosmic egg. Birth, then, is implied in the egg myths. And rebirth and resurrection. As all birth does, the egg implies what Robert Graves calls, "infinite potentiality" waiting to hatch out. [5] Like Easter eggs at Easter time, the hatching depends on the sun to do its warming work and bring about a new birth, just as the sun in fact hatches the eggs of snakes. Apparently in his vulnerability is the fact that Humpty was in no sense of the word a hard-boiled egg.

Woman is related to the Egg of the World in a special way. "The egg of the world is associated with the feminine principle," says one commentator. [6] The mother as All-Giver is implied in the World-Egg story. The mother goddesses of the Chaldeans, Greeks, Scandinavians, Hindus and Chinese take their stand on the myth that the origin of both the earth and moon "was a World Egg, the moon, which split in two parts, one remaining in the sky as moon and the other becoming the earth." Thus the "first World Egg *was* the mother from whom all things come" and the "earth is but a part of the great cosmic World Egg."[7] What is at stake here is, as Harding points out, a psychic truth—that birth without motherhood and eggs, of which mothers are something akin to experts, is not possible. No wonder the entire male retinue of all the king's horses and men were so stymied by how to save Humpty!

There is also implied in the Humpty Dumpty myth an entire story about dualism—we have seen this hinted at in the separation creation myths we have just considered. The Egyptians report that the universe was conceived "in the hour of the Great One of the dual force."[8] Perhaps it is because egg implies dualism that it is so fragile and vulnerable—or vice versa—and so subject to breaking. Perhaps the wall from which Humpty fell so tragically was the wall of dualisms. It was the compulsion to Either/Or reality that made the whole, the synergy, collapse into pieces and call out for salvation and holness. In other words, as both Meister Eckhart in the 14th century and Mary Daly in the 20th century suggest, original sin is not that original after all, but it is in fact our fall into separateness and dualisms. And the only healing is a recovery of the neglected side of our psyches on the one hand—named, for lack of a better one, the 'feminine'—i.e. the non-kingly, non-horsey side—and the recovery of dialectical perception on the other. Without this dialected perception we will only substitute a new wall for the old one, an equally demonic dualism to replace the one that has proven to be so violent toward Humpty already.

The Global Village as the New Mandala

God has laid an egg. A beautiful, delicate, organic, developing and life-filled egg. It is our home. We call it the global village. The global village is the new name for the world egg. Unlike any generation to precede us, we have taken a look at its beauty—in our times there has occurred an unprecedented breakthrough in our awareness and appreciation of the world egg. That breakthrough is in the form of photographs taken by astronauts miles from our global village. What we see through this picture no human beings in the entire history of the world have ever seen before. It is the oneness, the unity, the harmony and balance of our global village. It is truly a new mandala, this picture we all share of the globe on which we live. The word "mandala" comes from the Sanskrit word for circle or center.[10] A mandala is a sacred circle which is meant to heal us, make us whole and as holy as we truly are. Blair points out that DNA, the basis of all life, forms a mandala when it is seen from the top. DNA is a flat representation of a spiral.[11] There are many mandalas in our lives—atoms, the eye, the body, flowers, etc. To meditate on a mandala is to get in touch quite literally with our roots as living organisms since every cell is a mandala. Easterners and Westerners alike have recognized the power of mandala meditations. Long before C.J. Jung recovered the mandala as a device for therapeutic wholeness-making, our medieval ancestors displayed mandalas in the Rose windows of the Gothic cathedrals. These stained glass windows, in all their living, vibrating colors, were circular and symmetrical mandalas that were capable of rendering us sacred once again.

In the new mandala of the Global village we are—all of us—regardless of race, sex, religion, invited to sacred worship once again. It is a common worship of our sacred planet, our global village. And, like any true mandala, this global village is not merely 'out there' but is in us at the same time that we are in it.

Since, as we have seen previously, worship does not mean looking up but celebrating, the sacred celebration of the new mandala of the global village binds us all. In this sense it is the true religion of our time (religion being derived from the words *re-ligare*, to bind back) that calls us to bonding and to binding no matter what particular spiritual tradition and way we journey. For the issue of the preservation of this divinely made mandala, this global village, is a universal issue today. Some scientists feel it is already too late to change both our ways and the deadly direction the mandala is headed in. Others, like Buckminster Fuller, give us seven more years to change ourselves and our directions. Whatever the truest guess be, it is evident that time is rapidly running out or already has run out. Powerful negative energies are converging on our mandala. As Rosemary Ruether has put it, "all the crises of history are converging: racism, sexism, colonialism, the technological depletion of the earth." [12] Compassion understood in the critical and structural way we have defined it in this book is the only way out. It is the only glue for our cracking mandala.

It is for this reason that compassion is *not* altruistic but is a matter of the fullest self-interest. For we are all alike in our pain and we will suffer equally if the mandala self-destructs. As Paul warned: "All of you are Christ's body, and each one is part of it . . . If one part of the body suffers, all the other parts suffer with it" (1 Cor. 12.26f.). We love others *as* we love ourselves, and if we wish our own survival, then we wish others' survival and work to make it happen. This is not altruism—it is love, self-love and other-love. It is compassion, compassion toward others *and* compassion toward self and compassion toward the precarious world egg, lately named the global village. In a village interdependency becomes the basic law of life. It alone will preserve life. In such a situation of group survival there is no time for the trivial morality of philanthropy that altruism implies. For what Humpty reminds us is that without creative compassion the global village will perish; we will perish; God, insofar as God fully loves the global village and us, will perish. Perhaps it is this sense of necessity that will—finally—urge humanity to what it was meant to be: harmonious dancers of Sarah's circle, sharers of the good earth, creators all, justice-makers in interdependent political and economic systems, intelligent searchers of the universe, divine images of the Creator. Perhaps it will urge us to the true meaning of bonding, binding and religion which Silvano Arieti puts this way: "religion can be seen from its origin as a set of cognitive constructs that prolong hope in the survival of the individual and of the small social group to which he belongs. Later, of course, hope is expanded further and embraces the survival of the tribe, state, nation, or human race; or it is focused on the eternal survival (immortality) of at least a part of the individual (soul), or on general human progress and so on." [13] Humpty Dumpty beckons us from hope in the soul's survival to hope in the global village's survival and back again, as we shall see.

Humpty Dumpty as Cosmic Egg

Once one enters into the symbol of the World Egg, one cannot stop there, for every microcosm leads to its macrocosm. And so, in discussing Humpty Dumpty as World Egg, we have already alluded to Humpty as Cosmic Egg.

Bentov proposes the egg as the proper model of our universe since "the flow of matter in it resembles very much the shape of the electrical fields around a seed or an egg." The seed or egg represent potentiality, the gradual unfolding of an altered and more expanded consciousness, that emerges from its "meditative, hibernating state" and unfolds when the time is ripe. (115) To conceive of the cosmos as an egg is to understand it as ordered and not as chaos. Indeed, cosmos (from Greek *Kosmos*) *means* order. If order or kosmos is what the universe is, then chaos is driven out. Cosmos implies interconnections everywhere. The universe of such an egg is an organic and interdependent one—not a chaotic struggle between isolated independencies. A cosmos would mean that we are truly "part of a highly integrated system in the broadest sense of the word"—which is what contemporary science is teaching us. (Bentov, 43) Such a universe detects "a universal 'homeostasis', a dynamic equilibrium in which we are all integral cells: to 'interfere' with this at any point is literally to harm one's self." (Blair, 127) The law of a cosmos, as distinct from a chaos, is a synergy or a "system-behaviour" as opposed to "part-behavior." [14] Ours is a holistic, not a piece-meal universe. One egg, not many. In cosmos, as opposed to chaos, "we begin to sense . . . that our own individual feelings are part of the musical movements of the cosmos, and that we are one and the same Leviathan of Life." (Blair, 71) One egg. Very much alive.

Still another insight is implied in Humpty as World Egg and Cosmic Egg. J.E. Cirlot reports that implicit in the egg symbolism is also an appreciation of space—as distinct from place I would suggest—that lies at the center of things. The symbolic center that is implied in the architecture of cave temples or mountain caves or of domes is a matter of "the space at the center of things" that in turn is identified with "the ancient symbol of the 'world egg.' " (p. 16) A primary belief in an external form such as the pillar or menhir or omphalos is balanced by a belief in the internal form of emptiness as a primary force for creativity. The Fall of Humpty, then, is also a fall into externals and superficials and away from centering, spacefulness and fruitful nothingness. Authentic compassion implies an emptying and nothingness experience in order that the cosmos might truly be taken in, ingested, and not merely projected or even objectively treated as an outside object. Nothingness, then, lies at the very center and at the center-space experience of both the egg and of interrelations among the egg's energies. Perhaps, as Bentov suggests, the so-called "black holes" of space or the space within space is merely the obverse side of creation. White holes of creative fecundity depend on black holes, as fullness depends on emptiness.

Buckminster Fuller was once asked in a radio interview: "How do you get in contact with the Universe?" and his reply was: "You must get on the same frequency." [15] We need to "tune in," he insists, to what is cosmic and not merely world, or in his terms, to what is universe and not merely environment. He defines his terms this way: "By universe I mean: The aggregate of all of humanity's apprehended and communicated experiences." (15) A "scenario Universe" demands "a lot of sequence" and will not be possible with a mere "single frame affair." (17) In other words, our universe is growing with the growth in the knowledge of our universe. The egg, one might say, is as large as the boundaries of what we know—as large as our horizons. The egg then is more than an egg and much more than an object—it is a reflection of our consciousness, it is the parameter of our souls, it is as big—and as small—as we are. Thus Fuller actually defines universe as consciousness when he says: "Environment to each must be all that is that isn't me. Universe in turn must be, all that isn't me, and me." (18) Environment is the space in which we live; universe is that plus the space that lives in us. Humpty Dumpty becomes, then, an edge, a horizon of our consciousness and therefore the universe. And Humpty Dumpty also becomes the new word for soul.

HUMPTY DUMPTY AND THE SEARCH FOR THE HUMAN EGG OR SOUL

Is Humpty Dumpty dead? Apparently not. For the King's horses and the king's men came to put him together again and not to bury him. There is some life in the old fellow yet. Like a seed, though it die to the ground, it lives in another form, potentially speaking at least. What is evident, however, is that Humpty, being in so many irredeemable pieces, appears close to death and, with the failure of the kingly men to reconstitute him, his hopes of revival appear slim indeed. We might say that Humpty is on the edge of death, which is also to be on the edge of life. He is hovering between this life and the next, if there be a next, between mortality and immortality, between The End and The Beginning. There are very good reasons, as we shall see, why Humpty is so close to the edge. In some ways he *is* the edge, our edge.

Humpty Dumpty as the Edge

The word "egg" as a verb comes from the word for "edge" (ecg) in Old English. To "egg on" is to "edge on." There is even a connection between egg as noun and edges. A special dimension to an egg is that it lacks edges. You *lay* an egg, but eggs, of all beasties in the world, never *lie* in any predictable way. They have no identifiable edge on which to lie. It is, one might say, edge-less. How important is it to spiritual consciousness that Humpty Dumpty reminds us of edge and of edge-lessness? It is *all* important to spiritual consciousness for spirituality, the act of waking up, is an act of resisting the boundaries and edges that society has given us and that we sense are in fact making us edgy. Spirituality is learning to live on the edge without being edgy; to dare to live on the edge without hedging. When we use the term "egg on" we are employing an ancient use of the word edge— thus the edge eggs us on and invites us to balance sharply over its cutting edge. This demands utter wakefulness indeed—which is what all spirituality is about. Perhaps Humpty fell because the wall of dualism on which he sat so comfortably was *not* egging him on but was in fact making him sleepy and comfortable and fat and lazy. Maybe he fell because he was *not* pushed, not coaxed, not challenged, not opened up to his possible potential of unlimited horizons and universes.

William James suggests that the core of spiritual experience known as conversion is in fact an act of making the marginal central. Making the edge the center is the very heart of every religious experience and perhaps of every true spiritual teaching. Making compassion the center has been what this book is all about. Filling the void created by the flight from compassion with compassion. Filling the hole created by the divine absence with divinity. For compassion is very much on the edge of our society's energies and its remaining there is breaking up Humpty Dumpty—World Egg and Cosmic Egg. An important dimension to any true edge and any true egging on that deserves to be called spiritual is the fact that edge is not grabbable. For edge is not an object but a relation between interconnected realities. As the poet has put it:

The sun of poems is on the snow
    on the slope past the wood
to the pond.[16]

Edge is the horizon or what lies between the snow and the sky, between the snow and the slope, between here and there, between all and nothing, between God and us. As long as we remain materialists, that is people who think in subject/object or 'thing' terms, we will never be edge-people; therefore we will never be egged on or egg on others. We will remain spirit-less people, boring people, and sure to fall as Humpty did from our seemingly secure and comfortable walls of dualism. Which are in fact walls of edge-lessness. Barriers of boredom.

Humpty Dumpty as edge invites us to marginal living and to active harmonizing with the earth, air, fire and waters of our lives. He invites us to the edge where all interconnected or compassionate living thrives. He invites us to become edge-conscious and edge-hungry. To leave the middle, the boring, muddled, dualistic middle in search of a center—which center will have to be ingested from the edge. Like

roots of a tree that always seek an edge, we are invited to stretch ourselves to the edge to make it our center. And with this stretching will
come aliveness, Spirit and rebirth. Indeed, Humpty's story suggests
that perhaps people are edgy because they sense that they, sitting on
the wall of dualisms, have no roots or true center. We become on edge
and not on the edge. We are afraid to create and give encouragement
or courage to one another to create. For all creation eggs us on to the
edge . . . of birth and death, for example. Our fear of living and our
fear of dying keep us on the wall and thoroughly insecure, as any ladder dynamic is sure to do. We, like Humpty, could fall any time and
we know it.

The edge in Humpty Dumpty also brings to mind the edges of
history and how thoroughly we are part of those edges today. We
sense, consciously or unconsciously, that a certain spiritual era has
ended. We sense the loss of a past edge. The edge of past spiritualities
has become blunted and dull to many if not all of us. We announce
this dullness in phrases like "God is dead," "Churches are empty," or
"religious vocations are declining." But what we are really saying is
that yesterday's edge has grown so dull that no one is egged on any
more by it. There is little sharpness, brightness or illumination in
these dulled and dusty religious forms. We are edge-less. For the Constantinian era is dead and Neoplatonism is dead and Cartesian efforts
to buttress up faith are dead and the Christian faith insofar as it has
been known through these cultural patterns in the now dead-age of
pisces is dead. Some are scurrying to the East, others to the pagan
West, still others to a wandering agnosticism or hollow reutterance of
Christian formulas.

But to be at the edge of a dying and dulled spiritual era is also to
be at the edge of an emerging one. We live in a time of rare privilege:
a time when new edges and new horizons and new possibilities are
egging us on. If only we would, as Fuller recommends, tune into them
and get on their frequencies. If only we would truly, deeply and cen-
teredly "listen to the signs of our times." But to do this we need to
be edge-hungry people for we need the courage to leap what is not
a "leap of faith," as Kierkegaard saw it, but a leap from one edge to
another. From a wall to no wall at all. From dualism to dialectic. From
Either/Or to Both/And. From contemplation to compassion. From I to
We. From ladder to circle; from climbing to dancing; from control to
celebration; from Newton to Einstein; from Wealth of Nations economics to Poverty of the Globe economics; from home as nation to home
as global village.

In talking of edge, of universe, of consciousness, as we necessarily have been in talking of Humpty Dumpty, we are also talking of soul. Perhaps soul means edge. If we stand between two spiritual eras and two spiritual edges, then we also stand before a new meaning of soul. And a leaving of a former meaning for soul. We are leaving a dulled and dead understanding of soul and searching for a new one, one that truly eggs us on to become something greater and more divine. Every era that stretches to new spiritual horizons necessarily redefines the term "soul."

The History of the Meaning to 'Soul'

The word "soul" has a long and involved history that is itself a reflection of who humanity has thought it was and what it wanted to become through the ages. As Elmar Klinger has put it, "the coming-to-be of the soul is the substantial mirror of the coming-to-be of the finite world." [17] I would like to attempt a brief outline of the meaning of soul through history in order to better analyze what Humpty's fall might suggest for the meaning of soul in our time.

Otto Rank defines soul at one point as the "power of rebirth." Soul is the quest for edges, for immortality in the face of mortality, for the divine in the face of the all-too-human, for beauty in the face of dullness, for truth in the face of superficiality and cover-up, for depth in the face of shallowness. Rank believes that the Greek quest for soul reached its summit (and its demise) when the soul was localized with the head. When "the head became both the seat of the soul and of the highest human faculties—then, indeed, the culture culminated. Everything that was chthonian and animal was banished to the depths of Orcus to make way for the spiritual head-culture which appears personified in the works of Athenian poets, orators, and sculptors and later in their portrait busts." [18]

Gnosticism, lacking any saving grace or traces with cosmic thinking, reduced this head-culture to an understanding of soul that hates the "stinking body." [19] Soul for the gnostic tradition was the power that is lost to matter (Jonas, 222). Soul, a third principle torn between Spirit and Chaos, becomes easily immersed in the latter (67). Its only way out is to ascend and to climb up, up and away from all hint of matter, earth, nurturing. Thus the elaborate schemas developed for the *"ascent* of the soul" in gnostic traditions and even in Christian spiritualities that borrowed more than they thought from gnosticism. Indeed, it was Western mysticism that kept this portion of gnostic myth alive long after the disappearance of Gnosticism itself. It was kept alive in Neoplatonic and monastic mysticism, Jonas points out. (166) "The real *conceptual* elaboration of the whole idea of an inner ascent ending in mystical ecstasis, and its articulation into psychologically definable stages, was the work of no other than Plotinus and the Neoplatonic school after him . . . and, slightly later, of the monastic mystics of eastern Christianity (where the theoretical basis was derived from Origen)." (286) What was the result? Brown points out that sublimation in the quest of a soul produces "a displacement upward of the genital function." [20] The end of ladder climbing for the sake of soul-ascending would mean the end of sublimation as the basic spirituality of the West.

What made the tradition of ascent so profoundly introverted among Gnostics was its utter lack of cosmic awareness and concern—a flight from the universe that Plotinus, to his credit, severely castigated the Gnostics for preaching. The Gnostic God was an acosmic God and the Gnostic soul was an acosmic soul. "The stars too have souls" insisted Plotinus, yet the Gnostics who call "even the basest men" brothers refuse kinship with the universe. "With frenzied mouth they declare the sun, the stars in the heavens, and even the world-soul, unworthy to be called by them brothers." [21] Thus we see that a partial saving grace to Neoplatonic spirituality was its insistence on a cosmic connection between the soul and other aspects of creation—a connection that the Gnostics utterly rejected.

In this regard, it is of considerable interest to pose a question that will need still more investigating: to what extent is the scientism that isolated humanity from nature, and now the exaggerated Personalism that continues this isolation, in fact a mere repeat of Gnosticism in our day? Is compassion so dead because Gnosticism is still so popular? Is the fear of solitude, of space, of suspended time, of silence, of aloneness that so characterizes much of secular culture today a species of gnostic dread of chaos and of dread itself? Has the search for soul run into the dead-end that gnosticism once fell into?

Jewish and Christian faith contributed substantially to a new vision of soul. Christianity, as Rank points out, "democratized the immortal soul, which before had been the prerogative of kings, heroes, or creative people (artists)." (156). It was this democratization of soul that accounted for the artistic renaissances within Christianity. The Jewish, Biblical tradition, that assured believers that the universe is a cosmos and not a chaos also encouraged the quest for soul and for rebirth. Liberation in such a context does not mean liberation from the earth or from this world, as in Gnostic belief, but liberation from all that interferes with birth and rebirth. Liberation from Egypt as the symbol of slavery. Instead of an ascent of the soul to a God who is high above the earth, the deepest Biblical tradition of both Judaism and Christianity preaches the transparency of God.[22] "The Spirit of the Lord fills the whole world," shouts the Psalmist, and it is this sense of realized eschatology or of the edge already beginning—eternal life now and soul now—that Christianity, when it is not tainted by Gnosticism through Neoplatonism, teaches. This personalized panentheism is not guilty of that exaggerated personal*ism* that characterizes gnosticisms of old and of late.

In the Hebrew, Biblical tradition "the soul is the man. Indeed we should not say that man *has* a soul, but that he *is* a soul; nor consequently that he has a body, but that he is a body." [23] A living person is called "soul" (*nepes*) or "flesh" (*basar*) in Hebrew. What is distinguished in Biblical thought is *not* body and soul, but rather the living soul called human beings and the living spirit called God. In other words, soul and spirit are distinguishable but not soul and body. Sometimes God's spirit resides in human beings and sometimes it is absent. A person's spirit or *pneuma* is the divine within that person. Unfortunately, this notion of soul as person and spirited person as divine image and likeness has never played a very dominant role in the West.

In fact, until recently most translations of the Bible rendered the Hebrew word *nepes* as "soul" and a Greek eisegesis was performed on this word which, in fact, "reflects none of these ideas" of Greek understanding of soul. *Nepes* means the human person as he or she begins to live; "it is the self precisely as personal, as the conscious subject of action and passion . . . Consciousness is life, the manifestation of the *nepes*" and "can be signified by no single word in modern languages." The New Testament word, *psyche*, also shows "little or no effect of Greek philosophical concepts" and the New Testament "adds nothing to the Old Testament conception of *nepes*." By projecting Greek concepts of soul unto either of these two Biblical words, believers risk rendering the concept of salvation and eternal life into Platonic categories. It is in this context that the Bible says a unique thing about "soul": "The novelty of the New Testament belief does not arise from a new idea of the *nepes-psyche*, but from a radically new revelation of the meaning of life and salvation." [24] This radical new meaning of salvation is in fact the omnipresence of compassion and the nearness of human and divine compassion, the reality of the Creator's compassion and the compassion of those made in the Creator's image and likeness, the dependence of God upon humanity's compassionate alteration of human history. In this tradition Meister Eckhart declares, "just as I can do almost nothing without God, so God can accomplish nothing apart from me." History—salvation history—waits on humanity's becoming more compassionate, more in tune with the Spirit of the Lord that "fills the whole world" (Wis. 1.7).

Much of Christian theology fell under the strong influence of Neoplatonic philosophies concerning the "soul" and salvation and became introverted in the process and looked forward to immortality and life after death with greater zeal than it looked forward to the initiation of eternal life and compassion before death. It is interesting that Plato was far less involved in withdrawal and introspection than were the Neoplatonists; it was the ladder who most influenced Christianity. The "shift of emphasis from the outer world to the inner world is clearly seen in the Neoplatonism of Plotinus (205–270). Plato, like all the Greeks, was supremely interested in action, politics, and the external world . . . Plotinus, on the other hand, saw mystical contemplation and absorption in the One as an end in itself. Psychology therefore became harnessed to the exploration and mapping of inner experience."[26]

In the Middle Ages the rediscovery of Aristotle, especially as utilized by Thomas Aquinas, served as an antidote to the excessively subjected and introverted notion of soul that the Neoplatonists had dealt with. Aquinas rejected the Platonic theory of a person using a body and followed Aristotle's notion that the soul was the form of the body. Aquinas did not sacrifice the notion of *spirit* as passion, motion and vulnerability as rationalism has done in the modern era, however.[26] Yet, his world view was static and his understanding of realized eschatology was underdeveloped, and so he lost touch with Aristotle's sense of the soul's striving for a final end in this life, not in another.

The most important contribution of any civilization's quest for a meaning to soul invariably comes from those artists of experience whom the Middle Ages called mystics. Thus, for example, both Meister Eckhart and Julian of Norwich, writing in the fourteenth century and at the end of Medieval civilization, venture into a quest for a new language and a new meaning for 'soul.' Their quest was in many ways aborted, however, with Eckhart's condemnation (1328) and the virtual ignoring of Julian's spirituality and with the onslaught of nationalism, colonial expansionism, religious sectarianism, rationalism, scientism, industrialism, and modern materialism the quest for soul was effectively laid aside. In many ways this book takes up where Eckhart and Julian left off—only this time from the perspective of the felt demise of contemporary, modern culture. Today's recovery of interest in Western mystical writers— Eckhart and Julian in particular—parallels a growing awareness of our deeply-felt need for a new sense of soul.

What most characterized the modern era's grasping for a meaning of soul was the reduction of the concept to a purely subjective, private and mental activity. For Descartes, since body is machine, people are souls that are bodiless. The soul was *res cogitans* as distinct from *res extensa*. Like Plato, Descartes posited soul as distinct substance weighed down by body, saying, "our soul is in its nature entirely independent of the body." From his time on, "Western thought fell victim to a dualism of body and soul hitherto unknown" and soul was now considered exclusively as subjectivity. [27] Like all dualists, Descartes identified soul and spirit with the predictable result that rationalism, while enthroning reason, reduced spirit to an abstraction. Spirit now meant spiritualism: "A simple and massive body-soul dualism leads to the indentification of spirit and soul and announces the basic element of spiritualism." [28] Soul now became overly mental and highly privatized, so that since Descartes privacy became the keystone to psychological theories. "This stress on privacy as a hallmark of the mental was a far cry from Aristotle's view of soul as characterized by a self-originating tendency to pursue an end." [29]

Krister Stendahl has spoken out on the privatized consequences of the "soul game" in Christianity.

> In the Christian tradition, . . . we have played the 'soul game,' transforming practically all of the immense and ferocious drama of history that we read about in the Bible into the kind of pastoral counseling and consolation in which God's mercy overcomes the fear of judgment. That way of plowing such concepts under, and of applying overpowering and majestic words *to the intricacies of our little souls* has been one of the elements in what Bonhoeffer rightly called 'cheap grace,' and in what Marx and others rightly recognized as the 'opiate of the people.' (KS, p. 98, italics mine.)

One thinks, in reading these comments, of the definition of Christian ministry that prevailed for centuries as "the saving of souls."

Thus the modern contribution to the quest for soul as represented by Descartes for example, has been essentially the privatization of the soul. Like Gnosticism of old, soul came to mean something more and more subjective, more and more removed from the body, body politic and body cosmic. Privacy, not public purpose, was now the basis of mental activity. "Descartes' theory in this respect marked the culmination of a trend that can be traced back through St. Augustine and Plotinus to Philo" (Peters, p. 7).

HUMPTY DUMPTY AS THE NEW WORLD SOUL

The search for soul and its meaning continues into our own time. Charles Fair has written a book on his conviction that the soul is dying in our civilization. Humpty Dumpty dead, we might say. "It is always," he points out, "at the end of civilizations that notions of the soul begin to disintegrate" and with this disintegration the bonding myths that keep us with one another. I agree, though I also insist that, correlatively, it is at the beginning of new civilizations that new understandings of soul egg us on. Fair offers his own definition of soul: "There lay in all of us a further self, ready to be saved, dragged up by stern effort out of the perennial dark: in short, a soul." He senses the egg-like quality of the soul, namely its potentiality. "It corresponds to something potential in all of us—which is to say, potential ultimately in the structure and working principles of the human brain. It owes its hold, as an idea, to the fact that it releases new energies in us; not fancied powers, but real ones, even though in fact only a few ever came into full possession of them." And it is the emergence of a new notion of soul, he maintains, that gives birth to the rise of great civilizations. Soul, then, urges us on because of its being an egg so full of mysterious yet coiled new energies. "The idea of the soul appears in particular to those who are ready and eager to realize themselves but have not yet done so—men who sense but have not experienced 'transcendence.'" [30] A new meaning of soul, then, implies a new meaning to transcendence. Soul undergoes a re-definition when transcendence does. Atheism, for Fair, would mean denial of the soul, that is of all hope at transcendence. It would, I suppose, mean the refusal to come to Humpty Dumpty's aid.

Fair is not alone in his search for soul today. C.G. Jung's book, *Modern Man in Search of a Soul*, puts the issue bluntly in its title alone. Dr. J. Hillman, director of the Jungian Institute in Zurich, offers a kind of examination of the soul each day as sane therapy for our times. We should ask ourselves daily not "What happened today?"—as the news does for us so glibly—but rather, "What happened to the soul today?" This examination will assist in purifying our memories and putting us in healthy contact with our past and our origins, he suggests.[31] To reflect on the title of Jung's book is to awaken to the possibility that we do not have a soul. A soul that is truly human, i.e. compassionate, is something that needs to be carved, discovered, given birth to. Poet Robert Bly has spoken eloquently of the ancient tradition that teaches that the proper recipe for soul-making is spirit (masculine principle) plus body (feminine principle) and that only the marriage of the two will yield a soul. The equation might look as follows:

$$Body (B) + Spirit (S) > Soul$$

Bly also suggests that it is unlikely that such a holistic marriage can happen much before one is forty years old. It is an intriguing thesis for it helps to explain how soul-less so much of organized religion has become in the West and the spiritual price we have paid for too much patriarchy and our flight from body. It also underlies the immensity of the challenge that awaits those in search of a soul and a meaning for soul today.

R.D. Laing calls soul "experience," and Elmar Klinger testifies that "the key-word is now person and not soul." But Klinger's solution—which is in many ways the solution in the documents of Vatican II—runs the risk not only of abandoning the very search for soul but of abandoning the deeper meaning of this search which involves humanity's relation to *all* the cosmos and not just to other humans. It smacks precariously of the Personalism so characteristic of Gnosticism of old.

Humpty Dumpty as the Cracked World Soul

Constance Urdang has named the Global-Village crisis when she tells us that "the egg of the world is cracked." The egg of the world is indeed cracked into all the dualisms that we have dealt with in this book (and more). It is from the cracks that the poisoned tears rain upon us all. But to speak of the cracked egg and cracked edge is also to speak of the cracked soul.

This entire book has been, of course, about a new meaning to soul. A new birth of a new egg. Whose name is compassion. A soul named compassion. Such a soul would not suffer Humpty Dumpty's fate for it would not be sitting on a wall at all. First it would not be sitting as in sitting in an arm chair or sitting on the fact of 40% unemployment among minority youth or sitting on ever more horrible development of weaponry. It would be acting and dancing and urging and cajoling. Not sitting. And it would not be on a wall but off the wall, on the earth, dancing circle dances of laughter and celebration which are dances in which, if there is any falling to be done, no one is hurt and everyone easily and effortlessly assists one another. The falling is a falling *in*, as 'into the earth' or 'in love', and not a falling down or a falling from. (Jesus said his Kingdom and Queendom were not *from* this world.) Such a falling in is a fun falling. A falling in love with compassion, thus a falling in love with celebration and the sharing of celebration.

Everyone and every world has a soul—it is, as Jesus points out, wherever one's treasure is. That is our soul. Our treasure. Norman O. Brown says that money is the world's soul. (221) That may well be. For some, the ladder is their soul. Fuller has said in effect that muscle and might are today's world soul. My impression is that, in a ladder-culture that is so insecure, security becomes the culture's soul. All these souls are in fact alienating and alienated—they begin with cracks. Humpty reminds us that our soul ought to be where the crack is and where pain is. It ought to be at the edge.

Humpty Dumpty, then, extends us an invitation to a new meaning of soul—one that takes us beyond the compulsion to "save souls" or to redeem the private, individual soul. We are invited instead to enter the soul and allow soul to enter us. In this regard blacks, as oppressed groups are prone to do, have been on the cutting edge of recovering the true meaning of 'soul' which for them means spiritedness, aliveness, looseness, and capacity to celebrate and commiserate. In other words, soul as compassion. Soul in this sense is the opposite of up-tight. But the opposite of up-tight would be neither uppity nor tight and clinging. It would be Sarah circle and not ladder celebration and letting go instead of compulsion and control. We are invited from a preoccupation with redemption of an introverted and caged soul to the redemption of the world *which is itself a soul.* The world soul. The Cosmic Egg. The Universe. It is *our* soul and not merely my soul nor the soul of any isolated object whatsoever. Therefore, though vast, it is truly personable and a truly relational soul. It is a relative soul and not an absolute soul. For its salvation we might adapt an ancient prayer: "Glory be to the Father, to the Son and to the Holy Spirit as it was in the beginning, is now and ever shall be, world without *edge.* Amen." For if the world had no edge it would truly be soul-stretched to its horizons. It would become divinized with the grace of the Creator. It would be the divine soul. And it would be healed.

The Global Village: The New World Soul

Rosemary Ruether, among others, calls for a "new soul" which will comprise a "new social vision that would inspire the whole world." [32] I agree with her and I believe that Humpty Dumpty points the way to all who seek a new soul, a meaning for soul, or indeed a soul at all.

The new meaning of "soul" that Humpty Dumpty points to is world or Global Village. I propose that this is the "treasure" that the human race might share today. The Global Village is our common soul. And its survival is a matter of saving our souls. The Global Village is the New World Soul. It is a *world* soul because the whole world knows about it. Almost at once, in the current generation, a world-awareness has happened. The world-soul is a state of consciousness among the inhabitors of our planet. Technology, by its approaching the speed of light and sound through television, radio and rapid transportation has brought about the change in space-time consciousness that has unleashed a new world soul. It is not a world soul in Plato's sense or in the sense of a choice-less future for the world dictated by some outside fate. (It is the latter concept of world-soul that Christian churches have condemned for its lack of freedom and personal responsibility.) It is a world soul in the sense that interconnectedness teaches that the survival of one is the survival of all. We now know this to be the case. Compassion is a law of our universe. The new world soul will come about when we believe this law deeply enough to start acting on it. And doing it.

The New World Soul is as cracked as the Global Village itself because we do not yet believe in it. We are beginning to believe in it but we have a long way to go. Like Augustine, we want to pray, "give me belief—but not quite yet," because the responsibilities for our changing our ways are great. Buckminster Fuller says the survival of the planet is "touch and go" at this time. Barbara Ward and Rene Dubos warn that "the planet is not yet a center of rational loyalty for all mankind" and it is only this "ultimate loyalty to our single, beautiful, and vulnerable planet Earth" that gives us hope of survival.[33] The new soul and new meaning of soul is still new.

The new meaning of soul will no longer stumble on the dualism of body vs. soul where 'soul' has floundered and been dying for several centuries. Instead of the search for independent substance distinct from body, this meaning of soul will borrow from Meister Eckhart's insight that reverses the basic question. He says: "The soul is not in the body but the body is in the soul." True interdependence and not dualistic independence will characterize our new search for soul. Indeed, there is a precedent for our understanding world as soul in the thinking of Meister Eckhart who said: "The soul is called world." He also declared, as one must who has a cosmic consciousness that it is not a flight from the body, "the soul loves the body."

Our new search for soul will refuse to succumb to the era of sublimation and sexual repression; it will not look for ascents of the soul any longer. Instead, we will look for *extensions* of the soul—to become a 'world soul' and even a cosmic-souled people once again. Compassion has always been the first victim of ascent-of-soul spiritualisms, as we saw in Chapter Two. In soul-extension spiritualities, which will be consciousness-expansion spiritualities, compassion returns to human history once again. In fact, human history becomes salvation history or the history and story of compassion. The soul thus returns to its proper, nonprivate, cosmic home. The exile of soul is ended. And the exile of compassion. Humanity finds a home in the universe once again. The home is a verb, not a noun. Its name is compassion.

Religion will also return from its exile into the frivolous task of building empires or of sentimentalizing privatized lives. It will find its true origins as a way of life that heals. The word *re-ligare* means to bind back or to bind again. Religion will again mean to bind the wounds of a cracked people, a cracked world globe, a cracked world soul. It will accomplish this saving task of healing by making connections once again instead of freezing and isolating them. By re-connecting and re-binding the rift between God and humanity, which is also the rift between Spirit and soul. Thus a re-divinization of humanity will take place once again. Humanity will become spirited once again and ever so alive in order to itself heal the rift between itself and nature, itself and the planet, itself and the cosmos. Humanity as rational animal will no longer mean a dualistic rationalism but a harmonious animal (*ratio* originally meant harmony), one at its harmonious best *as* animal in search of harmony world-wide, self-wide and cosmos-wide. An animal, after all, cares profoundly about the survival of its species. A cosmic consciousness that lacks a body, as all species of Neoplatonism do, is contributing to Humpty's fall and not to Humpty's healing. At home with its own bodiliness, sensuality, and animality, as well as with its divinity, such a spirited animal will truly contribute to seeing that creation once again knows that it is filled with the spirit of God. Creation will truly dance to the divine music whose name is compassion.

HUMPTY DUMPTY AS THE DIVINE SOUL

It is no small matter that Buckminster Fuller, among others, testifies to how today's science is leading us to fuller appreciation of an intelligent Designer of this wonder-filled universe wherein no laws contradict any other laws. He confesses to being "overwhelmed" by the fact that there must be "a greater intellect operative in the Universe than that of humans." Why? Because the design of the parts of the universe all fit so workably. Our human minds actually have "access to an eternal design of the Universe" and "we are discovering a priori intellectual arrangement." (19f)

Does Humpty Dumpty, like contemporary science, also lead us to the ultimate edge whom we call God? Is Humpty Dumpty an intimation of the divine soul? Did the divine soul crack and break when Humpty fell? Is God dead if the human soul is dead, dulled, or dualistically strangled? If it is true that God suffers pain when his/her creation suffers pain, then the answer to these questions has got to be "Yes." Yes, God has known pain. And the sitting and the wailing and the dualizing that led to Humpty's fall is surely more painful to God than to Humpty, since God is more capable of pain—being more truly compassionate and sensitive—than is any other form of existence. Where Humpty lies in pieces, there also does God lie in pieces. Who will save Humpty? Who will save God? Christians would suggest that the Son of God, broken himself upon a cross, is such a saviour or healer of the divine/human pain. And that the healing comes in mending once again the broken distance between God and humanity. In short, in recognizing that Humpty is more than our souls, more than our worlds, more than our cosmos. That Humpty is also God. And when Humpty fell, God fell and was broken. Who will mend this broken God? Who will have compassion on God. And when? And how?

HUMPTY DUMPTY: THE SALVATION OF OUR SOULS: A SUMMARY

I have suggested that Humpty Dumpty, a symbol for our spiritual times, is many energies. Humpty is the divine soul broken with pain; Humpty is the human person, body and soul, in search of soul and spirit; Humpty is therefore the edge, the edge of the spirit, the horizon that calls and beckons us to divine potentials that an egg harbors; Humpty is Cosmic egg that we are now learning is an ordered, startlingly unified universe; Humpty is the World Egg, Global Village, fighting to breathe as a single organism, a unity struggling, like a newly hatched egg, to survive. The healing of the New Mandala—the Global Village known as the World Egg—takes place together with the healing of the human egg—the soul and the cosmic egg—or it does not take place at all.

All this means that Humpty Dumpty is us and more than us. Humpty is our known and our yet-to-be-known us. Humpty is our God. This is good news to a people who, like ourselves, have lost our way, lost our spirituality, and are adrift and in search of a sense of soul. It is the kind of good news that could resurrect our selves and our souls, preventing us from losing our souls. For what Humpty teaches us in our search for salvation is that what we formerly looked for in the word "soul", namely an inner substance, is today a false journey. Humpty teaches us that soul means psyche *plus* world. The world is our soul and our soul the world. That is why it is correct to say, as Monika Hellwig has put it, that the primary issue in spirituality is not redemption of the soul, but redemption of the world.[34] For we are both in the world and the world in us. To heal one is to heal the other. To redeem the one is to redeem the other. For what is the world if not a projection of our inner-selves? It is because we worship upness inside that we build skyscrapers outside. It is because we prefer aggression to gentleness inside that we invest so mightily in armaments and so punily in artists on the outside. Humpty teaches us how the inside is the outside and the outside is the inside. For better or for worse . . . until death do us part.

In the past in the West we have searched for a soul too inwardly, thus becoming myopically introspective and withdrawn from the cosmos.[35] And we have also searched for soul too much as a noun or a substance, thanks to the noun-like definitions of the search set up by Plato and reinforced by Neo-platonists like Augustine and mechanists like Descartes. But Humpty reminds us by his tragic fall that soul is not a noun but a verb—it is energies all interacting with one another. Soul, like the universe and the global village and the world and cosmic eggs and God, is a verb and not a noun. Good news, this. For in learning to dance our way to the edge and to soul once again as being outside and inside, as being verb and not noun, we may in fact do something about the poisoned tears that rain over Jakarta and all cities today. For the egg of our world is cracked indeed. The crack in the world egg, like the cracks in Humpty Dumpty, are reminders of the price we have paid for our fall into worshipping Jacob's ladder, dualistic competition, sterility, mechanistic scientism, and a nationalistic economic system.

But the hopeful news from Humpty Dumpty is this: that the soul we look for now has a home. Its home address is Compassion. Christianity, which once democratized the immortal soul, is now being called upon to contribute to the democratizing of the world soul or global village. Not to make it immortal but to make it interdependent—which may in the long run prove to be, by its beauty, a sort of immortality. This democratizing of the global village does not stop short of its economic systems. Indeed, all the religions of the world are called upon in these times to re-invite their global citizens to ways of living that are Spirit-filled in their devotion to celebration and the sharing of celebration by way of justice. That is, filled with compassion.

The alternative to this homecoming for the world soul is an un-imaginable and almost unmentionable option—but one that needs to be considered and meditated upon. With the times so pressing and the stakes so urgent, we cannot afford not to imagine the unmention-able alternative to compassion. What if it is indeed too late for the global village to survive? Poet Adrienne Rich has written what might be the proper epitaph for a global village that, out of lack of compassion, extinguishes itself. Is it possible that, in reading this epitaph before our funeral, we might postpone that extinction? Reading it would mean changing our lives and ways to being compassionate ones. Rich says:

> I would have loved to live in a world
> of women and men gaily
> in collusion with green leaves, stalks,
> building mineral cities, transparent domes,
> little huts of woven grass
> each with its own pattern—
> a conspiracy to coexist
> with the Crab Nebula, the exploding
> universe, the Mind—[36]

Is it possible that this epitaph may someday be preached to the universe? What does faith and hope say to that? Maybe indeed there is no putting Humpty together again. No salvation of the global village. If that be the case, if it is already too late after so brief a breath of human existence on this globe, then God would indeed have been a failure. God's unpredictable experiment of making an animal and pouring the divine image and likeness and potential for creativity into it—this egg that God has laid—has failed. So be it. A foolish, dangerous experiment that went up in smoke and poisoned tears. So be it. The universe might still survive without us.

But why did it fail, we would like to ask? My only response can be: because we did not believe it. We did not believe that we were creators, free to celebrate our global village with new visions of economic and political justice and distribution of the earth's good gifts.

Free to let go of our ladders, for instance, to let be and let the dialectic happen. Free to celebrate. We did not believe that heaven had begun. And fullness. And divinity—our own. The news was too good. It was Too Good News. And so it had to fail.

NOTES

PREFACE

[1] Rev. W. Sterling Cary, "Why They Remember the Holocaust," in *Chicago Sun-Times*, April 11, 1978, Section on "The Holocaust," p. 12.

[2] Robert Coles, "Lost Generation," *The New York Review of Books*, September 28, 1978, p. 50. His essay reviews Ned O'Gorman's book, *The Children Are Dying* (NY: Signet, 1978).

[3] Simone Weil, *Waiting on God* (London: Fontana, 1959), p. 116.

[4] Samuel H. Dressner, *Prayer, Humility and Compassion* (Philadelphia: Jewish Publ. Society, 1957), pp. 236f. Abbreviated D hereafter.

[5] Thomas Aquinas, *Super II Cor.*, ch. XI, 6; Abraham J. Heschel, *The Prophets* (NY: Harper and Row, 1962), p. 143.

[6] Matthew Fox and Kyra Kenny, *Meditations with Meister Eckhart* (1979); Matthew Fox, "Meister Eckhart and Karl Marx: The Mystic as Political Theologian," *Listening* (Fall, 1978), pp. 233–257; Matthew Fox, "Meister Eckhart on the 4-Fold Journey in a Creation-Centered Spirituality," in Matthew Fox, ed., *Western Spirituality: Historical Roots, Ecumenical Roots* (Notre Dame: Fides-Claretian Press, 1979).

CHAPTER ONE

[1] "Abraham Joshua Heschel Last Words: An Interview by Carl Stern," *Intellectual Digest* (June, 1973), p. 78.

[2] Frederick S. Perls, "Gestalt Therapy: Retroflection, Introjection, and Projection," *The Handbook of Gestalt Therapy*, Hatcher *et. al.*, eds. (NY: Jason Aronson, 1976), pp. 98f.

[3] Max Scheler, *The Nature of Sympathy* (Hamden, Ct.: Shoestring Press, Inc., 1973), pp. 138, 136.

[4] "Pity," in *The Universal Jewish Encyclopedia*, Isaac Landmon, ed. (NY: KTAV Publishers, 1969), VIII, p. 547.

[5] R. Brouillard, "Compassion," in *Catholicisme*, (Paris: Letovzey et Are, 1949), II, col. 1417.

[6] Francis Rapp, "La Compassion: Le culte du Christ douloroux," in *L'Eglise et la vie religieuse en occident à la fin du moyen age* (Paris: PUF, 1971), p. 148.

[7] Anne Douglas, *The Feminization of American Culture* (NY: Knopf, 1977), p. 254. Based on Douglas' analysis, I treat the "Seven Sins of Sentimentalism" in Matthew Fox, "On Desentimentalizing Spirituality," *Spirituality Today* (March 1978), pp. 64–76. Cf. Shirley C. Guthrie, Jr. "The Narcissism of American Piety: The Disease and the Cure," *The Journal of Pastoral Care* (Dec., 1977), pp. 220–229. *Baker's Dictionary of Theology*, Everett Harrison, ed. (Grand Rapids, Michigan: Baker Book House, 1969), says: "The Bible shows a preference for the use of the verb form rather than the noun" in speaking of compassion. (p. 132).

[8] Friedrich Nietzsche, *Anti-Christ* (London: T.N. Foulis, 1911), pp. 131, 134.

[9] Kazoh Kitamori, *Theology of the Pain of God* (Richmond, Va.: John Knox Press, 1965), p. 98. Abbreviated K hereafter.

[10] E.R. Achtemeir, "Mercy," *Interpreter's Dictionary of the Bible*, (NY: Abingdon Press, 1962), III, p. 353.

[11] Jose Miranda, *Being and the Messiah* (Maryknoll, NY: 1977), pp. 97f.

[12] For example, Rom. 12.13; Eph. 4.32; Col. 3.12; James 3.17; 1 Pet. 3.8; 1 Jn. 3.17; Mt. 9.13; 18.32f.; 2 Cor. 9. 6-13.

[13] Jose Miranda, *Marx and the Bible* (Maryknoll, NY: 1974), p. 61. Abbreviated hereafter as M.

[14] Claude Tresmontant, *A Study of Hebrew Thought* (NY: Desclee, 1960), p. 130.

[15] Hans Jonas, *The Gnostic Religion* (Boston: Beacon Press, 1963), p. 141.

[16] William Eckhardt, *Compassion: Toward a Science of Value* (Toronto: CPRI Press, 1973), p. 258.

[17] John E. Steinmueller and Kathryn Sullivan, "Justice," *Catholic Biblical Encyclopedia* (New York: Joseph F. Wagner, Inc., 1956), I, p. 607.

[18] Cited in Raphael Posner, "Charity," *Encyclopedia Judaica* (NY: Macmillan, 1971), V, col. 340.

[19] Cf. John L. McKenzie, *Dictionary of the Bible* (Milwaukee: Bruce, 1965,): *"Hesed* in the judgment is a part of the conception of the judge not as an arbiter but as a deliverer." (p. 565).

[20] Rabbi Harry A. Cohen, *A Basic Jewish Encyclopedia* (Hartford, Ct: Hartmore House, 1965), p. 71.

[21] Miranda, *Marx and the Bible,* pp. 46f. Miranda gives the following parallelisms between *hesed* and justice or right: Jer. 9.23; Is. 16.5; Mic. 6.8; Hos. 2.21f.; 6.6; 10.12; 12.7; Zech. 7.9; Pss. 25.9f.; 33.5; 36.6f.; 36.11; 40.11; 85.11; 88.12f.; 89.15; 98.2f.; 103.17; 119.62–64.

[22] Krister Stendahl, *Paul Among Jews and Gentiles* (Philadelphia: Fortress, 1978), pp. 100f., 107. Stendahl also points out that Philo turned the Hebraic concept of Yahweh as Compassion completely around because of his dependence on the Greek translation of the Old Testament. Philo translated Yahweh as *kyrios* suggesting sovereign judge and Elohim as *theos* suggesting mercy. (p. 98) Future references to this book will be abbreviated KS.

[23] Thomas Aquinas, *Summa Theologica,* III suppl., q. 94, a.2.

[24] Ernst Troeltsch, cited in *A Basic Jewish Encyclopedia,* ed. cit., pp. 62f. Kaufmann endorses this same opinion.

[25] "Compassion," in *The Encyclopedia of Jewish Religion,* R.J. Zwiwerblowsky, ed. (NY: Holt, Rinehart and Winston, 1965), p. 95. "Pity," in *Universal Jewish Encylcopedia,* ed. cit., p. 547.

[26] "Deus secundum scriptures irascitur, nec tamen ulla passione turbatur." St. Augustine, *The City of God Against the Pagans,* Bk. IX, Section V. *In the Loeb Classical Library Series* (Harvard Press, 1968), p. 170.

[27] Arturo Paoli, *Meditations on Saint Luke* (Maryknoll, NY: Orbis Books, 1977), pp. 8f., 6f., 4.

[28] Mary Richards, *Centering* (Middletown, Ct. Wesleyan Univ. Press, 1964), pp. 92, 115. Cf. Matthew Fox, "The Case for Extrovert Meditation," *Spirituality Today* (June, 1978), pp. 164–177.

[29] Thomas Aquinas, *In librum Beati Dionysii de Divinis Nominibus,* II, 1.4, #192; *In IV Sententiarum,* Dist. XV, q. 2, a. 1, ad 4. He also says that this kind of passion belongs to God (*Super II ad Cor.,* Ch. XI, lect. 6.).

[30] Thomas Merton, "Marxism and Monastic Perspectives," in John Moffitt, ed., *A New Charter for Monasticism* (Notre Dame: Univ. of Notre Dame Press, 1970), p. 80.

[31] James A. Christenson, "Religious Involvement, Values and Social Compassion," *Sociological Analysis* (1976: 37), p. 218. A cautionary note is in order, however, for this study is restricted to North Carolina which is uniquely Protestant with little Jewish or Catholic representation at the time of this study.

[32] In Cohen, *op. cit.,* pp. 60f.

[33] In *ibid.,* p. 74.

[34] Achtemeir, *loc. cit.*

[35] Cf. Miranda, *Marx and the Bible,* p. 225. Cf. Schweizer, "pneuma," *Kittel's Theological Dictionary of the New Testament,* VI, p. 431.

[36] Samuel H. Dressner, *Three Paths of God and Man* (NY: Harper and Row, 1960), p. 106.

[37] W.F. Albright, trans., *The Anchor Bible: Matthew* (Garden City, NY: Doubleday, 1971), pp. 71f.

CHAPTER TWO

[1] Beverly Wildung Harrison, "The New Consciousness of Women: A Sociological Political Resource," *Cross Currents* (Winter, 1975), p. 455. Italics hers. She is approving of Habermas' analysis.

[2] Erica Jong, "Visionary Anger," in Barbara Gelpi, ed., *Adrienne Rich's Poetry* (NY: Norton, 1975), p. 172. Says Jong: "By the feminine I mean the nurturant qualities of all people."

[3] Emile Gertaud, Andre Rayez, "Echelle Spirituelle," *Dictionaire de Spiritualite* (Paris: Beauchesne, 1961), IV, col. 78.

[4] "Jacob," *Encyclopedia Judaica*, ed. cit. IX, p. 1192.

[5] PL 101, 1208b.

[6] PG v. xliv, 1248D.

[7] *De oratione Dominica.* Cited in Anders Nygren, *Agape and Eros* (NY: Harper & Row, 1969), p. 443. Hereafter abbreviated N.

[8] *De beatitudine*, Or. ii, p. 1208.

[9] Paul Philippe, "La Contemplation au XIII Siecle," *DS*, III, col. 1987. Other theologians who were highly dependent on the ladder symbolism include Philo of Alexandria, who saw Abraham as standing for the first rung of contemplation, Jacob for those who progress further, and Isaac for the perfect. This kind of thinking takes one far afield from the salvation history that these persons depict in the Hebrew Bible. Origen (d. 253) was indebted to Philo for his emphasis on the ladder. He developed several ladders for the spiritual ascent. One had three rungs consisting of the purgative way (corresponding to the Book of Proverbs); the illuminative way (Book of Ecclesiastes); and the Unitive way (Song of Songs). Another ladder compared beginners to the Israelites; the progressing to the levites; the perfect to the priests. Some imaginative medieval theologians such as Alan of Lille employed the ladder to the advantage of new spiritual movements. Alan placed the new movement of preaching at the top of his ladder of perfection at the seventh degree, beyond the investigation of doubts and the exposition of sacred scripture which was Number Six. (*Summa de arte praedicatoria*, pref. PL, CCX, 111.) Chenu observes that the ladder images of St. Benedict, St. Bernard and Hugh of Saint-Victor, "though not identical, have in common their goal of personal perfection; whereas the ladder of Alan has a social orientation." (M.D. Chenu, *Nature, Man and Society in the Twelfth Century* [Chicago: Univ. of Chicago Press, 1968], p. 247, n. 7)

[10] *De modo bene vivendi* 53, PL 184, 1276bc.

[11] *De laudibus Beatae Mariae*, Jean Bogard, ed. (Anvers: 1625). In *DS*, IV, col. 73.

[12] Thorleif Boman, *Hebrew Thought Compared with Greek* (NY: Norton, 1960), p. 203, n. 3. Italics mine.

[13] "Stepping Backward", Adrienne Rich, *Poems: Selected and New*, (NY: Norton, 1975), p. 9.

[14] Karen Horney, *The Neurotic Personality of our Time* (NY: Norton, 1937), p. 201.

[15] Cf. p. 277 below.

[16] Cf. Jong, *art, cit.*, pp. 172, 171. See also Adrienne Rich, *Of Woman Born* (NY: Norton, 1976).

[17] "An Interview with Buckminster Fuller," *National Public Radio*, May 15, 1977, p. 11.

[18] Carole A. Etzler has put her own words to this same song in her album, *Sometimes I Wish* (Sisters Unlimited, Atlanta, Georgia, 1976). I was first introduced to this variation of Climbing Jacob's Ladder by an unnamed retreatant in the woods of Oregon. Wherever she is, I am grateful to her.

[19] Eckhart, *op. cit.*, p. 105.

[20] See Mary Daly, *Beyond God the Father* (Boston: Beacon Press, 1974); Rosemary Reuther, *New Woman, New Earth* (NY: Seabury, 1975). An especially powerful critique of sexism and spirituality is Rosemary Reuther, "Women's Liberation in Historical and Theological Perspective," in *Women's Liberation and the Church*, Doely, ed. (NY: Association Press, 1970), pp. 22–36. She lays bare the intrinsic dualism of an overly male spirituality. Eugene C. Bianchi, Rosemary Reuther, *From Machismo to Mutuality* (NY: Paulist, 1976); Sandra M. Schneiders, IHM, "Apostleship of Women in John's Gospel," *Catholic Charismatic* (Feb–March, 1977), pp. 16–20; Casey Miller and Kate Swift, "Women and the Language of Religion," in *Christian Century*, April 14, 1976, pp. 353–358.

[21] Barbara Varro, "A Sexual Profile of Men in Power," *Chicago Sun Times*, March 9, 1978, p. 69. Jane Fonda found a similar situation in living among New York prostitutes in preparation for her role in *Klute*: "I noticed in all of these women a terrible hardness. Many of them are sleeping with senators, executives of major corporations, of TV Networks. They told me names, and they told me unbelievable stories about sadomasochism. You can imagine the view that it gives them of the rulers of this country." (*Newsweek*, Oct. 10, 1977 p. 81).

[22] Chuck Lathrop, "In Search of a Roundtable," in *A Gentle Presence* (Washington, D.C.. ADOC 1977), pp. 5–8.

CHAPTER THREE

[1] Arthur T. Jersild, *The Psychology of Adolescence* (NY: Macmillan, 1957), p. 201.

[2] Horney, *op. cit.*, pp. 162–187.

[3] Cf. Eckhart, *op. cit.*, p. 111.

[4] Gene I. Maeroff, "Mental Health Centers Booming as Campus Competition Rises," *The New York Times*, Feb. 27, 1978, pp. 1,D7.

[5] Karen Horney, "Recoiling from Competition," *loc. cit.*, pp. 213f.

[6] Horney, *op. cit.*, p. 288.

[7] For more on creation-centered spirituality see Matthew Fox, *On Becoming a Musical Mystical Bear: Spirituality American Style* (NY: Paulist, 1976), pp. xxvii-xx and Matthew Fox, "Elements of a Biblical, Creation-Centered Spirituality," *Spirituality Today* (December, 1978), pp. 360–369.

[8] The astrological tradition depicting the end of the age of Pisces (symbolized by two fish swimming in opposite directions) and the beginning of the Age of Aquarius (symbolizing water or the mystical holistic experience available for all) sees a dualistic consciousness ending within twenty years. Cf. Matthew Fox, *Whee! We, wee All the Way Home: A Guide to the New Sensual Spirituality* (Gaithersburg, Md.: Consortium Books, 1976), pp. i–xii and *passim* and Lawrence Blair, *Rhythms of Vision* (NY: Schocken, 1976), pp. 230–234.

[9] Ernest Becker, *The Denial of Death* (NY: Macmillan, 1975).

[10] Robert E. Ornstein, *The Psychology of Consciousness* (San Francisco: W. H. Freeman, 1972), p. 139.

[11] One of the harshest critics of Ornstein, psychologist Howard Gardner, concedes nevertheless that his educated guess is that a "picture of differing, but complementary, contributions by the two hemispheres will hold as well for other realms of thought" as research is expanded and discovers "more ways in which the two hemispheres can interact." He admits our now knowing that the left hemisphere manifests a "clear advantage in dealing with language" and "assumes a more dominant role than the right in classifying objects into standard" categories. The right hemisphere seems "relatively more important in spatial tasks" and in "making fine sensory discriminations." He denies knowing what "consciousness" means and seeks a "definition." One wonders, however, if this quest is not a left brain one exclusively. (Howard Gardner, "What we know (and don't know) about the two halves of the brain," *Harvard Magazine* [March–April, 1978], pp. 24–27.)

[12] Joen Fagan, "The Gestalt Approach as 'Right Lobe' Therapy," in Edward Smith, ed., *The Growing Edge of Gestalt Therapy* (NY: Brumner/Mazel, Publishers, 1976), pp. 59, 67. One might speculate here on whether much of introvert meditation in the West has been left lobe spirituality and whether, with the interests in creativity, body expression of gesture and dance and the emergence of extrovert meditation, the West is now opening to the possible contributions from right lobe spirituality. See Claudio Naranjo & Robert Ornstein, *On the Psychology of Meditation* (NY: Viking Press, 1971) and Matthew Fox, "The Case for Extrovert Meditation," *Spirituality Today* (June, 1978), p. 164–177.

[13] Ornstein's contributions are found in Ornstein, *The Psychology of Consciousness, op. cit.*, p. 67.

[14] Cited in Dressner, *Three Paths, op. cit.*, p. 11.

[15] Tresmontant, *op. cit.*, p. 48.

[16] For more on time consciousness, see Matthew Fox, "Demonic vs. Sacred Time in American Culture," *Listening* (Fall, 1976), pp. 175–190.

[17] Andrew Weil, *The Natural Mind* (Boston: Houghton Mifflin Co., 1972), p. 135.

[18] Cf. Boman, *op. cit.*, pp. 27–55 for an important treatment of the Hebrew sense of dynamic being vs. the Greek sense of static being.

[19] Adrienne Rich, "Planetarium," in *Adrienne Rich's Poetry, ed. cit.*, p. 46.

[20] See my *Whee! We, wee All the Way Home, op. cit.*, pp. 210–216 where I have shared many of these games.

[21] For example, on the subject of dark and light, night and day, see Eulalio P. Baltazar, *The Dark Center: A Process Theology of Blackness* (Paramus: Paulist, 1973); on dialectical consciousness in a saint's life, see Eloi Leclerc, *The Canticle of Creatures: Symbols of Union* (Chicago: Franciscan Herald Press, 1977) who treats of Francis of Assisi's immensely richly developed dialectical consciousness.

[22] Cf. Matthew Fox, "Hermeneutic and hagiography": *Spirituality Today*, September, 1978, pp. 263–271.

[23] Bruce Vawter, J, Heuschen, "Forgiveness of Sin(s)" *Encyclopedic Dictionary of the Bible*, Louis Hartman, ed. (NY: McGraw Hill, 1963), col. 806.

CHAPTER FOUR

[1] Richards, *op. cit.*, p. 27.

[2] Carl Rogers, "Toward a Theory of Creativity," in Carl Rogers, *On Becoming a Person* (Boston: Houghton Mifflin, 1961), p. 348.

[3] Jose Arguelles, *The Transformative Vision* (Berkeley: Schambhala, 1975), p. 218.

[4] Otto Rank, *Art and Artist* (NY: Agathon Press, 1975), p. 427.

[5] Erich Fromm, *Sane Society* (NY: Holt, Rinehart & Winston, 1955), p. 301.

[6] Kenji Mijazawa, "Life as Art," a duplicated essay given to me by members of the Buddhist Temple of Chicago.

[7] Silvano Arieti, *Creativity: The Magic Synthesis* (NY: Basic Books, 1976), p. 38. I use Arieti, not because he is the final word on the subject of creativity, but because his seems to be a balanced account of numerous theories of creativity. The author betrays an inkling of being an artist himself, that is, of having experienced connections.

[8] Boman, *op. cit.*, p. 173.

[9]William Blake, "The Laocoon," *Complete Writings*, Geoffrey Keynes, ed. (London: Oxford University Press, 1969), p. 776.

[10] Thomas Merton, *Conjectures of a Guilty Bystander* (Garden City: Doubleday, 1968), pp. 101f.

[11] Adrienne Rich, *Of Woman Born, op. cit.*, pp. 188f.

[12] Lawrence Blair, *op. cit.*, pp. 46f. I am indebted to Mary Schmiel for her research on spirals as symbols for immortality.

[13] Karen Horney, *Our Inner Conflicts* (NY: Norton, 1945), p. 197.

[14] Karen Horney, *New Ways in Psychoanalysis* (NY: Norton, 1939), p. 255.

[15] Ernest Becker, *op. cit.*, p. 210.

[16] Cited in Gerald and Patricia Mische, *Toward a Human World Order* (NY: Paulist, 1977), p. 298.

[17] Anne Douglas, *op. cit.*, pp. 200–226 deals with the fascination with death in a sentimentalized culture and people.

[18] Carl Gustav Jung, "Psychology and Literature," in Brewster Ghiselin, ed., *The Creative Process* (NY: Mentor, 1952), p. 221.

[19] Henry Miller, *Tropic of Cancer* (NY: Grove Press, 1961), p. 253.

[20]Norman O. Brown, *Life Against Death* (Middletown, Ct.,: Wesleyan University Press, 1972), p. 60.

[21] Jung, *loc. cit.,* p. 222.

[22]Cited in John Ardoin, "Leonard Bernstein at Sixty," *High Fidelity* (August, 1978), p. 57. Italics mine.

[23] Robert Bly, *The Kabir Book* (Boston: Beacon Press, 1977) p. 11.

[24] Cf. Krister Stendahl, "The Apostle Paul and the Introspective Conscience of the West," in Wayne A. Meeds, ed., *The Writings of St. Paul* (NY: Norton, 1972), pp. 422–434.

[25] Bill Connolly, "Jesuit Spiritualities and the Struggle for Social Justice," *Studies in the Spirituality of Jesuits* (September, 1977), pp. 202–43. Reactions may be found in the September, 1978, issue of the same journal.

[26] Mary Richards, *op. cit.,* pp. 38f. For more on extrovert meditation, cf. Matthew Fox, "The Case for Extrovert Meditation," *art. cit.*

[27] Ornstein & Naranjo, *op. cit.,* p. 74.

[28] Norman O. Brown, *op. cit.*, p. 63. This entire chapter, "Art and Eros," (pp. 55–67) is worthy of every artist's careful attention.

[29] Miller, *op. cit.,* p. 257.

[30] Heschel, *The Prophets, op. cit.,* p. 309.

CHAPTER FIVE

[1] Buckminster Fuller, *loc. cit.,* p. 24.

[2] Albert Einstein, cited in Fritjof Capra, *The Tao of Physics* (Berkeley: Shambhala Press, 1975), p. 41.

[3] For much of this discussion I am indebted to James Kenney, lecturer at the Institute of Creation-Centered Spirituality, Mundelein College, Chicago and to a seminar conducted by Fritjof Capra.

[4] I have developed this theme in Matthew Fox, "The Meaning and Importance of Bodily Sacramentality," *Modern Liturgy* (Fall, 1979). The entire issue is dedicated to the subject of body and spirit.

[5] Blair, *op. cit.*, p. 234. A stimulating account of these interconnections is found peppered throughout Blair's book.

[6] Boman, *op. cit.*, p. 58. Cf. pp. 27–73.

[7] Cf. his numerous concerns in his book of essays, *Out of My Later Years* (Secausus, NJ: Citadel Press, 1974).

[8] Itzhak Bentov, *Stalking the Wild Pendulum* (NY: E.P. Dutton, 1977), p. 129.

[9] Bruce Vawter, J. de Fraine, "Freedom," *EDB, ed. cit.*, col. 819.

[10] Jonas, *op. cit.*, p. 140.

[11] Rene Dubos, *So Human an Animal* (NY: Charles Scribner's Sons, 1968), pp. 9, 27.

[12] Melvin A. Benarde, *Our Precarious Habitat* (NY: Norton, 1970), p. 25. Italics his.

[13] Lewis Thomas, *The Lives of a Cell* (NY: Bantam Books, 1975), p. 147.

[14] John M. Storer, *The Web of Life* (NY: Devin-Adair Co., 1953), p. 140.

[15] Victor Hugo, cited in John Vynyan, *The Dark Face of Science* (London: 1971), p. 105.

[16] Albert Schweitzer, *The Teaching of Reverence for Life* (NY: Holt, Rinehart & Winston, 1965), pp. 49f.

[17] "Rhesus Monkeys Sacrificed Needlessly for Research?" *Chicago Sun-Times*, Jan. 22, 1978, p. 64.

[18] Nergis Dalal, "Do Animals have Rights?" *Atlas World Press Review*, July, 1978, p. 44.

[19] See Mary Hunt and Mark Juergensmeyer, *Animal Ethics: An Annotated Bibliography* (Berkeley: Graduate Theological Union, n.d.).

[20] Cited in Vynyan, *op. cit.*, p. 108.

[21] E. F. Schumacher, *Small is Beautiful* (NY: Harper & Row, 1975) p. 108.

[22] This and the following two citations are from Marcia Keegan, "Indians Kept the Faith and Buffalo are Back" *Parade*, May 14, 1978, pp. 6–8.

[23] See John M. Rich, *Chief Seattle's Unanswered Challenge* (Seattle: Lowman & Hanford, 1947).

[24] Eric Salzman, "Avian Arias from Audubon," *Stereo Review* (Sept., 1978), p. 114.

[25] Becker, *op. cit.* p. 227.

[26] Ashley Montagu, *Touching* (NY: Harper & Row, 1972). Becker too comments on violence and lack of sensuality: "The modern world, after all, has wanted to deny the person even his own body, even his emanation from his animal center . . . with the result that if we don't have the omnipotence of gods, we at least can destroy like gods." (*op.*

cit., pp. 84f.); Neuropsychologist James W. Prescott has written on this subject in *The Futurist* (April, 1975) and *The Bulletin of Atomic Scientists* (November, 1975). See "Body Pleasure and the Origins of Violence," *Script,* June, 1977, p. 1. An excellent theological study on the importance of matter and human beings is: Conrad Bonifazi, *A Theology of Things* (NY: Lippincott Co., 1967).

[27] D. H. Lawrence, *Women in Love* (NY: Viking Press, 1974), "Foreword," p. vii.

[28] Rene Descartes, "Meditation on First Philosophy" (second meditation), in Elizabeth Anscombe and Peter Thomas Geach, ed., *Philosophical Writings* (Edinborough: Thomas Nelson & Son LTD, 1959), pp. 67f.

[29] Celano's *Second Life of St. Francis,* 214, p. 534.

[30] Eloi Leclerc, OFM, *The Canticle of Creatures: Symbols of Union* (Chicago: Franciscan Herald Press, 1977), pp. 154f.

[31] See John Rich, *ed. cit.,* p. 40.

[32] Jesus' soil-oriented Parables of the Kingdom include: The Sower and the Seed (Mt. 13.3–8; Mk. 4. 3–9; Lk. 8. 5–8); The Kingdom as the Seed (Mk. 4. 26–29); The Wheat and the Weeds (Mt. 13.24–30); The Mustard Seed (Mt. 13. 31f.; Mk. 4.30–32; Lk. 13. 18f.).

CHAPTER SIX

[1] Victor Ferkiss, *The Future of Technological Civilization* (NY: George Braziller, 1974).

[2] Musician Anton Webern has set this folk song to music. Its title is "Armer Sunder, du." (Opus 17, Webern).

[3] Herman E. Daly, "Introduction," in Herman E. Daly, ed., *Toward a Steady-State Economy* (San Francisco: W.H. Freeman & Co., 1973), p. 5.

[4] Cited in Schumacher, *op. cit.,* p. 100.

[5] In an "Interview with Dr. E.F. Schumacher" *Mother Earth News* (November, 1976), p. 11.

[6] Gregory Baum, *Religion and Alienation* (Paramus: Paulist, 1975)pp. 38f.

[7] Cf. E.P. Thompson, "Time, Work-Discipline, and Industrial Capitalism," *Past and Present* (1967, vol. 38), pp. 56–97.

[8] Boman, *op. cit.,* pp. 184, 188.

[9] Gerald and Patricia Mische, *op. cit.,* pp. 61, 37.

[10] Michael Harrington, *Socialism* (NY: Bantam, 1977), p. 344.

[11] Daly, *loc. cit.,* p. 13. Economists are relating the new physics to their science. Daly writes: "Economists must undergo a revolutionary paradigm shift and sacrifice large intellectual (and material?) vested interests in the perpetual growth theories and policies of the last thirty years before they can really come to grips with these questions. The advantage

of the physical scientists is that, unlike economists, they are viscerally convinced that the world is a finite, open system at balance in a steady state, and they have not all invested time and energy in economic growth models....Something of the physiocrats' basic vision, if not their specific theories, is badly needed in economics today." (*ibid.*, pp. 6, 19) Kenneth E. Boulding writes: "Economists in particular, for the most part, have failed to come to grips with the ultimate consequences of the transition from the open to the closed earth. . . . The closed earth of the future requires economic principles which are somewhat different from those of the open earth of the past. . . . The earth has become a single spaceship, without unlimited reservoirs of anything, either for extraction or for pollution, and in which, therefore, man must find his place in a cyclical ecological system. . . ." (Kenneth E. Boulding, "The Economics of the Coming Spaceship Earth," in *ibid*, pp. 122, 127.)

[12] N.O. Brown, *op. cit.*, pp. 228f., 221, 192.

[13] Pope Paul VI, *On Development of Peoples*, March 26, 1967, #830.

[14] *Ibid.*, #863, 837.

[15] Rosemary Reuther, *New Woman, New Earth*, p. 182.

[16] *Economic Report on Corporate Mergers*, (Bureau of Economics, Federal Trade Commission, Commerce Clearing House Edition), p. 3; *Fortune*, (May, 1971), pp. 172–178. See Eugene Toland, Thomas Fenton, Lawrence McCulloch, "World Justice and Peace: A Challenge to American Christians," (NY: Church Research & Information Projects, Oct. 1976).

[17] Einstein, *Out of My Later Years*, p. 34.

[18] George Will, "Enterprise Not So Private," *Chicago Sun-Times*, January 9, 1977, p. 6.

[19] Ernest Becker, *op. cit.*, p. 284.

[20] N.O. Brown, *op. cit.*, p. 268.

[21] Carroll Quigley, "The Search for a Solution to the World Crisis," *The Futurist* (February, 1975), p. 39.

[22] Daniel Goleman, "Breaking out of the Double Bind: An Interview with Gregory Bateson," *Psychology Today* (August, 1978), p. 44.

[23] Edward Joseph Holland, *Look At Yourself, America!* (Ambler, Pa: The Episcopal Church Publishing Co., n.d.), p. 7.

[24] *Northliner Gifts*, (Publication of North Central Airlines, n.d.), pp. 12, 7.

[25] "Former Exec Blasts Greed," *Chicago Daily News*, May 31, 1975, p. 23.

[26] "King Pong Inventor Makes Quite a Splash," *Chicago Sun-Times*, July 25, 1976, p. 76.

[27] Karen Horney, *Our Inner Conflicts, op. cit.*, pp. 207f.

[28] "Money? It's Ex-Spendable," *Chicago Sun-Times*, August 14, 1978, p. 29.

[29] Marie Augusta Neal, *A Socio-Theology of Letting Go* (NY: Paulist, 1977), pp. 6, 104.

[30] Studs Terkel, *Working* (NY: Avon, 1976), p. 534.

[31] Adrienne Rich, *Of Woman Born*, p. 67.

[32] Jose Miranda, *Marx and the Bible*, p. 113.

[33] Philip Stern, *The Great Treasury Raid*, Cited in *A Teacher's Handbook on Christian Values and Economics* (St. Paul: Center for Economic Education, College of St. Thomas, Preliminary Review Edition, 1977), p. 13.

[34] Alexander Cockburn & James Ridgeway, "How to Fix a Handout," *Village Voice*, August 21, 1978, pp. 15f.

[35] William O. Douglas, *Points of Rebellion* (NY: Vintage Books, 1970), p. 68.

[36] "Gaudium et Spes," (The Church in the Modern World), *Proceedings of the Second Vatican Council*, 1965, #672.

[37] "A Unique Competence, A Study of Employment Opportunity in the Bell System," (Washington, D.C.: Equal Opportunity Commission, 1971), pp. 59, 238, 173; *Fortune* (NY: March, 1972), p. 17.

[38] 1970 *Annual Report of A. T. & T.*

[39] Anne Douglas, *op. cit.*, p. 52.

[40] In Bianchi, Reuther, *op. cit.*, p. 51. Hereafter abbreviated *B*.

[41] "Estimated Advertising Expenditures in the U.S.," "Advertising Expenditures by Medium," in the *World Almanac and Book of Facts* (NY: Newspaper Enterprises Assoc., 1978), pp. 82, 425.

[42] Horney, *Our Inner Conflicts*, p. 196.

[43] Claude Steiner, "The Stroke Economy," in Claude Steiner, ed., *Readings in Radical Psychiatry* (NY: Grove Press, 1975), p. 33.

[44] Brian J. Kelly, "Monk is Top Salesman for Xerox," *Chicago Sun-Times*, April 3, 1977, p. 117.

[45] "50 Leading U.S. Advertisers, 1976," in *The World Almanac and Book of Facts*, ed. cit., p. 424.

[46] *Pocket Data Book, USA*, (U.S. Dept. of Commerce, 1971), p. 217.

[47] James L. Busey, ed., *Progress and Poverty by Henry George* (NY: Robert Schalkenbach Foundation, 1968).

[48] Frank McEachran, "Henry George and Karl Marx," Paper presented at the International Conference, London, Sept., 1936. (NY: Robert Schalkenback Foundation, n.d.), p. 6. Marx himself dismissed George as "capitalism's last ditch attempt to rear itself anew upon a firmer basis than its present one." (Letter from Karl Marx to a friend, June 20, 1881, reprinted in *The People*, June 5, 1892.)

[49] Jorgen Randers and Donella Meadows, "The Carrying Capacity of our Global Environment: A Look at the Ethical Alternatives," in Daly, ed. cit., p. 304.

[50] See Pat Ryan Greene, "Advocate of Poor Honored: Winner Sold Shares in Self," *National Catholic Reporter*, May 26, 1978, p. 1.

[51] C.J. Bullock, ed., "Introductory Note," to Adam Smith, *An Inquiry into the Nature and Causes of the Wealth of Nations* (NY: P.F. Collier & Sons, 1909), p. 3.

[52] Barbara Ward and Rene Dubos, *Only One Earth: The Care and Maintenance of A Small Planet* (NY: Norton, 1972), p. 29.

53 "Socialism: Trials and Errors," *Time*, March 13, 1978. Time is itself the 217th largest corporation in America according to its brother publication, *Fortune*, May, 1977.

54 Robert Bellah, "The American Taboo on Socialism," in *The Broken Covenant* (NY: Seabury, 1975), chapter five.

55 Cf. Ivan Illich, "Total consumption of medicine is largely independent of cost or the kind of practice that is prevalent, i.e. private or socialized." In other words, industrialization and consumption are ideologies that threaten both right and left-wing economic systems. Ivan Illich, *Medical Nemesis* (NY: Pantheon, 1976), p. 73, note 119.

CHAPTER SEVEN

1 Karl Marx, *The Holy Family* (Moscow: Foreign Languages Publishing House, 1956), p. 176.

2 Ivan Illich, *op. cit.*, p. 50, note 44.

3 *Sun Times: A Publication of the Solar Lobby*, August, 1978, p. 2

4 Ellen Frank, "The Whiz Kid Energycologist," *New Times* (August, 21, 1978), p. 44.

5 Robert Jungk, "The Menace of 'the Atom State,'" *Atlas World Press Review* (July, 1978), p. 52. Cf. Joel Kotkin and Bill Wallace, "Cops Spy on Anti-Nukites as the Atomic Backlash Sets In," *New Times*, (May 1, 1978), p. 17.

6 Frank, *art. cit.*, p. 37. Marlene Cimons, "The Goal of Sun Day: Solar Power," *Los Angeles Times*, Dec. 1, 1977, Part IV says: "The one thing solar energy does is offer a decentralized technology" in contrast to the bigness desired by big government and big business.

7 See "Nuclear Waste Watch: West Valley, N.Y. . . . 2,600,000 Gals.," in *New Times* (March 20, 1978), p. 19.

8 Illich, *op. cit.*, p. 48.

9 Ian Douglas-Wilson and Gordon McLachlan, eds., *Health Service Projects: An International Survey* (Boston: Little, Brown, 1973). Cited in Illich, p. 49, note 41.

10 Robert Charles D.C., "Bio-Energy Healing," (Unpublished paper: 1971), p. 1.

11 Robert Charles D.C., "The Language of Cells" (Unpublished paper, 1971), p. 1.

12 *Ibid.*, p. 2.

13 *Ibid.*, p. 5.

14 Mary Richards, *op. cit.*, p. 15.

15 Robert Bly, *op. cit.*, pp. 3, 13, 41.

16 *Small is Beautiful*, pp. 82–84.

17 Scheler, *op. cit.* pp. 105f.

[18] William Eckhardt argues such a case in *op. cit.*, pp. 2–11 as do the Misches, *op. cit.*, pp. 330–349. Still more thorough investigation is needed not only as to the fact of compassion being a universal religious value but as to the methods that religious cultures have developed for teaching compassion. Dr. D.T. Suzuki speaks of the Buddhist notion of interconnectedness which is so experiential. "The significance of the *Avatamsaka* and its philosophy is unintelligible unless we once experience . . . a state of complete dissolution where there is no more distinction between mind and body, subject and object. . . . We look around and perceive that every object is related to every other object . . . not only spatially, but temporally. . . . As a fact of pure experience, there is no space without time, no time without space; they are interpenetrating." (D.T. Suzuki, Preface to B.L. Suzuki, *Mahayana Buddhism* [London: Allen and Unwin, 1959], p. 33.) See also Garma C.C. Chang, *The Buddhist Teaching of Totality: The Philosophy of Hwa Yen Buddhism.* (University Park: Pennsylvania State Univ. Press, 1974).

[19] Cf. Jose Miranda, *Being and the Messiah*, *op. cit.*, p. 88.

[20] Martin McGuire, J. de Fraine, "Church," *EDB* col. 381.

[21] Capra, *op. cit.*, p. 305.

[22] For more on the mystical body, see McGuire, *loc. cit.*, col. 370ff.

[23] Rudolph Pesch, "Jesus Christ," *Sacramentum Mundi*, Karl Rahner, ed. (NY: Seabury, 1975). p. 740.

[24] McGuire, *loc. cit.*, col. 381.

[25] Wilhelm Bruening, "Communion of Saints," *Sacramentum Mundi, ed. cit.*, p. 276.

[26] See Bernard Cooke, *Ministry to Word and Sacraments* (Philadelphia: Fortress Press, 1976), pp. 645f.

CHAPTER EIGHT

[1] Constance Urdang, "Living in the Third World," *The American Poetry Review*, May, 1977, p. 48.

[2] Cited in Jonas, *op. cit.*, p. 322.

[3] Lewis, *op. cit.*, p. 117.

[4] Bentov, *op. cit.*, pp. 170, 4, 174.

[5] Robert Graves, *The White Goddess* (NY: Farrar, Straus & Giroux, 1974), pp. 248f.

[6] J.E. Cirlot, *A Dictionary of Symbols* (NY: Philosophical Library, 1962), p. 232.

[7] M. Esther Harding, *Woman's Mysteries Ancient and Modern* (NY: Harper and Row, 1976), pp. 95f.

[8] *Egyptian Ritual*, cited in Cirlot, *op. cit.*, p. 90.

[9] Mary Daly, *op. cit.*

[10] See Jose and Miriam Arguelles, *Mandala* (Berkeley: Shambhala, 1972).

[11] Blair, *op. cit.*, pp. 85f.

[12] *New Woman, New Earth*, p. 183.

[13] Arieti, *op. cit.*, p. 245.

[14] Cited in Blair, *op. cit.*, p. 152.

[15] Fuller, *loc. cit.*, p. 14.

[16] Jane Rohrer, "In the Kitchen Before Dinner," *The American Poetry Review*, Sept./Oct., 1977, p. 48.

[17] Elmar Klinger, "Soul," *Sacramentum Mundi, ed. cit.*, p. 1616.

[18] Otto Rank, *op. cit.*, pp. 128, 346.

[19] *Ginza, Der Schatz oder das Grosse Buch der Mandaer*, M. Lidzbarski, trans. (Gottigen, 1925). Cited in Jonas, *op. cit.* p. 63. Among the Gnostics, Jonas points out, "prison, ball and chain, bond and knot are frequent symbols for the body." (*ibid.*, note 16.) Sexuality and original sin are identical: "Sensual desire is the gnostic equivalent of original sin." (*ibid.*)

[20] N.O. Brown, *op. cit.*, pp. 196f.

[21] Plotinus, *Enneads*, II. 9.18. In Jonas, *op. cit.*, p. 263.

[22] Cf. Boman, *op. cit.*, pp. 190ff.

[23] Tresmontant, *op. cit.*, p. 94.

[24] McKenzie, *ed. cit.*, pp. 836–839.

[25] R.S. Peters, C.A. Mace, "Psychology," *The Encyclopedia of Philosophy*, VII, (NY: Collier Macmillan, 1972), p. 5.

[26] Thomas Aquinas, *Summa Theologica*, I, q. 36, a. 1 and q. 27, a. 4. Cf. I–II, q. 68, a. 1; *Contra gentiles*, IV, c. 23.

[27] Klinger, *loc. cit.*, p. 1617.

[28] M.D. Chenu, "Spiritus: Le vocabulaire de l'ame au XIIe siecle," *Revue des Sciences philosophiques et theologiques*, XLI (1957), pp. 232, 227.

[29] Peters, Mace, *art. cit.*, p. 4. Klinger (*loc. cit.*, p. 1617) points out that with Leibniz the soul became a self-contained monad, with Lessing an infinite striving, with Fichte the incomprehensibility of the absolute, with Hegel, the self-explication of the Idea, with Schelling a mystical potency, with Nietzsche the will to power, with Freud the difference between the ego and the super ego, with Jaspers existentiality, with Heidegger thereness or "being there", with Bloch the primordial realization of the future.

[30] Charles M. Fair, *The Dying Self* (Garden City, NY: Doubleday, 1970), p. 106.

[31] In Blair, *op. cit.*, p. 229.

[32] *New Woman, New Earth*, p. 210.

[33] Ward and Dubos, *op. cit.*, p. 220.

[34] Monika Hellwig, "Gifts from the Hasidism," *Listening* (Fall, 1978), p. 270.

[35] Cf. Krister Stendahl, "The Apostle Paul and the Introspective Conscience of the West," in Stendahl, *op. cit.*, pp. 78–96.

[36] Adrienne Rich, "The Phenomenology of Anger," (*Adrienne Rich's Poetry*, edited by Barbara Charlesworth Gelpi (Norton: New York, 1975) p. 71.